Magazine Design — *A hands-on guide*

ALSO FROM BLUEPRINT

Paper
Magazine and Journal Production
Litho Printing
Copy Prep
Typesetting and Composition
Inside Magazines
Graphic Reproduction Survival Manual
Introduction to Printing Processes
The Print and Production Manual
Desktop Publishing
Desktop Design
Desktop Publishing Design Basics
Word Processor to Printed Page
Pocket Glossary of Design and Typographic Terms
The Picture Researcher's Handbook

Ronald Walker

MAGAZINE DESIGN

A hands-on guide

BLUEPRINT
An Imprint of Chapman & Hall
London · New York · Tokyo · Melbourne · Madras

Published by Blueprint, an imprint of Chapman & Hall,
2-6 Boundary Row, London SE1 8HN

Chapman & Hall, 2-6 Boundary Row, London SE1 8HN, UK

Van Nostrand Reinhold Inc., 115 5th Avenue, New York NY10003, USA

Chapman & Hall Japan, Thomson Publishing Japan, Hirakawacho Nemoto Building,
7F, 1-7-11 Hirakawa-cho, Chiyoda-ku, Tokyo 102, Japan

Chapman & Hall Australia, Thomas Nelson Australia, 102 Dodds Street, South
Melbourne, Victoria 3205, Australia

Chapman & Hall India, R. Seshadri, 32 Second Main Road, CIT East,
Madras 600 035, India

First Edition 1992

Designed and typeset by Ronald Walker

Printed in England by Clays Ltd, St Ives plc

ISBN 0 948905 66 2

A catalogue record for this book is available from the British Library

Contents

Acknowledgements

My thanks are due to Roger Murphy FAIE, a freelance colleague, and to David Longbottom of the Periodicals Training Council, both of whom read early versions of the manuscript and made valuable suggestions. My thanks also to Liz Hughes whose eagle eyes came so effectively into play when my own glazed over from familiarity with the material and too many hours focused on the monitor screen.

For their courtesy in allowing me to reproduce pages from their publications I also thank the following:

Susanna van Langenberg, The National Magazine Company Limited; Geraldine Rudge, *Crafts*; Susannah Ward, World Publications; Lucy McCarry, *Elle*; Dee Nolan, *Metropolitan Home*; Susan Ross, *NatWest Magazine*; Keith Gretton, *BAT Industries Outlook*; Geoff Birtles, *High Magazine*; Roy Stemman, Company Communications; Tony Loynes, *UK Press Gazette*; Rosamund Casares, *Billiton Magazine*; Linda Davidson, *Nursing Times*; Jo Mattern, *Fortune*; Tony Judge, *Police*; Stuart Rock, *Director*; William Sieghart, Forward Publishing; Paul du Noyer, *Q*; Stuart Morrison, *Envoy*; Kevin Murray, Bayer UK; John Boswell, *Glaxo World*; Brendan Foley, *Hawker Siddeley World*; Stan Brooks, Jobson Publishing Corporation; C.W.Lavington, Chevron UK Ltd.; Alison Young, *M&S World*.

I owe particular thanks to *Naafi News,* the magazine of the British Navy, Army and Air Force Institutes, whose editor Patrick Breen allowed me unrestricted access to his archives – which were such a rich and accessible source of illustrations for many of the points I wished to make.

List of illustrations

Text set in italic indicates that the illustration is a page or spread from a magazine which will probably provide ideas beyond those indicated in the brief description.

Introduction

Our responses to magazine design are conditioned by the environment and times in which we grew up. But our tastes continue to develop and are influenced by changes in our environment and our circle of friends. Those of us who practise design find that our attitudes are further modified by our successes and our failures, by study and analysis, by watching reader reactions, by reading, and by attempting to summarize and present our experience and conclusions to new designers.

As a result, no two designers will have the same philosophy, advocate the same principles or follow the same rules – there are no tablets of stone for designers. But if you have picked up this book in the hope of learning something about magazine design, you must, initially, be prepared to accept my rules and follow my advice. Suspend argument, refute nothing until you begin to design pages: from that time on, inevitably, experience and inclination will lead you down an individual path which will diverge from mine and other designers' to a greater or lesser degree depending upon differences in taste, personality and experience.

Your progress will depend upon practice, your innate feel for design, and your application to the study and analysis of all the different elements that contribute to the whole. You can learn much from other people's mistakes and successes. You can listen to the advice of experienced designers and build upon their experiences. All of this will help you get started and speed up the learning process, but you will not learn to design unless you design.

You learn to ride a bicycle by getting into the saddle and persuading someone to give you a push while holding you steady for those first few wobbly attempts to remain upright while making forward progress. This book is meant to provide that initial push and the restraining, steadying hand for the aspiring designer.

Of course, there are a few desirable preconditions before the learner-cyclist should be allowed in the saddle: an appropriate space in which to practise, a safe bike, an appreciation that the handlebars are for steering and that pedalling provides the power, and an understanding of how to apply the brakes. A little knowledge of the highway code will not come amiss either. Control and confidence come from practice – and perhaps from falling off occasionally. Our approach to magazine design will be similar. We will cover the basics you need to get started, and will then move on to some of the finer points after you have got rolling.

Will you be a great designer by the end of the book? Not unless you were one when you picked it up. But if you follow its advice and heed its warnings you should find yourself on the right road, heading in the right direction. You will be steered away from many of the worst mistakes which lie in wait for the new designer, and you should be able to produce workable, acceptable page designs from the outset.

1 Why design?

Design is defined in the *Shorter Oxford Dictionary* as 'A plan or scheme . . . purpose, aim, intention'. In that sense the 'design' of any magazine is to attract readers and to encourage them to read from cover to cover. As an aspiring magazine designer you will need to keep that particular 'design' in mind. Your subjective view of 'good' and 'bad' design must be tempered by the evaluation of each page as a success or failure – with success being measured by how well the magazine is read.

Some of the best designers of magazines and newspapers are also writers or editors. As such, they have no difficulty in accepting that the prime function of page design is to get the copy read. They will reject any design ideas which could confuse, fatigue, or in any way hinder the reader's progress. They will do all they can to guide the reader's eye and help it move easily from sentence to sentence, from paragraph to paragraph.

Everyone who reads magazines, if only the weekend colour supplements, occasionally comes face to face with a page where the text is unreadable because of typeface distortions, unsuitable backgrounds, or eye-baffling colour combinations. Then there are those pages which demand such optical gymnastics from the reader that confusion leads to irritation and finally abandonment of the problem of discovering where on the page the eye is meant to leap to next. Argument about the artistic merit of such pages is pointless – if you cannot read the text because it engenders confusion, boredom or fatigue, the designer has failed; failed the writer, the editor, the publisher and you, the reader.

It will by now be obvious that the guiding

principle of this book will be: 'The text's the thing'. Publishers, editors, and writers have a right to expect that designers will employ their skills to persuade and help readers to absorb and understand the message. Photographers and illustrators will share that same objective, and their contributions can be among the designer's greatest aids.

Having accepted that the message is paramount, the designer must nevertheless make the design of each page or spread of the magazine as attractive (and appropriate to the subject matter) as possible. Although pages of unrelieved text place no obstacles in the reader's path, such deserts of unbroken grey tone will deter all but the most committed reader.

The designer's challenge is to stimulate readers to begin reading (by creating visual excitement, drama, humour, tranquillity or elegance as appropriate) and to retain their interest (by making it easy and pleasurable for them to continue reading).

Good design meets this challenge without making it obvious that a great deal of hard work was necessary to achieve success. Perhaps the best design is so transparent that the reader progresses directly to the message and its meaning unaware that a designer has been involved.

2 Familiarity breeds content

Designers have to steer a tricky course between providing an atmosphere of comfortable familiarity and inflicting one of boring uniformity. Regular readers do like to feel they know their magazine, that they can find their way around it as easily as they can move around their own homes. But even in their own homes they like to move the furniture around occasionally, add a few new cushions, hang a new picture, change the colour scheme.

The structure of the magazine comes from the positioning of its parts: covers, contents page, readers' letters, editorial, feature articles, news, regular departments or columns, advertisements and so on. Once established, this structure should not be changed without good reason: it provides that basis of familiarity which is a major step towards reader loyalty. It stands to reason therefore that the basic structure should be a matter for careful consideration from the very beginning.

How many pages of advertisements are the readers likely to accept before being allowed to get at the substance, their reason for picking up – and perhaps paying for – the magazine in the first place? It may be the kind of magazine where the advertisements are almost as important and interesting as the editorial. It may, on the other hand, be a matter of intense irritation to a reader to have to leaf through page after page of advertising before getting to the nitty gritty.

The relative importance of news pages, features, regular departments, letters, and so on needs to be assessed for every publication and their positioning, in relation to each other, given careful thought.

The grid (illustrated on page 40), typography,

colours can all reinforce the reader's feeling of familiarity and, at the same time, help build up that essential, distinctive personality which any successful magazine must possess. The character of a magazine stems from its editorial policy, content and style, but it is the designer who gives that character an instantly recognizable face. Something about every spread (with the exception of double-page advertisements) should remind the reader which magazine he or she is reading. And yet there must also be some stimulating differences from spread to spread and from issue to issue.

Of course, the personality of the magazine is not fixed forever. It can – and probably should – develop, and this will inevitably mean a change in the way the magazine presents itself. If editorial changes are gradual, design changes should keep pace. If the change stems from a change in policy, it will probably mean a complete re-styling, and that takes us on to Chapter 3. In those circumstances, the editor, designer and publisher should be aware that re-styling between one issue and the next, while pleasing some readers, will inevitably antagonize others. It should not be undertaken lightly.

Although visual variety and stimulation are essential to persuade readers to read, the basic conventions in design should not be ignored. Over the years readers become familiar with these conventions just as they become familiar with the positioning of material and with the typefaces used in their favourite magazine. It is a brave designer who sweepingly turns all these conventions on their head. It is usually wiser to provide your readers with a magazine with which they are familiar and comfortable (but do keep throwing in some surprises) and which is, at a basic level, constantly evolving.

3 Basic decisions

The opportunity to be in at the birth of a new magazine (or at the redesign of an established title) does not come the designer's way every day – and for new designers that day may be a long way off. But some understanding of what is involved, how and why certain decisions were taken, is essential even to the new designer working on the pages of an established magazine. That knowledge will not only explain some of the design restrictions that newcomers find already in place (and possibly irksome), but will also help them orientate themselves to maintain continuity and the original objectives.

The decision to publish a magazine is taken in the belief that there is a market for it (if it is a commercial publication) or a need for it (if it is, say, an association or company publication). In the former case the prime objective is to make a profit, in the latter it is to inform. In both cases there is a target readership. Like the editor, the designer needs to know who those prospective readers are, and what the publisher's objectives are. Ideally, therefore, the designer will be invited, at an early stage, to sit in on the planning of a new publication, to contribute to the decision-making process, and to gain the essential background knowledge of the publication's aims and objectives.

Take a magazine about to be launched by a large industrial concern. Is it to be aimed at staff, shareholders, customers, dealers or some other group? Is its prime purpose to inform, to educate or to entertain? Will it promote a particular business philosophy or is it intended to function as a two-way channel of communication? What kind of material will it carry – news, features, fiction, technical articles, learned treatises . . . ?

The marketing department should be able to provide a profile of the readership if the publication is aimed at customers or dealers. The staff department should be able to do the same if the publication is aimed at the company's workers. But statistical information covering a large number of people can be confusing. You might find it helpful to distil from the figures a mental picture of one, two, or (more probably) a small group of readers. Are they mostly young, middle-aged or elderly? Male or female? What sort of income groups are they from? What is their educational background? Are they shop-floor workers, administrators, technicians . . . ? Do they read the *Sun* or the *Financial Times*? *Q* or *Homes and Gardens*?

ON FIRST NAME TERMS

This mental picture should be as sharp and colourful as you can make it. You may even find it useful to complete the picture with names and personalities. It can be very helpful to ask yourself: will this particular spread appeal to Sharon, will Geoff quickly turn that page? You must be able to visualize your readers when the original design brief is being prepared, and as every page of every issue is laid out. A magazine aimed at teenagers working for a retail clothing chain will be different, right down to the size of typeface chosen for the text, from one aimed at executives in their fifties and sixties.

At the early planning meetings, decisions must be taken about budgets, formats, frequency, paper, staffing, content and so on. All of these decisions will have an influence on design – just as design decisions may have an effect upon, say, advertising or production. For example, although budgets do not directly impinge on the quality of the design effort (except as they influence the amount of time that can be devoted to it), they will affect paper quality, the production process, the availability of colour and other factors, and these will directly influence the design approach and the way in which the pages are eventually presented to the reader.

The type of content, too, will directly influence design (as a comparison of, say, *Time Magazine* and *Empire* will confirm). It may also influence page size: the international A4 size (210mm x 297mm) is still a popular magazine size but a larger page area is often preferred, particularly where photographic display is important, and news magazines can be found in a wide range of sizes.

The designer will certainly need to be involved in decisions about the number and width of columns. (The more columns the greater the flexibility with more possible variations of picture width, but there may be a typographic price to pay with fewer characters to the line.) The designer will obviously wish to influence the selection of typefaces, and to help establish the ground rules for the use of type ornamentation, the use of colour, the kind of illustration, the ratio of illustration to text, and so on. But even these decisions will not be based on mere whims of the designer, editor or publisher but will follow logically from careful consideration of content, budget, readership and so on. In other words they, too, will be affected by, and have an effect upon, many other decisions.

THE ADVERTISEMENT DIMENSION

The ratio of illustration to text is sure to have a bearing on the choice of paper. A cast-coated paper, a smooth high-gloss paper which might be preferred for a lavishly illustrated art publication, would be an unlikely choice for a news magazine which relied heavily on the text (where paper shine could prove a problem to the reader in some lighting conditions), but such a choice might be forced upon a publisher by the advertisers. And if an expensive art paper is chosen, its effect on the budget will be increasingly significant the larger the chosen page size and the longer the print run.

If advertisements are to be carried there must be an agreed policy defining the ratio of advertising to editorial, acceptable sizes for the advertisements, and which positions may be sold and which may not. Will advertisements be allowed on editorial pages, for example, or facing editorial pages (both will impinge on the designer's freedom), or will they be confined to purely advertising sections?

If the designer has to contend with advertisements booked to face editorial, will there be sufficient flexibility in the pagination plan to allow advertisements to be moved to face continuation pages rather than the opening pages of features?

If the magazine is to carry classified advertisements, a design and type specification will be needed which will allow the page or pages to look presentable and well organized while coping with a fluctuating number of bookings. Unless the classifieds are being carried as a reader service, the design will need to take account of the financial return expected from the page or pages. In other words, such pages must be able to carry enough advertising to produce a profit after the setting, paper and other costs have been met.

I am constantly surprised at how often magazines allow the outer columns of facing pages to be sold to advertisers. The outer areas of a spread are the dominant areas. They are particularly important on bookstall magazines because they are the areas browsers see as they flick through the pages. Allow too many half-

Spring/summer 90, right: swathes of chiffon and sculpted contours. This year, there's a greater emphasis on the navel, waist and hips.

Bouffant wigs, far right, are a playful dig at other designers' retro-mania. Linda Evangelista, bottom, in the autumn/winter 89/90 catalogue

mothers with dark, careworn beauty and iron wills.

The inspiration for Italy's hottest design duo comes from the peasant culture of the old Italian south – or at least how it was portrayed in the movies. Domenico Dolce and Stefano Gabbana grew up at different ends of Italy watching the same black and white films over and over again. They watched the work of Roberto Rossellini and Luchino Visconti, they fell in love with Anna Magnani's strength and steel, the proud and passionate Sophia Loren and every ample curve of Gina Lollobrigida.

They both adored the Roman movies made in the 50s and read the biographies of the stars who lived wild lives as wild cats there before they hit the big time in Hollywood. And they both had a fascination for Fellini. When Dolce and Gabbana met in 1980, they found they already shared a history.

They also shared a love for Sicily, the outpost of Italy that Gabbana describes as 'so passionate, so un-Italian, yet so archetypically Italian'. Born in Venice 28 years ago, Gabbana had never seen Sicily until he accompanied Dolce, 33, on his homecoming after several years of exile in Milan. The son of a Sicilian tailor, Dolce had grown up in Palermo and had found the reality of provincial life altogether less charming than it seems when condensed into a few delightful hours on celluloid as *Cinema Paradiso*, so he skipped out of university and escaped to the north. Only when he joined forces with Gabbana did he rediscover the pride of his heritage, and the appeal of the rustic and romantic clothes worn by the women who had surrounded him as a child.

Dolce & Gabbana clothes have their origins in the Sunday best dress of these Sicilians. And while their collections might include flame-red sheath dresses encrusted with glass lozenges – which are probably far too exotic for any party in Palermo – the basis of all their work is the Sicilian bustier.

'The bustier is an important symbol for us. The bust is the symbol both of maternity and sexuality. The bustier is a safety box half hiding something very potent which should only be opened in private. That's the key to sexuality in Sicily,' explains Dolce, who is one of the very few people at their Milan headquarters with a shirt buttoned up to the collar.

Gabbana is also dressed up to the neck, in a chenille Aran sweater, tight army-style trousers and battle boots, looking every inch the Italian stallion to the Gina Lollobrigida lookalikes who are milling around. That he happens to have the longest eyelashes is the only distraction from their visibly heaving curves.

The Dolce & Gabbana style has pervaded fashion's toughest capital like a warm summer breeze. The pair started their company in 1982, and after their first show in 1985, they were seen as part of a new mood, headed by Romeo Gigli, which proved that there was much more to Italian fashion design than a smart office suit. With Gigli now showing in Paris, the Dolce & Gabbana show has become the grooviest ticket in Milan fashion week.

This month, their fans will have another chance to see their work. Stefano Gabbano and Domenico Dolce are now signed up to design Complice, a mainstream label from the Milanese manufacturing giant Girombelli, a similar deal to Gianni Versace's designs for Genny and Romeo Gigli's revamped Callaghan. The contract is a sign that ▷

HENRY BOURNE

STEVEN MEISEL

At first glance this full-page advertisement, facing a continuation page in Elle, *seems to be part of the editorial feature.*

WOMEN'S REALMS

FROM GENDERLESS UTOPIAS TO SHARED CHILD CARE, WOMEN'S VISIONS OF THE FUTURE FOCUS ON LOVE AND BIRTH RATHER THAN VIOLENCE AND DEATH. ROSEMARY BAILEY LOOKS AT THE ALTERNATIVES OF FEMALE SCIENCE FICTION

Imagine a world where men can breast-feed; where babies gestate in tanks and have three mothers of either sex appointed to them at birth; where adolescents experience a traditional rite of passage, spending time alone in the wilderness to choose their own names and decide who they want to be.

Imagine a world where young children's sexual experiments are regarded as innocent play. Or where individuals can become male or female, and the 'mother' stays female only until she has finished breast-feeding. Or where men are the sexual slaves of women, their sole purpose to serve, entertain and sexually satisfy their owners. Or consider a future time when the triumph of religious fundamentalism has returned women to the status of sexual chattels, exploited for their child-bearing capacity by a ruling elite that has lost the capacity to procreate. All are alternative realities proposed by women science fiction writers in a genre that is gradually being recognised as an inspiring way to propose radical blueprints for the future of the planet.

The future is already here for computer science, which has created computer simulated Virtual Realities. As we increasingly dehumanise ourselves with realities like these, perhaps it is time to consider what kind of alternative we really want. So far, let's face it, we have made a monumental balls-up of running the planet: much of it is in toxic shock, a lot of it at war. Despite the fact that there is enough food for all, many are starving, many more deprived of the basic necessities. And that's only today; the prognosis for the future if things continue as they are doesn't bear contemplation.

For a brief halcyon period in 1990 it began to look as if sanity was possible. The Berlin Wall finally came down, Eastern Europe was liberated, the Soviet Union showed a human face. Until, that is, we found another war to fight. The armies whose role we had begun to question, even to reduce, rediscovered their virility. However legitimate the cause in immediate political terms, militarism is never going to benefit the course of world history.

BRAVE NEW WORLDS

If men can claim that brute strength gives them the right to rule the planet, surely the capacity for giving life rather than destroying it should give women some say. Women have had little opportunity to demonstrate the kind of world they might create, but their literature abounds in inspiration. The other worlds and alternative realities of science fiction create an opportunity to speculate about the way society has to be constructed.

Most science fiction, however, which is to say most SF written by men, has concentrated on scientific development and galactic exploration rather than on the sexual construction of society, its family structures and gender roles. As that notorious misogynist Kingsley Amis wrote as early as 1960: 'Though it may go against the grain to admit it, science fiction writers are evidently satisfied with the sexual status quo.'

But as Sarah Lefanu suggested in her survey of feminist science fiction, *In The Chinks Of The World Machine*, 'The stock conventions of science fiction – time travel, alternate worlds, entropy, relativism, the search for a unified field theory – are all powerful ways of exploring the construction of "woman".'

Women's visions of the future cover a wide spectrum. Some are near-perfect utopias while others predict a nightmare world such as that envisaged in Margaret Atwood's *The Handmaid's Tale*, where women are enslaved as sexual chattels by men to act as child-bearers. Doris Lessing's visions of a post-apocalyptic future in *Memoirs Of A Survivor* and *The Four-Gated City* are equally chilling. Others, like Marge Piercy's *Woman On The Edge Of Time*, present a grim present reality but glorious – and often hilarious – possibilities for the future.

Feminist utopias often share similar characteristics, based on righting the perceived wrongs of patriarchal society. They are often communally based with loose, non-authoritarian kinds of government, and demonstrate great concern for health and the environment.

But the most crucial difference between men's and women's future worlds is ▷

50

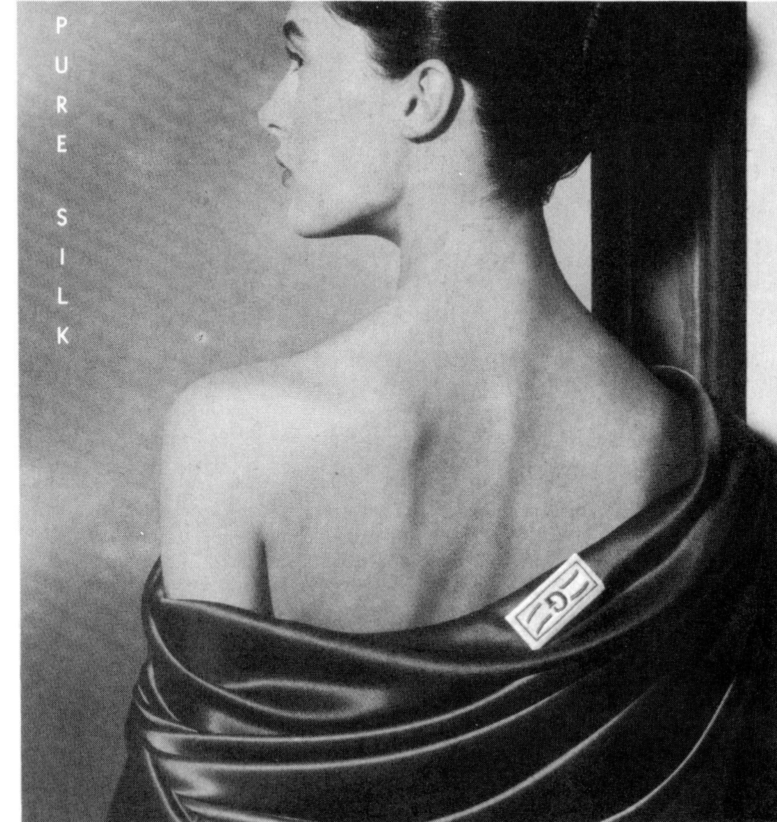

The lack of illustration in this two-and-a-half-page feature 'Women's Realms', also from Elle, *is alleviated by the simple expedient of facing each editorial page (the first is illustrated above) with a sympathetic full-page advertisement.*

Design discipline on Director copes equally well with full-page and multiple-ad pages facing editorial, and with half-page ads next to editorial.

Pages of brief news items or informative material (such as the review pages of Q, left) are a useful foil for complex page advertisements. A simpler advertisement (below) allows the facing editorial page to be more assertive without either page suffering.

page verticals in addition to the usual full pages of advertising, and browsers may well get a false impression of the ratio of advertisements to editorial.

Does this mean that the interests of advertisers and those of the editorial and design team are constantly in conflict? I think not. With few exceptions readers buy magazines for their editorial content. It follows that a quarter-page advertisement placed below an attractive feature stands a better chance of being read than one which effectively destroys the design of a spread and causes the reader to turn the page with no more than a glance. The advertising industry is not unaware of this, hence the increasing popularity of the double-page ad which gives the advertisement designer the freedom to express the client's message in the most appropriate form without problems of fighting for attention with other material.

So, all planning decisions must be based on reliable information, and they must be reached long before the designer puts pencil to paper (or mouse to mouse-mat if designing on screen) on issue one. They should be drawn together and set down as a policy document incorporating a set of objectives and a design brief. Although it will need to be reassessed and updated from time to time, that document will help to provide continuity and invaluable guidance for successive editorial, advertising and design staff.

4 About type

Anyone with a serious interest in print design will find it necessary to make a more detailed study of type than can be catered for in a book attempting to provide a general introduction to the broad subject of magazine design. This chapter is intended to provide no more than the essential groundwork needed to enable you to start designing pages.

But even at an elementary stage you will need, at least, to distinguish between typefaces with serifs (the text you are reading) and those without (sans serif – as used for the captions). Serifs are the short finishing strokes found at the ends of the character strokes (stems, arms and legs). Serif faces will generally, like handwriting with a traditional nibbed pen, have thin upstrokes and horizontals, and thicker downstrokes; sans serif faces will have strokes of even thickness – but there are exceptions.

Serif faces have a traditional look; sans serif, modern. Serif faces are generally thought to provide easier reading and to be less tiring than sans serif. Sans serif letters are vertically orientated, so the argument goes, while serifs provide a certain horizontal momentum which helps tie the letters of a word together and helps the eye move smoothly along the line. But choice of typeface, type size, line length and other things we have yet to discuss, each play their part in readability.

A vast and, to new designers, bewildering number of different typefaces is available, but on any particular project you will probably be restricted (or would be well advised to restrict yourself) to the range available from the printer who has the contract for the job. If your favourite display typeface is not among those on offer,

A A

Below left: A serif typeface. Right: Sans serif.

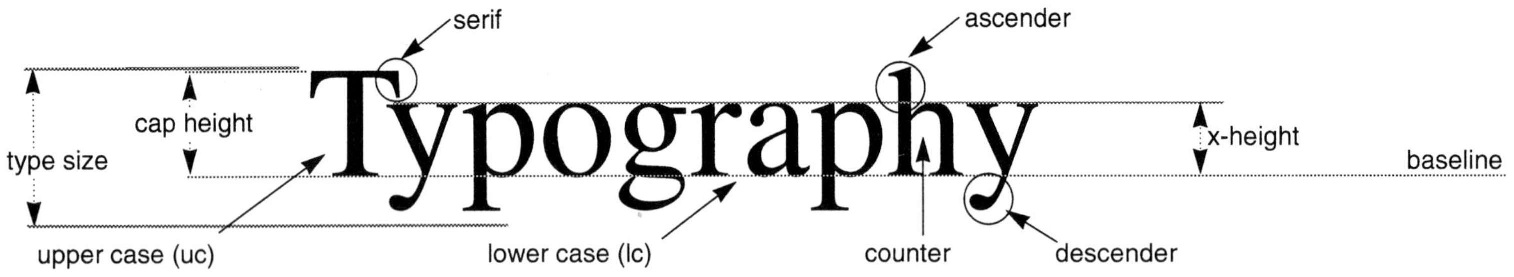

remember that the face is less important than the way in which it is used.

It makes sense to study and become familiar with the typefaces that are immediately and easily available before moving on to the study of others.

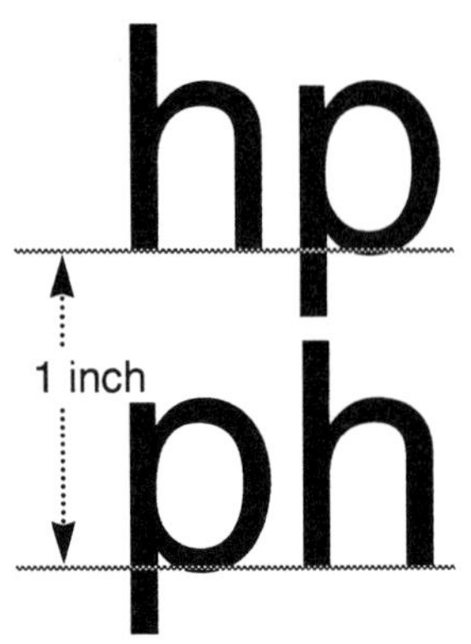

Above: 72 pt. Helvetica. Your ruler will show that it is just under 1 inch tall from the top of the 'h' to the foot of the 'p' but baseline to baseline will measure 1 inch.

TYPE SIZE

In the UK and the USA types sizes are specified in 'points'. There are 12 points to the pica, and 6 picas or 72 pt. to the inch (25.4mm) – 'pt.' is the abbreviation for point(s). You might therefore expect that 72 pt. type would measure one inch from the top of an ascender to the foot of a descender, but if you test that theory with a ruler you will find it falls a little short of an inch. Measure, instead, from one baseline to the baseline above or below on 72 pt. type set solid (that is, without any extra space between the lines) and that will prove to be one inch. In other words the point size covers the letters plus a little space which is built into the letter design to ensure that lines of type do not touch the lines above or below.

Before a numerical system of measurement was introduced, type sizes were distinguished by names: 48 pt. type was called Canon, 18 pt. was called Great Primer, and so on. The 12 pt. size was called Pica, which is the only one of these names to survive and is used, in the graphics and printing world, as verbal shorthand for 'pica em', in other words a 12 pt. em. Unfortunately, it is sometimes erroneously and misleadingly referred to simply as an 'em'. This can be dangerous. The 'em' (without the qualifying 'pica') is, in fact, a variable measure: the square of the width of the letter 'm' in whatever type size you happen to be working. A

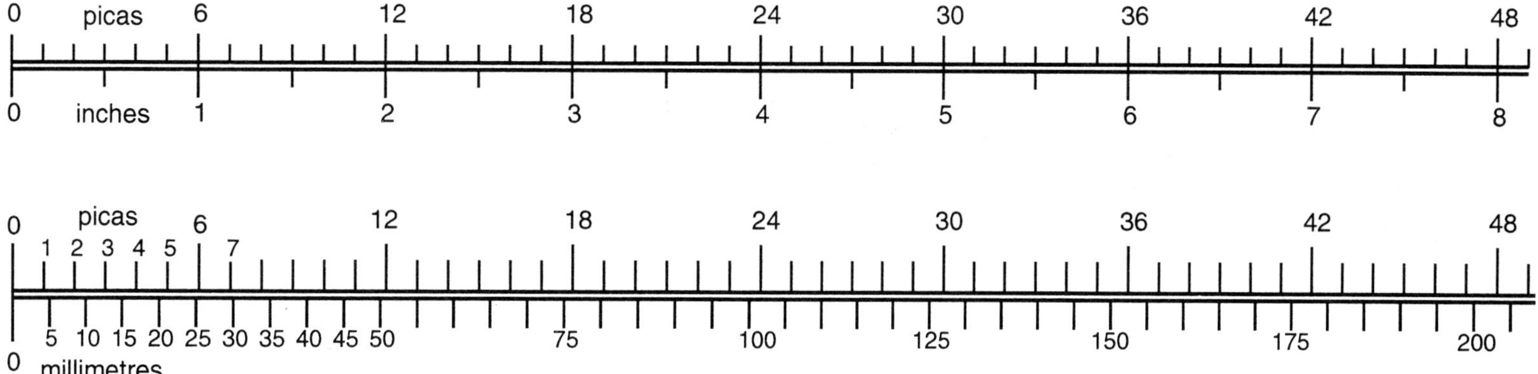

Converting from points and picas into inches (or vice versa) is easy. Points and millimetres are less compatible.

pica (or pica em) is always 12 pt. Because the pica is used to specify column widths, margins, gutters (the space between the columns), and so on, it is important to cultivate the habit of calling it a ‘pica’ and not an ‘em’.

The point size denotes the size of the letter but is almost invariably combined with a second point measure (the leading, pronounced ‘ledding’) which, in effect, specifies the amount of space to be placed between lines of type on the page. Thus 10 on 12 pt. (usually written 10/12 pt.) would specify a 10 pt. letter on a 12 pt. body – which would provide for 2 pt. of extra space between the lines, in addition to the small amount of space designed into that fount.

In traditional typesetting a fount is a set of characters, numerals, etc., of one size in one typeface. In DTP (desktop publishing is discussed in Chapter 15) the word and the meaning have been corrupted so that ‘font’ (the American word for fount) is used to refer to the whole range of sizes of a typeface. Inter-line spacing is called ‘leading’ simply because it used to be achieved by placing thin strips of lead between the lines of type when type itself was cast in lead. In those hot metal days it was usually referred to as ‘extra leading’ for the obvious reason.

The leading of text is critical to readability, but the amount of space needed varies from one typeface to another and from one size to another within the same face.

SIZE ANOMALIES

To further complicate matters, type of the same nominal size taken from different typefaces will vary in the actual size of letter as it appears on the printed page because of differences in

Different typefaces will seem to be of different sizes even when the same size and leading has been nominated throughout. All these examples are set 10/11 pt.
Times roman

Different typefaces will seem to be of different sizes even when the same size and leading has been nominated throughout. All these examples are set 10/11 pt.
Avant Garde

Different typefaces will seem to be of different sizes even when the same size and leading has been nominated throughout. All these examples are set 10/11 pt.
New Century Schoolbook

Different typefaces will seem to be of different sizes even when the same size and leading has been nominated throughout. All these examples are set 10/11 pt.
Helvetica

Different typefaces will seem to be of different sizes even when the same size and leading has been nominated throughout. All these examples are set 10/11 pt.
Bookman

Different typefaces will seem to be of different sizes even when the same size and leading has been nominated throughout. All these examples are set 10/11 pt.
Palatino

Short lines set justified will undoubtedly require type to be set in the smaller sizes if awkward word- and letter-spacing is to be avoided.

Some improvement should be possible if hyphenation is employed but its success cannot be guaranteed and obtaining good hyphenation can be time-consuming.

The best answer, if not too much text is involved, would be to set the text ranged left or right, as this produces the optimum word-spacing.

design. Variations in the x-height and in the length of ascenders and descenders will not only affect the apparent size of the type but also the amount of space between the lines. What is more, the character count for a given line length will also vary from face to face because the set (width) of the characters, and the amount of space between them, also changes from one design to the next.

What size of type, in your chosen face, you decide to use for the body text will depend upon a number of factors, including the age of the intended reader. Magazines for the very young at one end of the scale and elderly people (a rapidly growing market, which explains the popularity of large print books) at the other should use larger sizes than would be necessary for readers from the age groups in between.

READING COMFORT

As a rule of thumb, aim for between 38 and 50 characters to a line for teen- to middle-aged magazine readers. This should not be taken as a universal guide to readability however; a tabloid newspaper would have a lower character count, while a novel could have considerably more.

The lower the character count per line, the more uneven will be the word-spacing in justified text and the more prone the text will become to distracting ‘rivers’ of white spaces running down the column. An improvement can be achieved by hyphenating, but the lower the character count the more word-breaks (and, therefore, hyphens) you are likely to find at the end of lines. The longer the line for the same size of type, the higher the character count, the fewer the end-of-line word-breaks, the better the word-spacing but, beyond a certain point, the more difficult it becomes for the eye to move smoothly from the end of one line to the beginning of the next. Think of how often you have found yourself missing out a line of text when reading, or perhaps reading the same line twice. That was probably the result of lines which were too long, or which lacked sufficient inter-line spacing.

Bodoni (the late 18th early 19th century Italian typographer) recommended that leading should be set at one-third of the type size. That might seem a little generous in most situations today, but if you are unsure what leading to specify for body text in magazine columns try 20% of the type size and adjust it if necessary after seeing a test piece.

The designer should always seek that happy combination of type size, line length and leading which is not only easy to read but which produces a good-looking even tone on the page. However, the fact that time is a cost must not be lost sight of; the time and effort expended by the designer and the typesetter must be kept

This is 12 pt. Times roman set solid (i.e. 12/12 pt.). If the book text was set like this it would quickly prove very tiring for the average reader.

This is 12 pt. Times roman on a 13 pt. body (i.e. 12/13 pt.). Even 1 extra point of white space makes reading easier and improves the look and tone of the text.

This is 12 pt. Times roman on a 14 pt. body (i.e. 12/14 pt.), the setting used for the general text of this book, which should prove comfortable for most readers.

This is 12 pt. Times roman on a 16 pt. body (i.e. 12/16 pt.) which is the spacing recommended by Bodoni. It is elegant (on a longer line) if a trifle extravagant.

This is 12 pt. Times roman on a 24 pt. body (i.e. 12/24 pt.) which is well over the top for continuous reading but such extra leading has its uses in the presentation of non-continuous information.

Letter-spacing

L e t t e r - s p a c i n g

Letter-spacing added to lower case type destroys the shapes of the word and slows down comprehension. The first line shows normal spacing.

L E T T E R - S P A C I N G

LETTER-SPACING

LETTER-SPACING

Letter-spacing of all-cap titles (first of the three lines above) looks better than letter-spaced lower case (and cap words have little shape in any case) but extreme letter-spacing has become a fashion fad. Reducing letter-space (third line) quickly runs into trouble. The middle line is normally spaced.

within the budget. Commercial economics are a fact of life with which designers and typographers must come to terms. Costs must not be pushed beyond what the targeted reader will bear.

Because reading speed and comfort are largely controlled by our ability to recognize word shapes, lower case setting should normally be preferred, for continuous reading, to text set throughout in capitals. All-caps words create rectangles rather than recognizable shapes.

Each typeface is available in a number of styles: roman, italic and bold are common, but light, extra bold, condensed, outline, and others may also be on offer.

Type can be set justified, ranged left (also known as 'ragged right'), ranged right (or 'ragged left'), or centred.

The thousands of possible permutations of typeface, style, size, leading and letter- and word-spacing account for the variations of tone which can be achieved between one block of text and another. They can also lead to typographic disasters.

The thousands of possible permutations of typeface, style, size, leading and letter- and word-spacing account for the variations of tone which can be achieved between one block of text and another.

The thousands of possible permutations of typeface, style, size, leading and letter- and word-spacing account for the variations of tone which can be achieved between one block of text and another.

The thousands of possible permutations of typeface, style, size, leading and letter- and word-spacing account for the variations of tone which can be achieved between one block of text and another.

The thousands of possible permutations of typeface, style, size, leading and letter- and word-spacing account for the variations of tone which can be achieved between one block of text and another.

The thousands of possible permutations of typeface, style, size, leading and letter- and word-spacing account for the variations of tone which can be achieved between one block of text and another.

The tonal variations in these paragraphs (left) have all been achieved without changing the type family. They are simply the roman, bold and italic versions of Times, with only slight variation in sizes and with different amounts of leading. More variation can be achieved with typeface changes. Right, from the top: Univers Black , Futura Light, Cooper Black, Galliard.

The thousands of possible permutations of typeface, style, size, leading and letter- and word-spacing account for the variations of tone which can be achieved between one block of text and another.

The thousands of possible permutations of typeface, style, size, leading and letter- and word-spacing account for the variations of tone which can be achieved between one block of text and another.

The thousands of possible permutations of typeface, style, size, leading and letter- and word-spacing account for the variations of tone which can be achieved between one block of text and another.

The thousands of possible permutations of typeface, style, size, leading and letter- and word-spacing account for the variations of tone which can be achieved between one block of text and another.

Justified type is read more easily and more quickly than ragged setting in the same face, size, line-length and leading, but there are occasions when ragged settings can be used to good effect.

Justified setting

Justified type is read more easily and more
quickly than ragged setting in the same
face, size, line-length and leading, but
there are occasions when ragged settings
can be used to good effect.

Ranged left (ragged right)

Justified type is read more easily and more
quickly than ragged setting in the same
face, size, line-length and leading, but
there are occasions when ragged settings
can be used to good effect.

Ranged right (ragged left)

Justified type is read more easily and more
quickly than ragged setting in the same
face, size, line-length and leading, but
there are occasions when ragged settings
can be used to good effect.

Centred

5 Preparation

Even designers who propose to practise their craft on a computer screen will find it beneficial to begin with pencil and paper. This will allow them to concentrate on design matters, avoiding the distractions of the technology, and the experience will help them understand why electronic page make-up software works in the way it does.

The essential materials and tools needed to begin designing are minimal and inexpensive. They are: an A3 layout pad, an A4 pad of tracing paper, masking tape, a selection of soft lead and chinagraph pencils, a plastic type-scale, a clear plastic setsquare, a pair of L-shaped cardboard masks (ideally, cut from card which is black on one side and white on the other – paste black and white together if necessary), and a type book or specimen sheets (usually supplied by your printer but if you do

A basic toolkit for designers.

Examples of different margin and column schemes for two-page spreads showing possible one, two, three and four columns per page. Note the extra wide margin (upper right), the introduction of a narrower column (lower left and lower right), and the lowering of the type horizon (lower right) as methods of introducing white space.

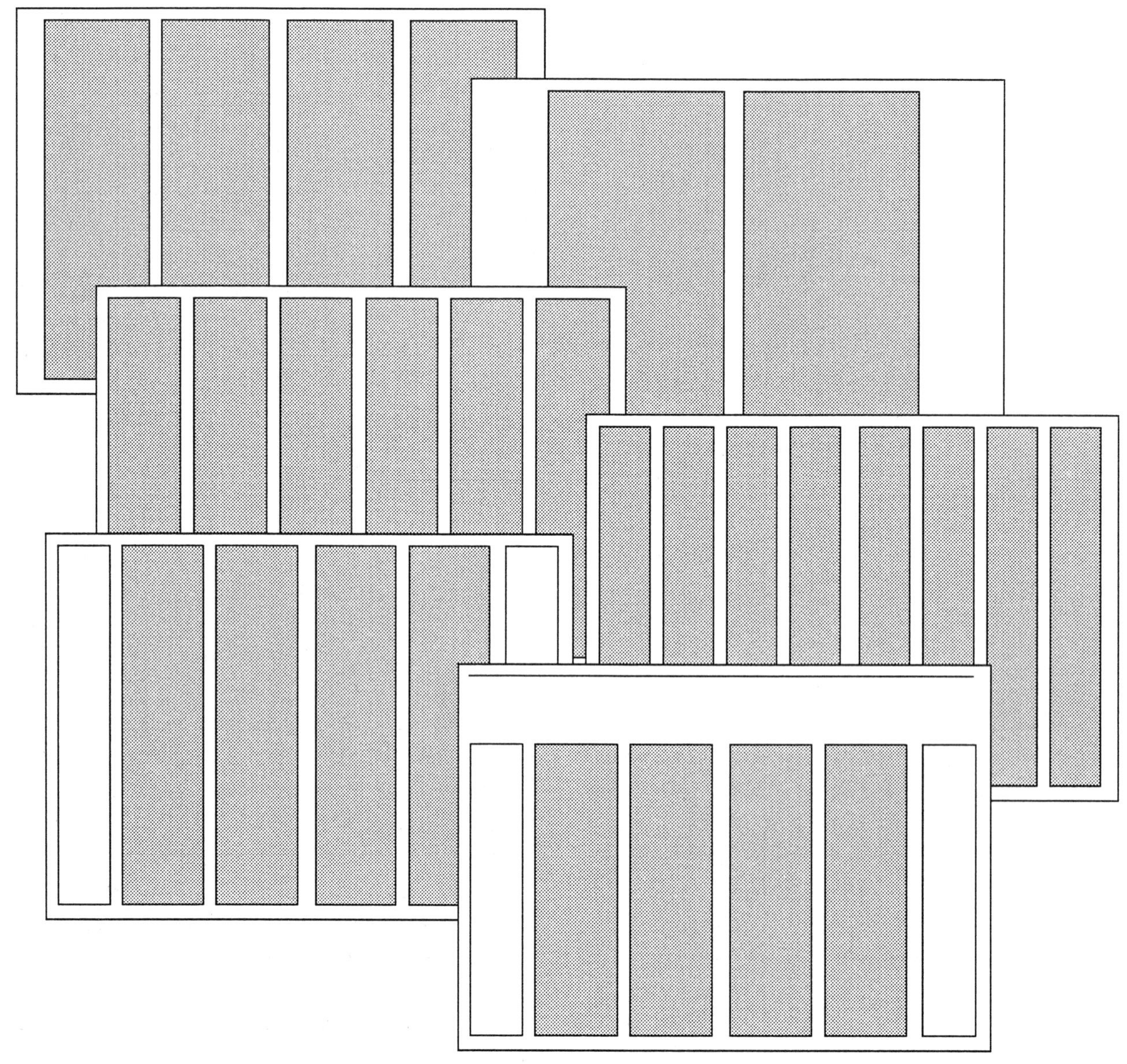

not yet have access to a printer, a Letraset catalogue will serve for practice). Most of the above can be bought at good artists' materials shops. You will also need a suitable (large) surface to work on.

The type-scale will prove particularly useful. Inches, millimetres and points are all still in use in the graphics and printing industry; the type-scale shows all three and makes conversion quick and easy.

Throughout this book I propose to use points as the main system of measurement. It will undoubtedly be used to specify sizes in your type book or specimen sheets and it will be less confusing to use the same system for all other measurements on the page. If you prefer to work in millimetres or inches, simply use your type-scale to make the conversion.

ON THE GRID

Printed grid sheets should be available if you are working on an established magazine. These 'skeletons' of the printed page will usually show the page area, margins, columns and gutters (the space between the columns) of a two-page spread. The lines of text may be indicated by lighter ruled lines. Some grids also show divisions of the column depths to indicate the position of titles, pictures and so on.

Margin, column, and gutter schemes can vary widely and will, to a considerable degree, determine the general appearance of the publication. Tight margins will give an overall dark cast to pages. A lighter look can be built in by using wider margins, or perhaps adding a narrow column which could be used for sideheads, pictures, graphics or captions. The position of this narrow column may be constant (in which case it will usually be the outer column) or it may be varied and used, for example, to separate two features placed on the same spread, thus providing more variety from spread to spread.

Dropping the type horizon down the page can also ensure built-in white space. Such deviations from the more commonplace margin schemes and standard two-, three-, or four-column grids contribute to a publication's individuality. As you browse through other magazines keep an eye open for original 'bone structures' and study the effect of this basic skeleton over the whole publication.

It is usually best to maintain the same top and bottom margins throughout a publication but left and right, or inside and outside, margins can sometimes be changed to good effect – perhaps to distinguish different sections of the magazine. This will mean changing the column structure too. The number and width of columns can, of course, also be varied without affecting the margins.

Be wary of overburdening the basic grid with

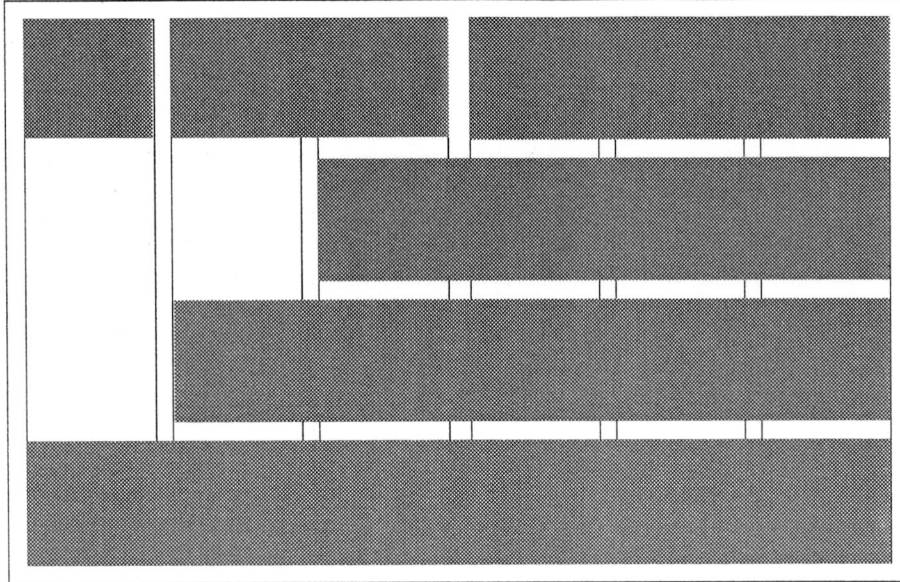

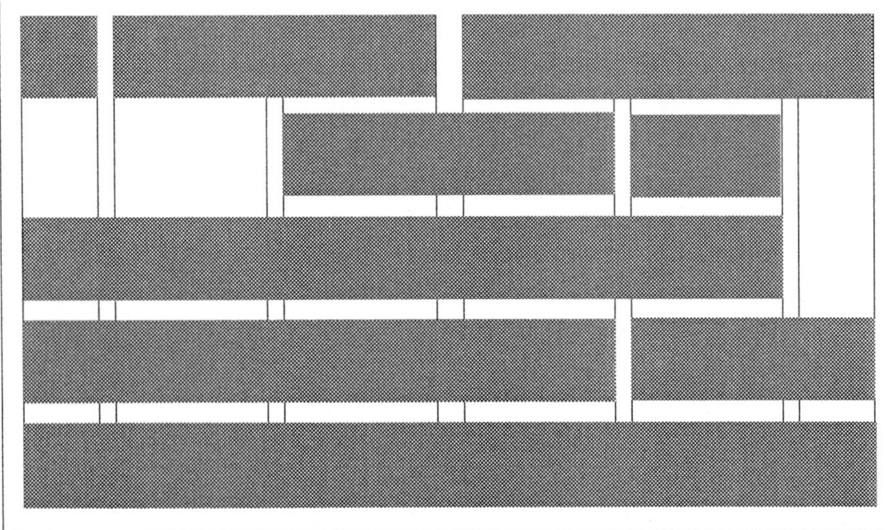

boxes and rules. Boxes (or sometimes hoods) around the type area are a current fashion; they can be very restricting when the designer gets down to the practicalities of individual page layouts, but they are well suited to annual reports, brochures and the like. Think carefully too about the position of headers, footers, folios and so on.

The more columns to the page, the greater the flexibility, with pictures capable of being sized over a greater variety of widths. Still more variety is added if one of the columns is of a different width to the others, as can be seen in the illustration (lower left). In both examples further variation can be obtained by adding bleeds to pictures. Pictures can also be sized so that they do not fit neatly into the column structure, but this needs great care if ugly text setting is to be avoided.

The greater design flexibility achieved by increasing the number of columns needs to be carefully weighed against the possible adverse effects on text setting.

If a printed grid sheet is not already available, ask your printer to provide one (most printers will do so without charge) or draw one up taking the measurements from the printed pages of the magazine or from the original design specification if available. If you are not currently working on a magazine, use the measurements in the illustration on page 40.

You require two more 'tools' before you can begin to design: the ability to cast off type (work out how much space the writer's manuscript will take up on the page when typeset), and the ability to scale illustrations (work out how much space and what shape your illustrations will take if you enlarge or reduce them).

Mechanical aids are available for both these operations but the ability to use manual methods is a necessary fail-safe even for those who prefer to use slide-rule or calculator.

A MEASURE OF COPY

I can offer you two easy methods of casting off copy. In each of these the first step is to calculate the average character count per line of text in the columns of your magazine. You do this by counting the number of characters in ten lines of printed text (including all punctuation marks and spaces between words) and dividing the total by ten.

Now, if you are able to specify how copy will be presented to you, simply arrange to have all typewriters or wordprocessors set so that they produce lines with that average character count. From that point on the number of lines in each manuscript will be equal to the number of lines which will be produced when the text is typeset. If you can also arrange for all the pages to have an identical line count, then the simple multiplication of number of pages by lines per page gives an even quicker result.

If the character count per line is low, you can, of course, set the typewriter or word-processor to produce lines with twice the number of characters. This will mean that you must double the number of manuscript lines to arrive at the line count for the printed page.

If you cannot arrange for manuscripts to be

Copy 2 Magazine Design

If you cannot arrange for manuscripts to be
presented in this way, adopt the second method.
Hold your type-scale or ruler, on its edge,
parallel to the right-hand edge of the manuscript.
Now move it so that any line-ends which show to
the right of the ruler are roughly matched in
length by the spaces produced by those lines which
fall short of the ruler (ignoring paragraph ends).
Draw a line down the page at this point. Count the
number of characters in one of the longer lines of
text starting at the left margin and stopping at
the pencil line. (Remember to include all spaces
and punctuation in the count.) This gives you the
character count in an average line of the
manuscript; multiply it by the number of lines in
the manuscript and divide the result by the
character count for a line of text in the magazine.

Left: Casting off copy by the second of the two methods described in the text.
Opposite: More columns mean greater flexibility in picture sizes. One odd-sized column also introduces greater flexibility.

presented in this way, adopt the second method.

Hold your type-scale or ruler, on its edge, parallel to the right-hand edge of the manuscript. Now move it so that any line-ends which show to the right of the ruler are roughly matched in length by the spaces produced by those lines which fall short of the ruler (ignoring paragraph ends). Draw a line down the page at this point. Count the number of characters in one of the longer lines of text starting at the left margin and stopping at the pencil line. (Remember to include all spaces and punctuation in the count.) This gives you the character count in an average line of the manuscript; multiply it by the number of lines in the manuscript and divide the result by the character count for a line of text in the magazine. This is the number of lines the copy will make in the magazine.

If the original typing is reasonably neat, both methods will be accurate to within a line or two on the average feature.

You will undoubtedly come across other methods of casting off copy: try them all and use the one which works best for you.

GETTING THE MEASURE OF PICTURES

To scale a photograph, or any other piece of flat reflective (as opposed to transparent) artwork, place it under a sheet of tracing paper close to the lower left corner. Ensure that neither photograph nor tracing paper move as you work by holding them down on your desk or drawing board with masking tape. Line up your type-scale (or ruler) on the tracing paper from the bottom left corner (point A) of the illustration and the bottom right corner (B) and lightly draw a line from A to the edge of the tracing paper (C). Now draw a second line which extends from A through the upper right corner of the illustration (D) to the edge of the paper (E).

Let us assume that you wish to reduce your photograph so that the picture on the printed page will be 18 picas (3 in.) wide.

From point A measure 18 picas along the line AC and mark this point (F). Using your set-square draw a vertical line from F until it cuts line AE (at point G). Measure the line FG. This will be the height of your picture when it is reduced to 18 picas wide.

The diagonal line AE shows how the photograph can be enlarged or reduced in proportion: lines drawn from any point on this diagonal to meet the original baseline AC at right angles will provide measurements which maintain the original's ratio of height to width.

If you wish to print the picture enlarged, follow the same procedure. Point F will this time appear between points B and C and the vertical will cut the diagonal between D and E.

It will be obvious that if the available height of the printed picture is predetermined, then the width can be ascertained by marking off the

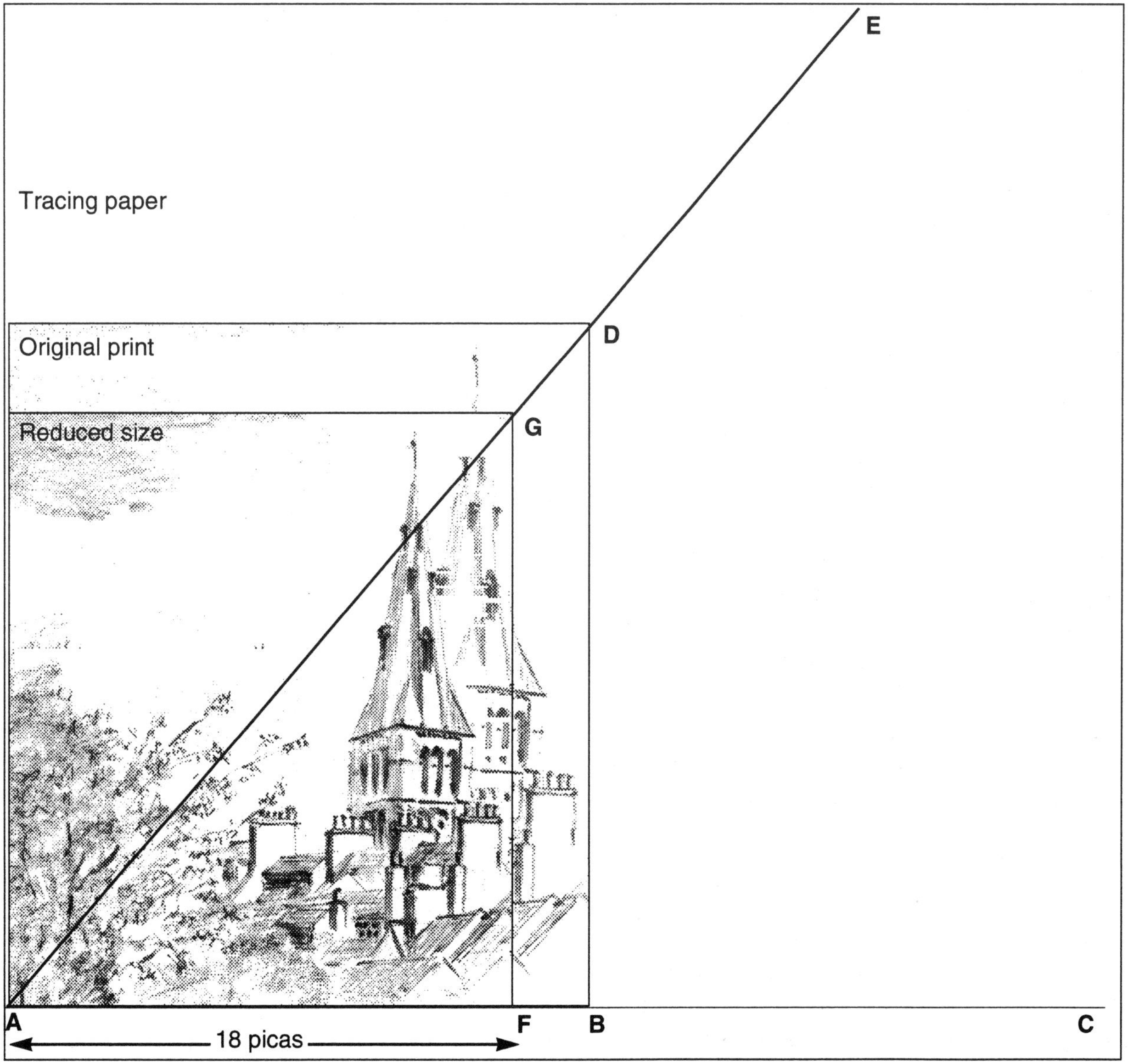

E

Tracing paper

D

Original print

G

Reduced size

A F B C

18 picas

Scaling a picture by the diagonal line method.

required height along the left side of the picture and then measuring at right angles from that point to the diagonal.

The same procedure can be used to determine where any point on the original will appear on an enlarged or reduced reproduction. This is explained in detail in Chapter 13.

Some designers prefer to work directly on the back of the photographic print rather than on tracing paper. To use this method you must place the photograph, image side down, on a light box and use a soft lead or chinagraph pencil (many modern photographic materials will not accept lead pencil). This provides a slight saving in time and is adequate for simple squared-up half-tone enlargement, or reduction, on publication-owned prints, but for anything more complex, and when using returnable prints, the tracing paper method is preferable.

The above methods work well for black-and-white or colour prints or other flat artwork but colour transparencies may require a different approach. The ideal, of course, is to have prints (black-and-white prints will serve) produced from the transparencies. These can be used to to indicate crops, cut-outs etc. in the usual way and must accompany the transparencies to the printer or repro house (where the pictures will be photographically or electronically copied).

Unfortunately time (or budgets) will not always allow for the production of prints. The solution depends upon the resources available. A well-equipped studio will have the means to project a transparency on to a ground glass screen, adjustable so that the image can be fine-tuned to the desired size and then traced. But even when such equipment is not to hand, with a little ingenuity, an ordinary projector can be used to produce tracings from 35mm transparencies. Project the image on to a sheet of paper on which the required size is already marked, adjust the image to fit and then trace it. For larger transparencies a light box (or even a window) will enable you to make same-size tracings. The tracings will then, of course, be treated as if they were prints.

If there are to be no crops, or if the crops are simple straightforward trims, it may not be necessary to make tracings at all. On mounted transparencies the crops can be indicated on the mounts. Take great care to avoid marking the emulsion side of the transparency – and that includes marking with the print of a finger or thumb. In the case of transparencies within protective clear plastic sleeves, the crop marks can be shown on the sleeve using chinagraph pencil. In addition, provide registration marks for the corners of the transparency in case it should move within its sleeve. There should be no need to take the transparency out of its protective sleeve.

6 Shapes on the page

To produce successful page design you must first understand the elements available to you.

The first is provided by the paper itself – or, at least, those areas of the paper which are not impressed with ink: in other words, white space.

Three further elements are provided by the application of black ink to the paper: the even grey tone of the text, the areas of varied tone provided by photographs or artwork, and the blacks of headlines, heavy rules, borders, and so on. (We will leave other colours of inks or papers out of our considerations for the moment.)

White, black and a range of greys may seem a limited palette from which to conjure an infinite number of interesting designs, but a browse at any magazine stand will reveal how wrong that view would be. Take, for example, the grey tone of the text; note how the 'colour' varies from one magazine to another, from page to page within one magazine, or between different areas of text on a single page. (If the variations in tone are not immediately apparent try looking at the pages through narrowed eyelids.) We can control these variations by the way we specify typeface, style, size, weight, leading and letter- and word-spacing.

Note also how often those areas of grey tone make up large simple shapes (usually rectangles) with photographs, line artwork and white space providing areas of contrasting shape and tone.

Because you are restricted to those four elements, you should not scatter them about the page. This produces weak, spotty, undistinguished and disorganized pages; an optical obstacle course for those eyes attempting to read the text. Mass each element to create strong bold designs with shapes of contrasting weight, proportion and direction.

The more you analyse magazine pages, the more you will be able to appreciate the infinite permutations made possible by variations of size, proportion, direction, weight and position of simple shapes. You will note that square shapes are generally less interesting than rectangles (although they can be useful for contrast purposes), that the use of an exaggerated rectangle (whether vertical or horizontal) adds extra interest, and that further interest comes from contrasting vertical and horizontal shapes.

PAGE ARCHITECTURE

The shapes of the different elements are the foundation stones of page design. A page which fails because of bad foundations cannot be propped up by the application of ornamentation. Because of the fundamental importance of these basic shapes, time spent in studying their relationship on the pages of magazines is never wasted. Note the interaction, study how balance has been achieved, pay particular attention to the white space, cut up pages and rearrange them, see how a simple change of position of one element can transform a design.

Further study and analysis of the most pleasing designs could lead you to the simple guidelines opposite.

The first element is the white space provided by a blank spread (right) to which is added the grey tone of the text (below).

A remote village on the windswept moorland of Cumbria is an appropriate place to find the major supplier of Naafi's fastest growing range – adventure training clothing and equipment.

Morland village is the home of Survival Aids, a company set up just seven years ago in an unheated barn near Carlisle, which now has a mailing list of over 100,000; uses a sophisticated minicomputer to handle orders, stock control, despatch, marketing, office procedures and accounts; employs 35 staff; runs two shops; and commands 80 per cent of the market in the supply of equipment for survival against the rigours of the elements.

'As recently as 1979 good quality survival equipment was hard to find' said Nick Steven, managing director of Survival Aids ' – as I discovered when I was in the Army. My plan was to fill the gap – and I had to develop the market from scratch.'

The first product, a survival ration pack, was the starting point in what developed into a range of over 500 items.

Many of the products are made locally by sub-contractors. Residents of two local disabled centres are employed assembling the range of own-brand packs, and most of the 'Gore-Tex' products are made on a cottage-industry basis. Naafi lists just 26 of the items in the Survival Aids range.

'Although the range you deal in is small compared to our total stock' said Mr. Steven, 'the Naafi business is worth 4% of our total sales. You are our single most important customer, with orders of around £110,000 over the past year.

Good for morale

'Survival Aids and Naafi together provide an important service. The goods we sell are important to the morale of the individual Serviceman. That's not to say issue equipment is no good. I think the British soldier is one of the best equipped soldiers in the world; he gets the best kit for the money available – but that money is limited.'

Naafi's range of adventure training gear – which includes clothing and equipment from other suppliers such as Berghaus – was introduced to Naafi's customers in a specialist catalogue in 1985, and in the first year turnover reached £89,000, establishing a strong demand.

In the three months up to November 1986, total sales were £73,000 – £47,000 in the UK and £26,000 overseas.

'The large volume of sales in the first year didn't come as a total surprise to us' said John Milcham, assistant to manager UK trading (marketing). 'We had been getting feed-back from district and shop managers that soldiers were going out and spending quite large amounts of money on gear for training and exercises, and so we thought "why not try to get that business?" We did, and the market is still growing.

'We are constantly reviewing our range and keeping it up to date. We seem to have read the market, and most of the 36 lines are selling well. Sometimes we will consider removing a slow seller from the range, but it pays not to be too hasty. A little while ago, demand for the mini survival tool almost disappeared but, just as it was being reviewed, sales climbed back to a healthy level.'

The best selling lines include a 'bivi bag' (lightweight sleeping bag cover), camouflage bungees (elasticated hooked cords), and a camouflage wallet – all supplied by Survival Aids. The Crusader rucksack, retailing at around £120, has been a huge success. This is supplied direct from the manufacturer, Berghaus.

'Surprisingly, we were selling around 25 sets of thermal underwear a month in the summer' said Mr. Milcham ' – it should be really popular in the winter.'

Among recent additions to the range – a waterproof notebook and refill, insect repellent spray, camouflage tee-shirt, and a Norwegian army shirt.

From the supplier's point of view, Mr. Steven is conscious that sales staff should be aware of the qualities of the products in the range. 'The shop assistant needs to know the difference between different fabrics, like Gore-Tex, which is waterproof and ideal for outer-wear, and Meraklon, suited for use in thermal underwear. The goods have to be ordered through a catalogue and the soldier may not be fully aware of what he is buying and turn to the Naafi staff for advice.'

Valuable tip

'There are always problems buying goods through a catalogue' says Mr. Milcham, 'but I think most of our customers – being familiar with survival equipment through their work – are aware of the qualities of the kit they intend to buy. The thing that most concerns them is the waiting period before the goods are delivered. So we are trying to encourage those shops near training camps, or where there are visiting units like the TAs, to carry a small range in the shop against chance purchases. That way the customer is satisfied and we make a firm sale on demand.'

'We value our connection with Naafi' said Mr. Steven 'and look forward to extending the range we supply to you. If an item is available on the market, Survival Aids will do its utmost to provide it.

'Strange requests? We've had a few, but nothing we couldn't handle – the odd shark repellent kit, that kind of thing....'

The mixed tones of the illustrations are added and, finally, the 'line' elements complete the spread.

Moving in the right direction

Adding adventure training gear to Naafi's range has helped sales – Helen Walkey reports

The guidelines

Keep each element to a bold but simple shape.

Contrast one shape with another by varying their sizes, proportions, and directions.

SEEDS OF SUCCESS

In the middle of the 1970s, Chile adopted a market economy in place of the previously nationalised economy. Within this new business environment the Group's local tobacco subsidiary began a programme of diversification, initially into the snack foods sector and subsequently into fruit juices and tinned foods. The latest venture is in biotechnology, as Pedro Jullian, General Manager of Empresas CCT now outlines.

A consistent economic policy has enabled Chile to overcome the world recession and to meet all the liabilities of her large external debt. The changing economic scene in the 70s and 80s has yielded many benefits including the impressive growth in non-traditional exports; in 1973, for example, 80 per cent of income from Chilean exports came from copper, today only 42 per cent.

Through research and development the quality of Chilean tobacco has been improved so that today it enjoys access to international markets. In 1981 the first export of 100 tons of Burley leaf to the USA took place, with in 1985, exports to Japan. In 1987 a total of 1,700 tons were exported and over 2,000 tons will be the target in 1988.

The development and growth of oriental tobacco has enabled progress to be made in areas of limited agricultural potential where the economy lacks alternative crops and other sources of income. The company has also initiated a vast reafforestation plan in tobacco growing areas.

Today, Empresas CCT enjoys the biggest share of the domestic cigarette market, despite competition from local manufacturers and many imported brands. Our market leaders are American-type filter cigarettes such as *Derby, Record, Advance, Hilton* and *Belmont* and among the international brands produced by Chiletabacos are *Viceroy, Lucky Strike, Kent, Pall Mall, Barclay* and *JPS*.

1985 was a very special year for the company. Compania Chilena de Tabacos became Empresas CCT, to lead our present group. The prime objective of Empresas CCT is to consider new investments, provide services and advice to subsidiary companies, and enable them to achieve greater productivity and efficiency.

In September of that year, Chiletabacos was set up as a tobacco subsidiary. Recently, a new cigarette factory has been opened in Casablanca — to replace an older building in Valparaiso which had been severely affected by three earthquakes and a fire in its 50 year history.

The climate and the soil of the central region of Chile are good for agriculture and both natural and industrially processed Chilean products are very popular overseas. With this export potential, Empresas CCT acquired a consortium known as Consorcio Agroindustrial de Malloa, the country's leading canning group.

Its products, such as tomato sauce, ketchup, jams, fruit juices and tinned vegetables, are undisputed market leaders in the Chilean food market. However, because of the limited size of the local market, the main growth potential for Malloa is export.

Malloa currently exports to 21 countries with the USA and Japan the main markets for tomato concentrate and pure apple juice. Exports of both fresh and tinned asparagus are now being made to the USA and, while Malloa is also consolidating its share of the Latin American market, it is also opening up new markets in Indonesia, Malaysia, the Philippines and Korea.

The management of Malloa has enjoyed a particularly successful relationship with the 400 farmers who provide the raw materials. The technical and financial advice and assistance has enabled land supervised by Malloa to produce an average of 72 tons of tomatoes per hectare, a yield which is considered one of the highest in the world. ▷

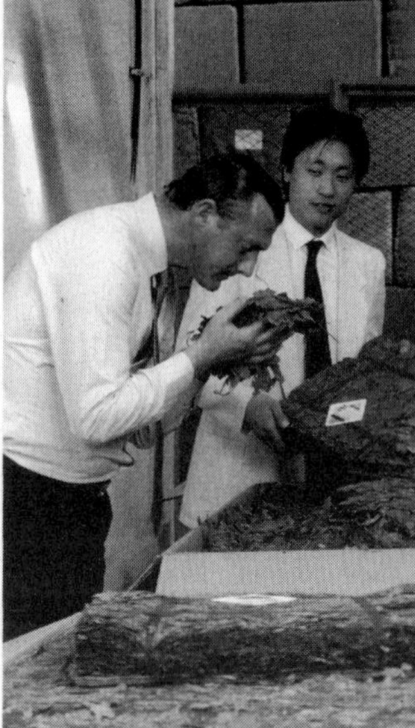

***Far left:* Malloa has the capacity to process 2,000 tons of tomato concentrate a day.**

***Left:* A Japanese client inspects Chilean Burley leaf before its export.**

***Below:* The Bioplant operation involves intense research activity.**

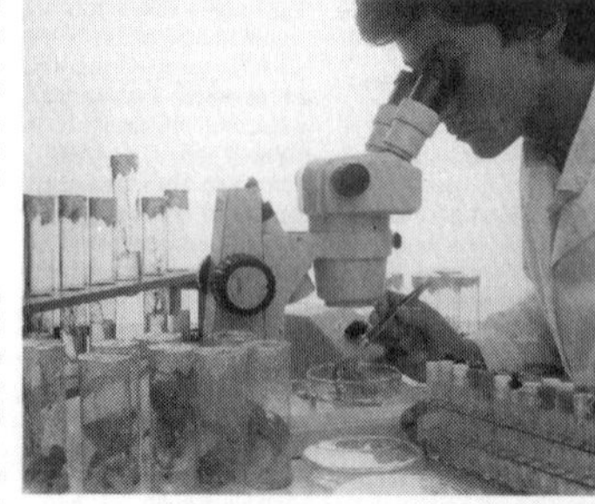

18 19

Note the opposing directional stresses of the two main pictures in this feature opening from BAT Industries' Outlook. *Making the upright picture more dominant would have given the spread more impact.*

David Perritt, president of D'Allaird's and of Peoples

a colourful atmosphere.

In the same building lies the key to another of the company's successes: its manufacturing arm Modes D'Allaird's. This supplies 40 per cent of D'Allaird's merchandise as well as supplying some lines to M&S Canada.

The large, air conditioned factory is just a few steps away from the offices – so liaison between selectors and manufacturers could not be easier.

All 300 staff at Modes D'Allaird's are skilled operators able to switch from making dresses to jackets or skirts according to demand.

"The work is labour intensive and standards are very high," said Denys Williamson, vice-president of Modes D'Allaird's and general manager of all manufacturing operations.

"We are able to produce development samples quickly and can be flexible with orders. We advise selectors on things such as cost implications and, if necessary, suggest modifications. Any money we save stays in the same company."

A close check is kept on quality control at every stage of production and D'Allaird's has its own laboratories to test fabrics.

Many of the fabrics used by Modes D'Allaird's are bought in Canada, but goods are also sourced from the Far East, Europe, the UK and the US.

The factory has a computerised pattern design system and employs six designers. It is spread over three floors – a different operation on each.

Goods from the factory floor travel only a short distance to the 75,000 sq ft distribution centre on the fifth floor. This operation has been speeded up with a new, computerised system for automated allocation and distribution.

Physical distribution presents a challenge in Canada as stores are widely spread out. D'Allaird's has one vehicle for local deliveries and is considering a second. The bulk of transportation is carried out by outside companies with 45 per cent of the work done in conjunction with M&S Canada.

D'Allaird's employs its own programmers and analysts and has some ambitious plans for new information technology systems. "We want to react more quickly to trends," said Stephen White, senior manager, central operations.

"There will also be changes at point of sale (POS) terminals with the introduction of a new taxation system in Canada in January 1991."

All D'Allaird's stores have POS tills and supply daily sales figures to head office. This data is consolidated at the end of each week on the corporate mainframe computer in Toronto which supplies D'Allaird's with weekly updates.

Not content with its present loyal customers, D'Allaird's is keen to extend its appeal and is currently upgrading its merchandise.

Selectors have been working closely with internal designers to develop new ranges in upgraded fabrics and more fashionable styles. Fashion colours such as magenta, purple, gold and jade have also made an impact in the latest collections. Areas such as casual wear and two-piece dresses have proved big successes and selectors are always looking at new resources and suppliers.

They work hand in hand with outside suppliers to agree specifications for garments such as coats and knitwear. An emphasis is placed on conformity of size and fit and all merchandise bears D'Allaird's own label.

To complement the upgraded merchandise, a store modernisation programme is being implemented over the next two to three years. Display techniques have been updated and stores given a warmer look with the use of wood and new lighting and fittings.

Store operations liaise regularly with store staff to get feedback from them and customers.

Eight store managers work as regional managers reporting directly to head office.

D'Allaird's employs a total of 1,300 people and its high standards of benefits and training mirror those of Marks & Spencer.

A recent staff initiative is an environmental committee consisting of representatives from across the business. Schemes already in place include recycling of cans and plastic clothes hangers.

The company retains a family feel and although stores are spread out, staff keep in regular contact. At head office, aerobic classes, baseball games parties and outings ensure that fun is always on the agenda.

Looking to the future, David Perritt said: "We aim to continue to enhance our market share by offering our customers the styles, colours and fabrics they want and ensuring that shopping at D'Allaird's is always a pleasure." M&S

— 32 —

Above, Hubert Street store, Montreal. Below left and right, customers browse through the autumn collection featuring new fashion colours in Place Vertu.

— 33 —

A continuation spread from M&S World, *the Marks & Spencer management magazine, which uses four pictures but varies shapes and sizes and makes one picture dominate as a focal point. Rules and small graphics (here a maple leaf) act as continuation symbols.*

Above, left: A Naafi mobile goes ashore on the Falklands; centre: carrying out a routine service; right: a supplies drop to a shop.

Far right: Checking out at an Army camp after a delivery

Below: Ken Matthews, manager transport department

Keeping Naafi on the move

Finding out about the transport operation with Eleonore Kostur

THE wheels of Naafi's worldwide business are kept turning by a fleet of 1,148 vehicles ranging from the heaviest of articulated trucks to a humble scooter.

They roll through the green lanes of England and the motorways of central Europe, the tropical scenery of the Far East, and the muddy roads of the Falkland Islands.

'The problems vary from one country to another' says Ken Matthews, manager of transport department, whose responsibilities encompass all four of Naafi's trading departments.

'Singapore's intense humidity brings corrosion problems, and the exceptional congestion and traffic restrictions led to us using a scooter to collect the mail from the town centre.

'In Gibraltar some 22,000 motorists drive around on two-and-a-half square miles of road, causing congestion and heavy fuel consumption. In Cyprus we need specially-built vehicles to meet the unusual regulations governing width and height. The climate and roads of Belize lead to many breakdowns – but spare parts are often unavailable.'

Among the key figures helping Mr. Matthews overcome these obstacles are his two assistant managers Peter Putt and Arthur Dicker, together with Ron Tadd, the expert on budgeting, and Bob Haywood and Margaret Statham, who look after insurance and accident processing.

Mr. Putt's special responsibilities include planning, utilisation, performance and accountability. He sees the vehicles as the life-blood of the corporation. 'Not much happens without the need for transport' he claims 'and a lot of money is involved.'

He estimates that if the whole fleet was wiped out it would cost £11 million to replace – and operational costs run into millions of pounds a year.

'When you see a Naafi "artic" on the road with a full load it represents anything up to £90,000 in corporation assets' he added.

'When a seven-ton temperature-controlled vehicle costs over £25,000 a year to operate in the UK, it is hardly surprising if we sometimes seem to be a little pre-occupied with costs and the continual search for systems improvement.

'Every effort is made to utilise the space on vehicles returning to warehouses after deliveries are made – even an empty container costs money. In the interests of economy vehicles should be loaded both ways.'

In Germany, the transport branch, under the control of Tony Wellbelove, operates a system where hundreds of cans of beer and minerals are collected each week for direct delivery to clubs and shops, by-passing the need for warehousing. All the scheduling, customs papers etcetera are processed by transport staff.

Naafi lorries also run a daily shuttle service to import milk from Denmark.

In all, the European Service fleet covers around four million miles a year delivering some 300,000 tonnes of merchandise.

Frequent inter-warehouse trips are now made from Germany to England. Naafi lorries leave the Continent with, for example, wine from the Mosel and electrical products from Holland before returning with British goods from Amesbury.

Local responsibility for transport in the UK is divided between three regional transport managers – Martin Everett, Len Dore and Peter Davies – with depots and workshops in London, Amesbury, Aldershot, Plymouth, Portsmouth, Darlington, Lincoln and Soham in Cambridgeshire.

A severe test of their staff and vehicles was provided by the Falklands dispute. 'That really did stretch us' said Mr. Matthews. 'There were deadlines to meet at ports and airfields – often with only minutes to spare – but we met every commitment.'

Lincoln, a typical UK depot, serves establishments in Lincolnshire, Yorkshire, the Midlands and East Anglia. Eight HGV3 vehicles make its seven daily runs, leaving one behind as a reserve.

The working day begins when most people are still asleep and the vehicles cover 6,900 miles, making 510 drops each week.

'All the drivers know each other's routes as they work on a rota,' explained Alan Collins, the depot foreman. 'It combats boredom, and means that, in an emergency, any driver can take over any route.'

About half the total UK fleet comprises passenger-carrying vehicles and vans, ranging from cars for field officials to shop delivery vans and the estates required by furnishing and vending branches.

Looking after the vehicles is a team of maintenance staff and fitters.

'A fitter's job is highly skilled and responsible,' said Mr. Dicker. 'A slip-up could result in a major accident.

'In our workshops we undertake virtually everything from major repairs to routine servicing. The quarterly maintenance bill for the UK fleet alone is £100,000.'

The commercial vehicles are serviced every 6,000 miles or every two months. They also undergo stringent tests at MOT testing centres.

'But commercial vehicles can be stopped at any time by the Ministry of Transport' Mr. Dicker said. 'If an inspector finds any defects he is empowered to order the vehicle off the road – an expensive temporary loss of the vehicle.'

8

9

council from discussing its report into Rechem, but also stopping it from carrying out further tests on the company.

Torfaen argues that it is not using Rechem as a political stick with which to beat the Welsh Office, but is dealing with an issue of legitimate public concern - which, it says, has reached a point where it should be allayed. The main tenet of the council's argument is that the plant should never have been sited at its Pontypool location in the first place - a problem best solved by the secretary of state through a public enquiry.

Rechem rejects most of the council's arguments with as much gusto as the council puts them - and the verbal ping pong will no doubt continue for some time yet - with the lawyers the main beneficiaries.

"In the early eighties the issues being thrown at us involved claims about deformed cows, deformed children and affected crops in Scotland. Then it moved down to Wales. But one by one we've knocked them all on the head," says Lee.

The company does seem to be on safe ground. As a result of allegations levelled at Rechem, the government has been forced in the past into carrying out independent investigations in both Scotland and Wales. The results of these have shown unequivocally that either no problem exists at all, or else the problem is a known veterinary or other ailment that is no worse near Rechem's plants than anywhere else in the country.

"People get very emotional and feel guilty if they or their children have a problem - or if they are farmers, if they lose some cattle. If someone comes along and puts the thought in their minds that Rechem could be the cause they latch onto that. It's human nature and you can understand that."

Rechem responded by paying for people to take their children to specialists where they have been told that ailments or deformities have nothing to do with any environmental issues. "We've worked very hard on that and I think we've more or less killed that issue," says Lee.

Lee maintains that even environmentally aware countries such as Sweden where high temperature incineration was halted for a year while it was investigated, have agreed that it is safe to use the method. Sweden has a state incineration scheme, but nevertheless it cannot handle certain materials and sends them to Rechem in the UK.

Lee warms to the job of defending his company: "The leading expert in dioxins in the world - the guy who discovered in the mid-seventies that dioxins can be formed as a by-product of combustion - has thoroughly investigated us and has been on television in the UK saying what a wonderful job we do," he maintains.

"No one else does air monitoring or monitoring off the plant as we do. We've even embarrassed the government into starting to do it, because they didn't have a clue. They didn't even know that PCBs and dioxins were ubiquitous.

"All the way down the line we have bent over backwards to prove that what we do is entirely safe."

Lee argues that people also exaggerate the problem because of the word "waste." He

60

Graham Searle, a founding member of Friends of the Earth and now a non-executive director of Rechem. Today he berates some pressure groups for their lack of knowledge of toxic waste

maintains that the waste Rechem is dealing with is less noxious than many raw materials that are used in manufacturing, such as concentrated sulphuric acid - or even petrol.

"These things are going round the world all day, every day," says Lee. "Waste represents a tiny percentage of the hazardous materials on the road. People just don't appreciate this."

Rechem, founded in 1968, has always specialised in the incineration of hazardous waste. Bought by BET in 1972, it constructed three new high temperature plants in the early seventies - at Pontypool, Fawley near Southampton and Bonnybridge in Scotland. Several other companies also built such plants in the wake of the 1972 Deposit of Poisonous Waste Act. The act was the first legislation controlling the waste disposal industry and a response to scares about indiscriminate dumping. Seen by some as panic legislation, it was soon followed by the 1974 Control of Pollution Act which also tied in with the restructuring of local government.

"Everyone in the waste disposal industry got very excited thinking there were going to be great new opportunities," says Lee. "Specifically, they thought that many of the toxic materials that were going to landfill would have to be treated. They went rushing round buying effluent treatment companies and trying to get planning permission to build incinerators. I built one myself at the time for a company in Wakefield.

"But as it turned out, co-disposal of toxic and non-toxic waste in landfill sites continued to be quite successful and perfectly legal. The controls that the legislation was putting on the industry didn't have the effect of taking many materials out of landfill sites. The industry had jumped prematurely."

Because there were too many incinerators chasing too little business, a price-cutting war ensued. But there was no way incineration plants costing millions of pounds to build and operate could compete with landfill that cost about £5 a ton. The predictable outcome was a severe rationalisation of the industry and a series of plant closures.

The situation in the early eighties was that there were only four high temperature plants left in the country. Cleanaway had - and still retains - one at Ellesmere Port, while Rechem had the other three. It was at this point that public concern over the environment began to gain ground.

Rechem started to come in for criticism for burning toxic waste, but at the same time people did not want landfill sites near them either - it was the start of the so-called nimby syndrome, "not in my back yard."

The opposition became louder and in 1984 it culminated in a massive campaign by the public and the media against Rechem's Bonnybridge plant. "It got to the point of mass hysteria," says Lee. "If anything nasty happened in Scotland, Rechem was accused of being to blame for it. The local community was coming out with ridiculous statements - such as cows being born with two heads - and they were being fired up by the media."

Simultaneously, Rechem was in financial trouble, losing some £110,000 in 1984. Until then it had kept its head above water, and despite the rationalisation of the industry it had been determined to keep three plants

DIRECTOR NOVEMBER 1989

Waste adhesive - a standard disposal problem. "If you want all the benefits of modern society, one of the payments you make is toxic waste," says Lee

open. But Bonnybridge had never made any money - the Scottish market had failed to develop and it was too far away from the larger markets of the south. Now, with the added broadside of damaging publicity, it was taking up a vast amount of Rechem's money and management resources. Finally, BET decided to close the plant.

"They should have made that decision years before," says Lee. "But the company was still run by the two scientists who had started it in 1968. Their hearts were in the right place, but they weren't what you'd call businessmen. They were running it more like a university department and they felt it was sacrosanct to have three plants. In the end performance got so bad they had to close and it helped to gear demand closer to supply."

In 1984, Lee was involved in BET"s landfill company, Biffa. There he worked with Richard Biffa, a member of the family that had originally set up the Biffa company, who was subsequently to partner him in a buy-out of Rechem.

Lee was asked to take over the management of Rechem on January 1, 1985, in addition to his responsibilities at Biffa. The incumbent managing director had had enough and wanted to take early retirement.

"We decided that the make or break time had come for Rechem," says Lee. "There was such a lot of effort and management resources going into it that unless it was going to make real money, we were just wasting our time, which would be better served elsewhere where we were making a lot of money."

Lee went through a period of consultation with customers and organisations such as the Confederation of British Industry and the Chemical Industries Association. The result was an ultimatum to customers.

"We said to them quite bluntly: 'you either pay a fair rate for this service that allows us to do the job properly and safely and enables us to invest in new technology for the future, or forget it. You must support us or we'll close.'

"We put in some pretty big price increases and brought in more salesmen and new senior management and we changed the philosophy of the company. We continued to provide technical excellence, but we became much more market orientated.

"We reduced the volume and concentrated on waste that could *only* be incinerated and got the necessary revenue from that."

On the back of the new environmental awareness felt by companies not wishing to alienate suppliers, customers, shareholders and employees, the business started to take off. Later on in 1985 BET decided that it was going to concentrate only on core areas of its business where it could dominate.

"Rechem didn't fit in with this new strategy," says Lee. "To BET it represented a load of problems, especially always being in the newspaper - even though we were starting to do well. It just wasn't worth the management's time for them."

Lee and Richard Biffa bought the company in December 1985, with funds raised from City buy-out financiers. Rejoicing in their new freedom from the shackles of a parent group policy they drove the business forward. For example they invested about £2m in a new scrubbing section at Pontypool, which gave Rechem a boost in the volume it could handle of the difficult waste that commands the highest prices and for which industry was crying out for disposal.

"There is no doubt that part of our success has been down to timing," concedes Lee. "Especially since 1986, big multinationals have been taking their responsibilities very seriously, even to the point of forming world environ-

DIRECTOR NOVEMBER 1989

61

Above: Continuation pages from Director, *which make use of a blank column for the personality picture in this article on pollution. Opposite: A multiple-picture spread with lots of size, shape and direction variations accentuated by white space. Note the 'tyre-track' rules.*

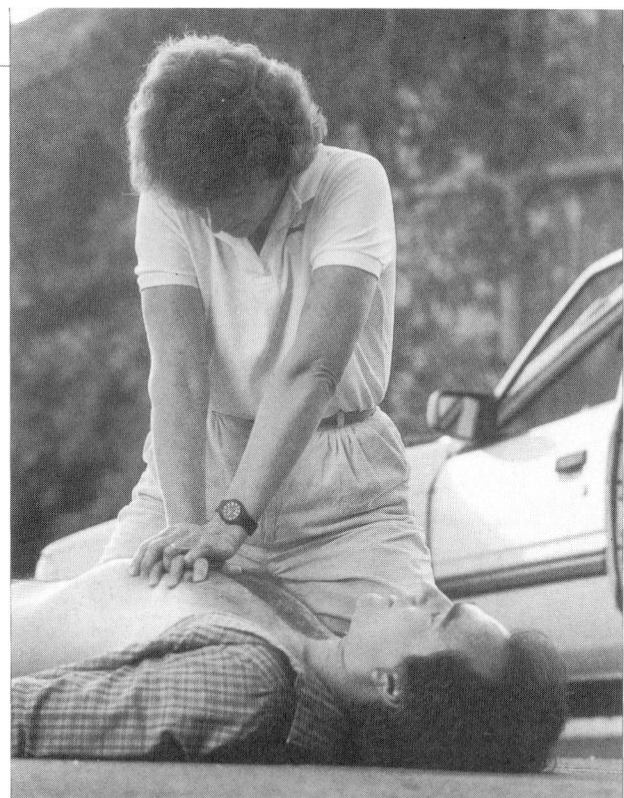

Will you die of a broken heart?

Heart disease is now the primary killer in the Western world. Certain people are more vulnerable than others. How can *you* protect yourself? And what can we all learn from the Scottish experience?

For thousands of years mankind has recognised the central role of the heart, many civilisations seeing it as the very centre of the soul. From the cruel sacrifices of the Aztecs to modern images for St Valentine's Day, (even in the phrase "broken-hearted") there is a deeply rooted conviction that the heart is much more than just a vital organ of the body.

Vital indeed; the heart is without doubt the most hard-working organ. Every day it beats more than 100,000 times and pumps some 7,500 litres of blood to provide nutrients and remove waste to and from every cell in the body. But, as with machines, without careful maintenance problems can arise. It is a disturbing thought that the average Westerner spends more time and money on his car than keeping his body in the best possible condition.

> It is a disturbing thought that the average Westerner spends more time and money on his car than keeping his body in the best possible condition.

This attitude is beginning to change as the health culture started in the 1980s really takes hold. Preventative medicine in all its forms is now entrenched into the modern lifestyle but, with most infectious diseases in the Western world kept under control through drugs, better food, housing and general public health, heart disease is now the West's number one killer. It is particularly rife in the United Kingdom as a whole and *especially in Scotland*.

Some people, it must be said, have an inherent disposition towards heart troubles. For once, nature is on the side of women who in general suffer fewer heart problems, especially before the menopause as oestrogens have a protective influence. There are always people who break all the rules and live to a ripe old age but for most of us, particularly if it is " in your genes", we need all the help we can get.

To help yourself avoid heart trouble you should avoid stress, obesity, a high fat diet, alcohol and, if you smoke, give it up; choose a well-balanced diet, eat more fibre and eat dairy products in moderation, avoid sugar, red meat and fatty foods; exercise in moderation, try to raise your heart rate for about twenty minutes each day (a brisk walk is best).

Stress has been called "the disease of modern living". If you have a highly stressed life-style, if you are a "born worrier" or a perfectionist or you are subjected to stress-inducing pressures, you could be a candidate for heart disease. Stress increases the heart's work-rate; it raises adrenalin levels, making the heart beat faster and, if this happens too often, damage to the circulatory system can result.

If you are over-weight, your heart has to work harder to enable you to lead a normal life. Weight is often directly associated with diet and lack of exercise; eating the "wrong" foods can not only result in increased weight but also in increased cholesterol levels (see adjacent article), which has a direct bearing on the narrowing of the arteries. Exercise helps to keep one's body-weight proportional but also develops the heart muscle, so that it becomes more able to bear additional loads from time to time.

It used to be only the Chancellor of the Exchequer who used to clobber the smokers and drinkers on a regular basis; now it is the medical profession too for entirely different reasons. In this context, both smoking and excessive drinking make important, harmful contributions. Alcohol can contribute to obesity; it also encourages the deposit of cholesterol, increases the heart-rate and blood pressure; it can also combine disastrously with medication. Nicotine stimulates the production of adrenalin, increases the heart-beat and also promotes cholesterol build-up. The other harmful substance in tobacco smoke is carbon monoxide; this reduces the oxygen level in the blood. Both nicotine and carbon monoxide encourage thrombosis (blood clotting).

What is heart disease?

Usually, excepting congenital defects, most heart disease is caused by a hardening or narrowing of the coronary arteries by fatty deposits resulting from an excess of cholesterol in the blood. This narrowing restricts the blood supply to the heart muscle, causing the heart to labour without its proper supply of oxygen. This painful condition is known as angina.

The condition becomes serious if the coronary artery becomes completely blocked, usually because a blood clot seals up an already constricted blood vessel; when this happens and an area of the heart muscle is deprived of all oxygen, the result is popularly known as a heart attack. This may vary in severity depending on how much of the heart muscle is affected; it can, of course, be fatal.

Angina can be relieved using a range of pharmaceutical products mainly designed to lower the blood pressure by a variety of different means. In addition, there is another class of pharmaceutical treatment which will reduce or prevent blood clotting and so minimise the risk of heart attack.

Bayer has specialised in cardio-vascular and cerebrovascular treatments for many years. The most spectacular break-through came in the early 1970s when the chemical substance known as nifedipine was evaluated in clinical tests; it has shown that in 70–80% of cases, with patients suffering from angina, attacks either became much less frequent or stopped altogether. In recent years Bayer has introduced a number of modifications as well as important new drugs to add further sophistication to the treatment of angina, hypertension, thrombosis and other heart-related conditions.

This special interest in affairs of the heart led Bayer to sponsor a special campaign in Scotland, which has the highest incidence of heart disease in the world. Between 1986-1989, 11 million working days were lost in Scotland through coronary heart disease and other diseases of the circulatory system at an estimated cost of £450 million.

> Why Scotland should lead the world in heart disease is attributed to a coincidence of all the worst contributory causes.

It has been estimated that 90% of Scots have some degree of atheroma, the underlying pathological condition in cardiovascular disease, and that one Scot dies every hour from cigarette smoking. Such statistics led a Scottish GP, Dr Shirley McEwan, to band together with some of her colleagues to form SHARP – the Scottish Heart and Arterial disease

Zebulon Record *editor Keith Taylor: Only one dissension.*

Rose Atkinson: Sense of security.

friends and their teachers could hardly believe their good fortune.

'Zebulon has never had a corporation like Glaxo to call on for funds,' said Laura Spell, the school's law and politics teacher. 'The company has been overly generous.'

But the staff at Zebulon High recognize that Glaxo's contribution to the student community can be counted in more than dollars. Before Glaxo moved in, two years ago, the only industry in the predominantly farming area was textiles, and there was little incentive for high school students to bother with further education. But according to Laura Spell, Glaxo's presence is changing all that: 'Having hi-tech industry on the doorstep is opening the children's eyes to the kind of jobs there are in the world: it is encouraging them to go on with studying.'

For Amy Caulder, Angel Branoff and their fellow students who travelled to Washington, the workings of the capital – and the deliberations on Capitol Hill – opened their eyes still further. 'I never bothered to pay attention to the news before I went to Washington,' admitted Amy. 'Now it all makes so much more sense. And I learned what our Representatives in Congress can do for us – especially for our farmers.'

Many Carolina farmers are giving up any hope of their Congressmen doing anything for them as prices for their staple crops continue to fall and government subsidies fail to fill the gap. Rose and Ed Atkinson have been struggling with the rest of them. Their 160-acre farm in Johnston County, just a short ride from Zebulon, produces 39,900 lb of tobacco. But prices at auction have never been worse, and their small profits on the soybean, corn and cucumbers are only just enough to keep the farm viable.

Rose worked all hours to keep the farm going and look after their three children while her husband took to driving a truck across America to help make ends meet. When a job at Glaxo came up, Rose jumped at it. 'It's so different from anything I've done before,' she said. 'It is so clean and well-organized. It's hard work, but compared with 14-hour days on the farm it's a holiday.'

She started work on the packaging line at Zebulon and was quickly promoted to line leader. 'Running a farm teaches you to be disciplined, highly disciplined. That experience has helped me in this job. We had people working for us and that has helped me understand the problems of the people I report to.

'There are personality clashes which were never a feature of life on the farm, but you can understand why they happen and that helps you cope with them. What I get most of all, working for a company of this size, is a sense of security – and that's something you really appreciate after working for yourself.'

The local labour force around Zebulon clearly has some outstanding qualities and no one appreciates that better than Glaxo Inc.'s director of Human Resources, Ron McCord. 'The people of North Carolina were brought up on farms,' he explained. 'They were hard working, conscientious and determined. A tremendous work ethic is still around today: they are loyal, dependable, independent-minded folk,' he said.

Building from scratch, McCord had to go further afield for some of the professional staff – people with experience in the pharmaceutical business. A total of 379 people work at the Zebulon factory and another 685 at the Research Triangle Park headquarters. And there is no shortage of aspirant employees at headquarters. McCord receives several hundred unsolicited job applications every week. In Zebulon there is a waiting list of around 2,000.

Adds Plant Human Resources manager Rick Mark: 'Zebulon has a lot of talented people. Many of them had industrial experience before we came along. Some commuted into Raleigh every day, driving bumper ⇨

20

Police chief Wendel Perry: Aura of authority.

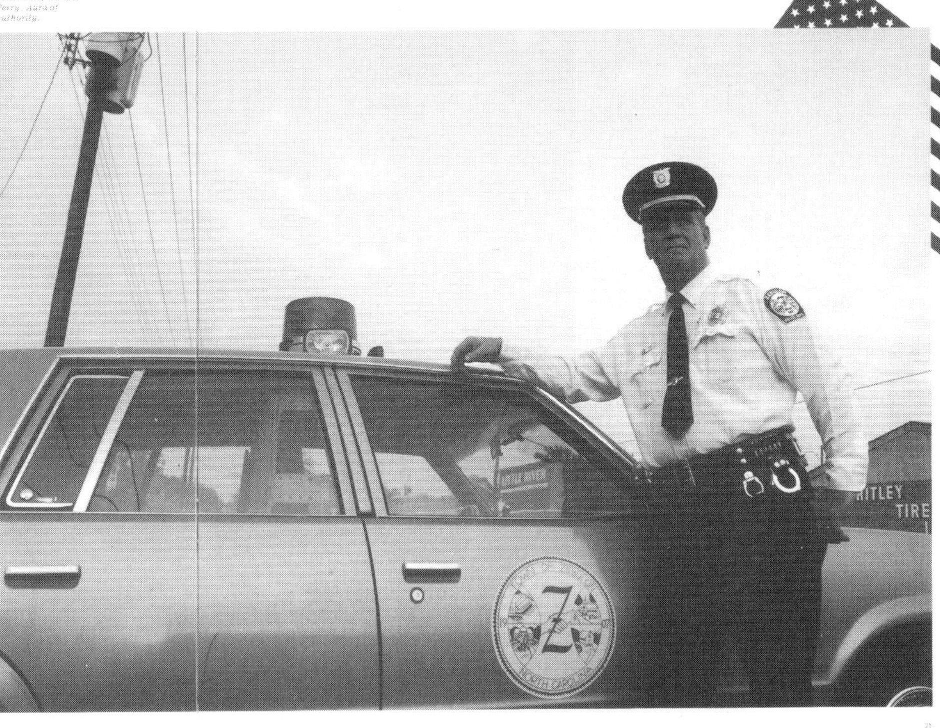

21

Above: A continuation spread from Glaxo World, *which makes excellent use of contrasting shapes and a dropped horizon.*

Opposite: Opening pages of a feature in Crosslink *(journal of the Bayer Group) in which the large upright photograph contrasts with the small horizontal drawing.*

Below: Medical representative Anita Flükiger details Dr Thomas Berther, a dermatologist in private practice
Right: Medical representative Ian Butler visiting a doctor's practice in Diemtigtal.
Bottom: Hospital sales representative Pierre Cruchaud (right) in discussion with Professor L.H. Blumgart (centre), Director of Intestinal and Transplantational Surgery, University Hospital of Berne, and Senior Registrar Dr Baer.

leadership by a major marketing effort, shaped by the need to meet local conditions (the 'local' market also includes Liechtenstein). There is no national health service in Switzerland, but practically the entire population (99 per cent, and moving towards 100 per cent) of 6.4 million has medical insurance. Some 90 per cent of costs are reimbursed to the patient.

Operating in such a business climate, and with a product portfolio of prescription medicines (and one OTC product – a basic Betnovate cream), Glaxo sells through wholesalers to doctors, retail pharmacists and hospitals. That is a statutory requirement. Some 50 per cent of the Swiss market is taken up by ethical and hospital sales, the rest by self-medication products, a considerable market segment in which Glaxo does not participate.

Up to now, Vock and his marketing team have naturally targeted doctors and hospital pharmacists. Glaxo has made little impact with the general public. However, that may have to change. Vock points out that there are about 350,000 people who suffer from migraine. Most have resigned themselves to living with the condition for the rest of their lives.

'We will have to make them aware that effective treatment is now available.'

However, he adds that the process must be handled carefully so that doctors do not feel that a pharmaceutical company is usurping its role. 'We have to remember that the doctors are our customers, not the patients.'

So the likely approach is to extend an existing marketing focus – helping doctors to be more competitive. And doctoring is a highly competitive business in this outstanding example of a free market economy – the ratio of patients to doctor (in own practice) is only 605:1.

Glaxo AG has been very active in providing help to doctors, beyond the provision of drugs and the essential related information. A move has been made towards providing treatment 'packages', so that patients can be provided with a Glaxo product plus, say, a general treatment booklet, anti-stress cassettes, diet sheet, or even such free aids as bed-raising blocks for sufferers from reflux oesophagitis.

In a country where four languages are in everyday use a good deal of effort goes into information. All Glaxo products are marketed and packaged in the two main languages, German and French, and many in the third official language, Italian. The fourth Swiss language, Romansch, although now officially encouraged, is still very much a minority tongue and not included by Glaxo.

Ironically, just at a time when the company might be about to adopt a higher public profile, it is distancing itself from the media men – physically, that is. Up to now the company has been based in the premises of the national broadcasting and television company.

However, expansion year-by-year has meant that Glaxo AG has outgrown its original home, and it is now planning a move to just outside Berne, to premises which will be able to support the company's continuing growth.

In 1974, the company sold just 14 different products. The number is now 32. Meanwhile, the original staff complement of 15 has grown to 67. This includes the addition of a second retail sales force and the expanded hospital sales team.

The sales resource was increased to cover the widened product range in late 1988. Vock's plans include a continuation of the growth of the number of sales forces and the creation of a trading subsidiary to Glaxo AG. 'Recruiting people is difficult in Switzerland, but we are luckier at Glaxo than most, as people stay with us for a long time,' he says.

Glaxo AG is now getting to a size when the way the company is managed must change. 'I still communicate directly with people as much as possible, but it is getting more difficult,' explains Vock. 'The management style of the company is changing. There is much more delegation.'

For the immediate future, great emphasis is being given to clinical trials of the various new products in the pipeline. Specially appointed clinical research associates will manage the trials for the new compounds, and possibly others – maybe even some licensed-in products if a suitable package can be put together. After, say, 18 ◄

Photographs by Geoff Tompkinson

26 27

Another spread from Glaxo World *following the same principle of using pics of different sizes and proportions while demonstrating a different design permutation. The flags provide an effective continuation symbol.*

7 Getting started

In almost any endeavour, the first step is usually the most difficult. To sit, pencil in hand, looking at a blank white page of the layout pad can induce a blankness of mind that rivals that of the paper.

This chapter offers a simple, almost mechanical method of getting those first vital marks on to the virgin sheet – on the principle that it is easier to improve an existing design than to produce a masterpiece at the first attempt.

To simplify the demonstration of the method, you will work on a two-page feature article for an A4 magazine with a three-column grid. The body text is to be set 10 on 12 pt. Times (six lines of text to every column inch) and your columns will contain 64 lines. It is a simple matter to transfer the method, once grasped, to any other grid and type specification.

You will need the materials and tools listed in Chapter 5 and an A3 grid sheet matching that in the illustration on page 40. Draw this up, using your type-scale and setsquare, on heavy paper or light card. Use bold lines in black ink to outline the page and column areas and lighter lines to mark off text lines. If you prefer, you need only mark off the text lines at ten-line (i.e. 10 pica or 1⅔ in.) increments.

Use a reducing photocopier to produce eight one-eighth size copies of the grid and mount them on the reverse of the original (as illustrated on page 41). It is worth producing a similar aid for any magazine you work on. Such masters will last for years if you cover both sides with clear adhesive film.

When the master is placed under the first page of your A3 layout pad with the eight mini-grids uppermost, the grids will be visible

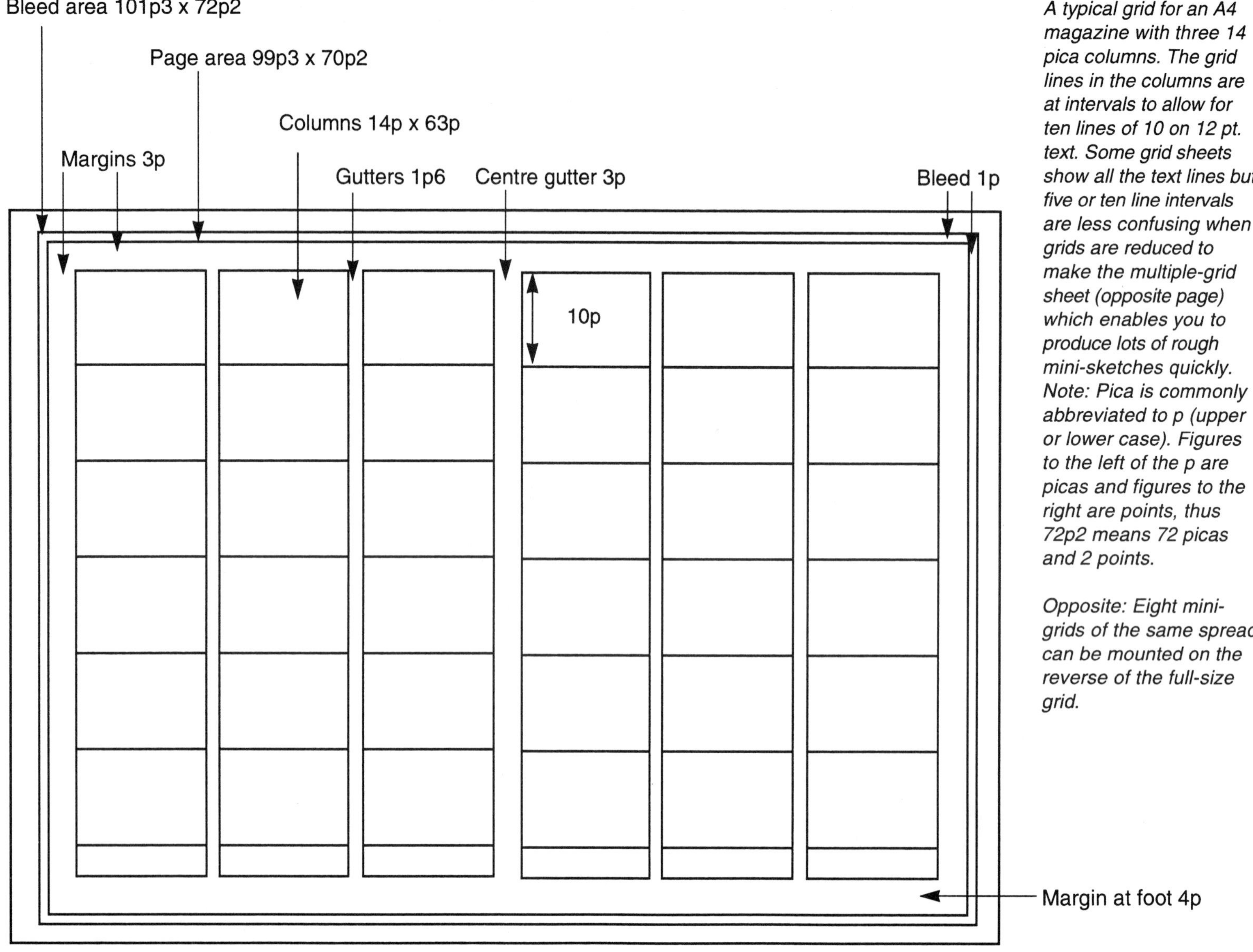

A typical grid for an A4 magazine with three 14 pica columns. The grid lines in the columns are at intervals to allow for ten lines of 10 on 12 pt. text. Some grid sheets show all the text lines but five or ten line intervals are less confusing when grids are reduced to make the multiple-grid sheet (opposite page) which enables you to produce lots of rough mini-sketches quickly. Note: Pica is commonly abbreviated to p (upper or lower case). Figures to the left of the p are picas and figures to the right are points, thus 72p2 means 72 picas and 2 points.

Opposite: Eight mini-grids of the same spread can be mounted on the reverse of the full-size grid.

through the layout paper. Mark the four corners of each spread on the layout paper.

For this exercise you will need copy and pictures for a two-page feature. (If you do not have manuscript and photographic prints to work with, cut suitable material from any magazine.)

KNOWING THE SUBJECT

Before you can begin to design the pages you must have an understanding of the subject matter so that you can produce a design which is appropriate. The typography and design which would suit a feature on Paris couture are unlikely to look right for a piece on the digging of the Channel Tunnel. So, read the copy and study the pictures. If, in the real world, you do not have the luxury of sufficient time to read every feature in full, you must either get a brief from the writer or your editor, or scan enough to understand the main thrust of the writer's message.

If, as often happens, you are expected to write the title and any straplines, standfirsts, crossheads, etc., understanding the subject is doubly important. If this should be one of your responsibilities, a useful tip is to make a note of key words from the text as you read; your list can prove a useful shortcut to an appropriate title, strapline or whatever is required.

Now you must cast off the copy as explained

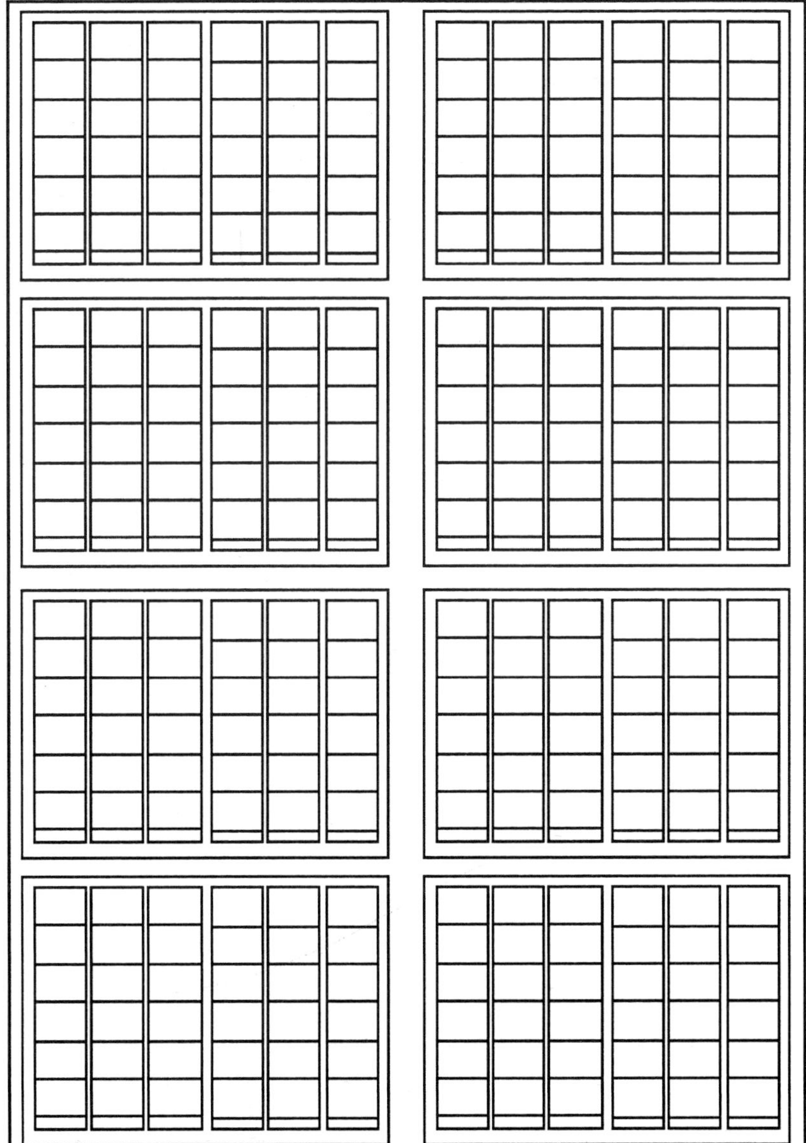

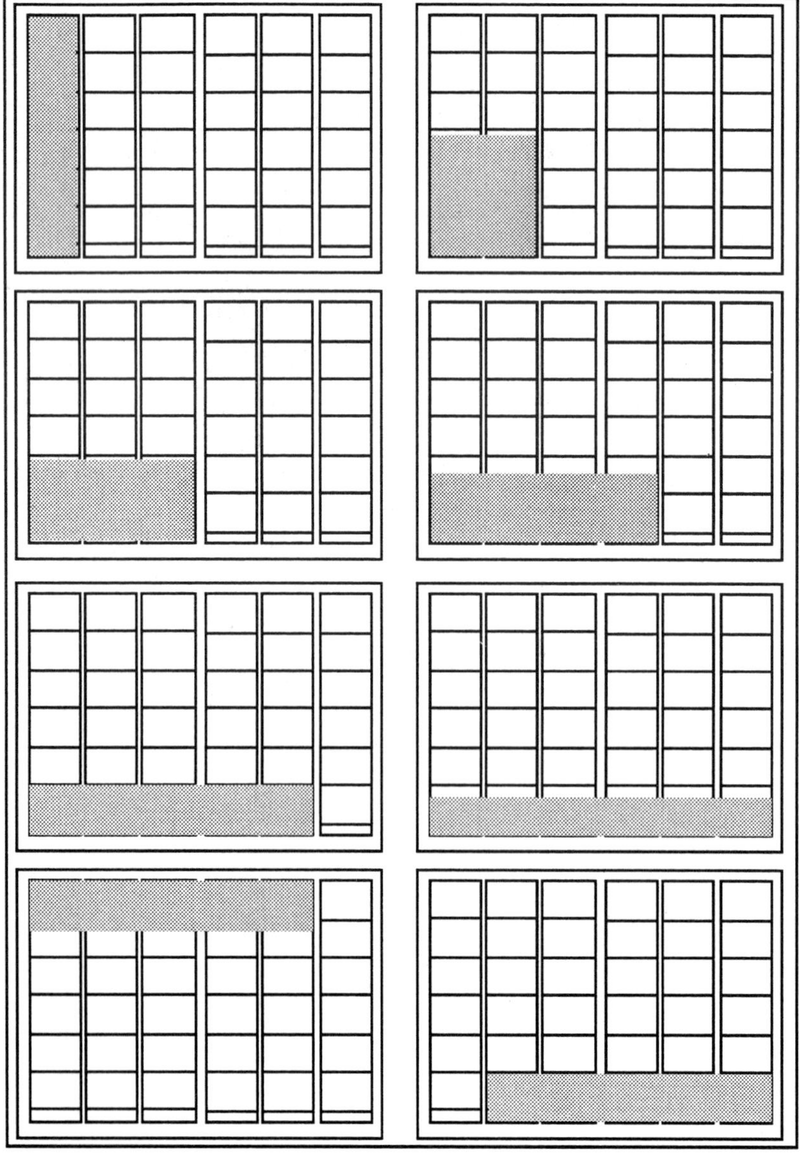

in Chapter 5. How many lines of type will the manuscript make on your pages? Make a note of that number on the first sheet of the manuscript and, for good measure, on the layout sheet too.

Progress from one mini-grid to the next on the layout sheet marking off, as you go, the areas the copy would take up if the number of lines was to be divided evenly between various numbers of columns. If, for example, the copy would fill one column, mark off a column on the first mini-grid. The same text would half-fill each of two columns, a third of three columns, and so on through to one-sixth of six columns. Mark up the mini-grids to show these areas.

TEXT ON THE MOVE

Although in the illustration the copy shapes have been marked in at the left and foot in each of the first six mini-grids, the position may be changed. The single column of text may be moved across to the right. The copy placed across four columns in the lower left of the grid could be moved to upper left, upper right, or lower right. In other words, you have defined shape possibilities for one of the elements in your design, but the shape itself can be moved around the page to any desired position.

Tear this sheet from the layout pad and place it where it can easily be referred to (the floor can sometimes prove useful if there is not too much traffic over it, or stick it on a pinboard or the wall).

Now you can turn your attention to the photographs. Frequently there will be more photographs than can be accommodated in the space available. In Chapter 13 we shall discuss illustrations in more detail but, for now, accept that fewer and bigger photographs will usually create more impact and be more appropriate than a greater number of small ones. (A number of small photographs will also cost more to reproduce than one large photograph covering the same area.) The next task may therefore be to make an appropriate selection from the available prints.

You may find it helpful to begin the selection by a process of elimination. Remove any prints which are badly exposed, out of focus, or in any other way of dubious technical quality – but do not confuse deliberate soft focus, graininess, or other effects produced to create or add to a particular mood or atmosphere, with poor technical quality. Photographs which lack any sense of scale, such as pieces of machinery without an operator, are best avoided, and you should reject visual non sequiturs such as the personality shot which shows the sitter apparently wearing a lampshade.

Eliminate those photographic clichés which you have seen time after time in magazines and newspapers.

Above: Sorting pictures into 'prime pic', 'must use', 'possibles' and discards.

Opposite: Mark out possible shapes for the text and then try different positions on the page.

Where's Old So-and-So?

The onset of winter brought a smile to the face of district manager **Dick Murray**. He left colleagues in Norwich preparing for cold weather while he headed off to the sunnier climes of Cyprus to replace **David Smith**.

Colin Holyoak also had something to smile about: the former club and shop manager successfully completed his DM training. He picked up the reins in Stamford district from **Jim Menzies**.

Down South, **Hammelore Anderton** took over the Zouch Farm families shop in Tidworth; **Megain Charles** is managing the Lucknow Barracks club nearby.

Also in South Central Region is **Dawn Taylor** following her promotion to manager at the Hotel Quebec Club, Erskine Barracks, Wilton.

In neighbouring London Region, **Irene Young** left the Adhara Road shop, Northwood, Middlesex, to manage the staff shop at headquarters Imperial Court.

She replaced **Rendle Cocks**, now at Chelsea Barracks from which **Richard Johnson** departed to manage the Nimrod Drive shop, Gosport, Hampshire.

The messing store at Woolwich has a new manager in **Michael Connolley**, formerly at the Sandhurst shop, Camberley, Surrey.

Susan Buckley – newly promoted to shop manager – moved from Beech Grove, Brookwood, Surrey to Broom Farm Estate, Windsor, Berkshire.

Also promoted – but to club manager – were: **Ian Davidson**, at the Collingwood Club, HMS Collingwood, Fareham; **Michael Stanfield**, now at Regents Park Barracks, London; **Kay Cooper**, at Rapier Barracks, Kirton-in-Lindsey, Lincolnshire; and **Carol Strudwick**, now at Garats Hay, Woodhouse, Leicestershire.

A departure from HMS Cambridge, Wembury, Devon, took manager **Dwaiyn Peace** to McMullen Barracks, Marchwood, Southampton.

The new manager at HMS Cambridge is **Deniece Moore**, formerly at the Flying Fish Club, HMS Osprey, Portland, Dorset.

In Western Region, **Susan Thow** is managing the Weeton Barracks club, Preston, Lancashire.

Across the water – in Northern Ireland - **Angela Shaw** took over at the Alexander Barracks club, Aldergrove, County Antrim, and **Robert Owens** is now the manager at the Ordnance Depot club at Kinnegar.

At sea, **Ron Leacy** is now managing the canteen aboard HMS Challenger, currently undergoing refit at Immingham.

Alec Brown joined HMS Phoebe on completion of her refit.

Mike Downey took over the canteen on HMS Penelope.

Gary Murphy travelled from Plymouth to Rosyth to take charge of the canteen on HMS Abdiel.

Andrew Stones, canteen manager, and **Andrew Stringfellow**, canteen assistant, transferred from HMS Jupiter (now under refit) to HMS Charybdis.

Major Bob Randerson, Officer Commanding the RAOC EFI, displays his MBE presented at Buckingham Palace by HM The Queen. With him are his wife, Camilla, and sons Martin (left) and Roderick.

Staff at Krefeld warehouse in Germany display their 25-year awards (from third left to right): Elfride Deus, Marie Trude Heinen, Adalbret Lehmann, Stan Barlow, Margret Doering and Klaus Behrendt. Presenting the awards were (left and second left) Bill Cunningham, supervisor of warehouses, and Peter Heinrich, administrator, European Service.

Bodo Schmidt (right), baker at Krefeld in Germany, receives his 25-year award from John Perry.

Friends and colleagues gave Mr. Schmidt an ornamental vase, presented by Evelyn Winkmann, assistant to bakery manager, Krefeld.

Horst Nitsch (right), receives his 25-year award at a presentation performed by Bob McGirr, food buyer European Service, to whom he was assistant.

Brigitte Christian, clerk, Gutersloh 'Å' Complex in Germany, receives her 25-year award and gifts from Ron Day, trading director.

Margot Rogiers, clerk at Wolfenbuttel in Germany, accepts her 25-year award from Colin Foster, assistant manager European Service.

Tang Kai Fai (left) chargehand at Cassino Lines, Hong Kong, receives his 25-year award from Colonel Denton, Army director, on his visit to Hong Kong.

Way Back When

First night surprise at hostel

I wonder how many Naafi-ites have had the pleasure of seeing one of our new Naafi hostels?

I was amazed and surprised when I walked into one: we ought to be very proud and thankful of the way the female staff's welfare is looked after.

When we arrived at the Bulford hostel I stood awhile and gazed at the new red brick building I was soon to enter as my home for a while. What did I perceive? Double gates each side of the garden with a drive leading up to the porch, four or five windows each side of the porch and about eight or nine windows above, giving the idea of plenty of fresh air and light.

I walked to the porch and rang the bell; I handed in my introduction letter to the smartly dressed girl in white and was told I was expected and would I wait in the lounge for matron. I could hardly get over my surprise at what had met my eye when walking through the door – the restful colour of the walls, the seat at the side ready for the weary and tired – the whole atmosphere gave one the feeling that this was a haven of rest.

Refreshing tea

I proceeded to the lounge and made my way to one of the easy chairs which I noticed were drawn close to the low red-bricked fireplace. While sitting there I glanced round and saw small tables down each side of the room, with wicker chairs placed round, and daffodils in vases on the tables; on the floor was a thick carpet; there was a large dining table in the centre; in the corner was a wireless, while a book cabinet was on one side of the fireplace and a sideboard on the other side. There were also some easy chairs placed here and there, just ready for someone to sit in them. I was just glancing at the pictures on the walls when matron came in with tea on a tray.

After a refreshing cup of tea, matron asked me if I would like to go upstairs. I was making my way across the hall when I espied an open door leading into the kitchen, I ventured in, asking matron if I might. The first thing I saw was the glass sliding doors of a dresser with the serving articles in, which I thought was a splendid idea for keeping the dust off. On the kitchen shelves were tins painted the same colour as the kitchen and the name of the ingredients in white, and then I found the stove with its bright steel work shining. Tucked into the corner was a wicker chair to rest those tired feet. I guessed the table in the centre had seen plenty of scrub and elbow grease, and I saw another stove for heating the hot water.

Marvellous view

I then made my way upstairs, and noticed everywhere was painted in the same delicate hue. As I was shown into a room I had to turn around and exclaim 'What a lovely room!'. There were three bedsteads of the latest design in wood with spring mattresses; three swing glass mirrors and glass-top dressing-tables; a large-size wardrobe; chairs; a carpet beside each bed; a washing basin with hot and cold water taps; a red bricked fireplace and, last but not least, three large windows with curtains draped down, giving one a marvellous view of the fields and plains. Matron asked me the next morning if I slept well and I said 'I awoke and thought I was at The Ritz'.

Imperial Club Magazine 1937

Bernhardine Jacobs, restaurant manager, Stelten warehouse in Germany, admires a book of signatures presented on her retirement after 17 years, by Colin Foster, assistant manager ES.

Joan Deverill, manager, Zouch Farm families shop at Tidworth, celebrates her retirement after 40 years. Saying their farewells are (from left) David Singleton, district manager Tidworth, Frank Johnson , district auditor, and Mike Mantle, regional manager South Central, who presented Miss Deverill with a piano stool on behalf of colleagues.

Retiring after 51 years is Arthur Licence (right), regional auditor, Amesbury warehouse, Salisbury, in Wiltshire.

Pictured with him is his wife, Agnes. Peter Dean, manager audit services, Nottingham, presented the pair with flowers, a cheque, and a silver tea-service and tray from friends and colleagues at a farewell celebration.

14

15

☐ The presentation with the smiling protagonists shaking hands and holding the gift, certificate, bouquet, cup or whatever (known as the 'cophold' shot because the presenter could be saying 'Here, cop hold of this').
☐ The staff, team, VIP visitors or other line-up (the 'firing squad' shot, because the photographer has lined them up against a wall and shot them).
☐ The executive pointing to a sales chart or the map on the wall.
☐ The committee gathered around the conference table.
☐ The giant cheque for charity.

These pictures will not only fail to interest your readers, they will discourage them from reading.

You can now evaluate the remaining prints. Relevance, topicality, impact, composition, humour, pathos, movement, tranquillity, elegance, emotion – these, and a variety of other attributes, could affect your final choice.

BIG IS BEST

One picture should be selected to dominate the spread. It might be the most appropriate to the story, the most atmospheric, the most dramatic, or one which combines with the title to make a strong point.

Use your first-choice picture big. It may be the only picture you need to use. If more

'This is my day' says Tommy Gore, regional manager for Northern Ireland, on his way to Buckingham Palace to be invested with the MBE awarded him in the New Year Honours List.

Opposite: Typical cliché presentation pictures, submitted snapshots of varying quality. Compare the investiture photograph (at the top right of the spread) with the imaginative treatment on this back cover (right).

Scaling a picture this way (described opposite) enables you to see at a glance the height it makes at various column widths. If the picture is to bleed, begin the keyline and the diagonal at the corner of the bleed area, not the page area. If you want the picture to fill the type area, a diagonal drawn from A to the opposite corner (D) will show (BE) how much should be trimmed from the picture.

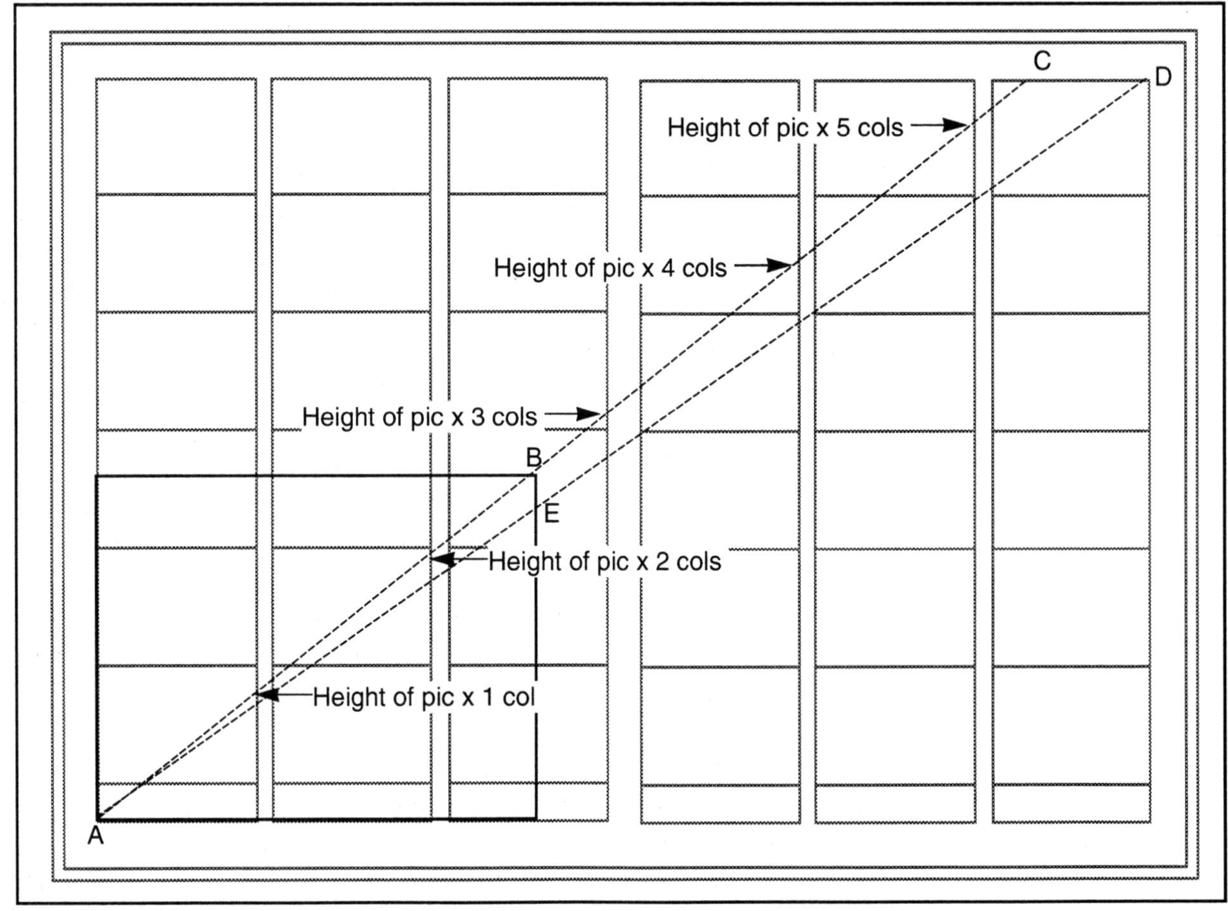

pictures are used they should play a supporting role. They should not only be smaller but, if possible, different in proportion and stress. In other words, mix landscape and portrait shapes and vary the ratios of height to width as much as is feasible (see illustrations on pages 36 - 38).

Place your mini-grids beneath a new layout sheet and again mark the corners of each spread. Measure the width and height of your chosen picture (or of the area of the picture you propose to use) and draw a rectangle to represent it in the lower left corner of the type area of the first grid (see opposite page). To accommodate large pictures on your mini-grid you can measure the picture area in inches but use, say, centimetres or picas when transferring those measurements to the layout pad. Draw a diagonal line from the bottom left corner (A) to the top right corner of this rectangle (B) and extend it to the edge of the type area (C). From this diagonal you can mark off the depth of the picture at each column width – or anywhere in between. Do the same, on other grids on the same layout sheet, for any other pictures you propose to use.

Place this sheet of picture shapes beside your sheet of text shapes. You can now see at a glance the relative sizes and shapes which can be made from text and pictures and you can begin to experiment with various combinations and juxtapositions of the different shapes of these two major elements of your design.

Place your mini-grids master under the next sheet in the layout pad. Try various combinations of the text and picture shapes, remembering to make allowances for the title, straps, standfirsts, captions and any other additional items you may wish to include. Don't forget the important fourth element – white space.

BE FAST AND FLEXIBLE

Do not be unduly worried at this stage about precision; produce lots of quick freehand roughs as you look for the right combination of shapes that fits the material on the spread in a well-balanced way. Remember that although the area taken up by the text is fixed, its shape and position are not. The pictures too, can be moved about the page and their shape can be changed (by changing the cropping as discussed in Chapter 13), but they have the additional flexibility that their area can also be increased or decreased.

Layout paper is cheap. Do not attempt to erase and correct your sketches – simply move on to the next grid or the next sheet. Do not throw away any of these sheets of roughs until you have decided on your preferred design. If you occasionally look back over rejected sketches, you might well see how a new idea could combine with some aspect of an earlier

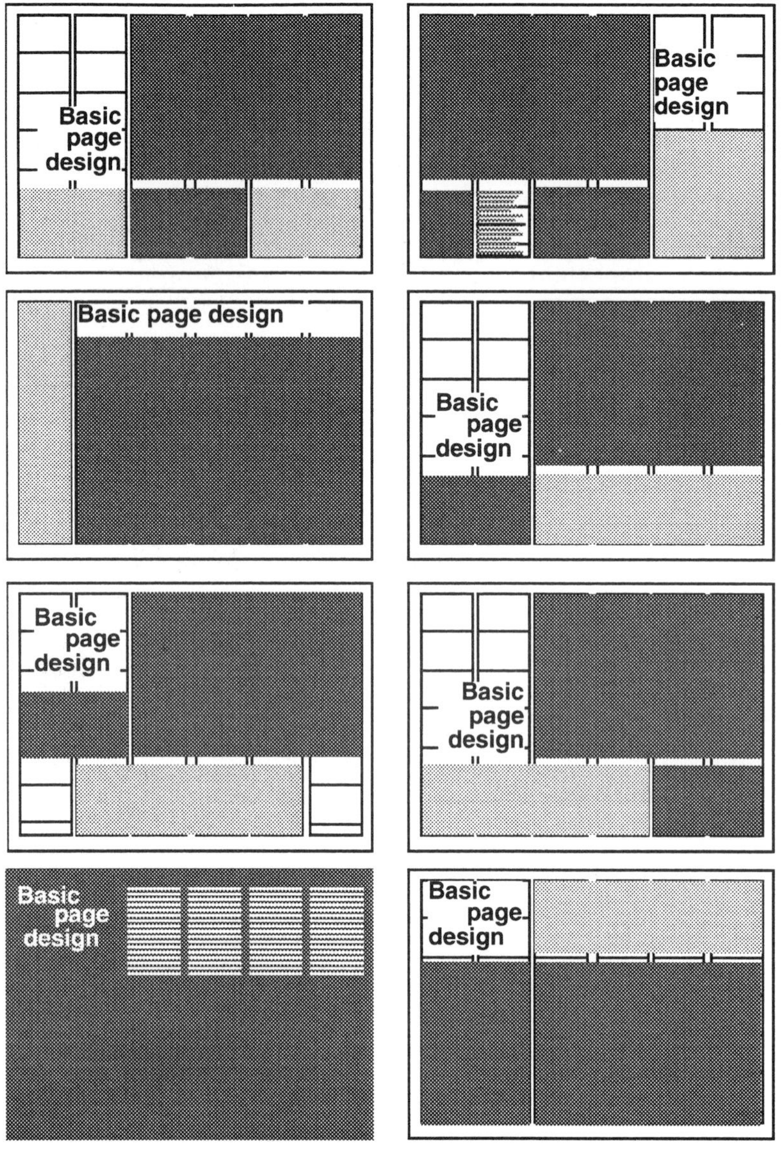

layout to produce the ideal design.

The illustration (left) shows some examples of how the copy and pictures for a feature might be used to produce different layouts.

You can now see how well-spent was the time you gave to preparing your master grid sheet. It allows you to move quickly from one idea to another. Columns, margins and text area are all accurately proportioned, providing an advantage which will become apparent when you transfer your chosen design to a full-size grid.

USING WHITE SPACE

At first, students of design tend to be tentative about the use of white space. In some publications, budget restraints might make it difficult to deploy this element effectively. But white space can add elegance to a spread, it allows the design to breathe, it can direct attention to an important aspect of the message – however, it can be difficult to get it right. Avoid trapping white space (it can look like a hole in the page); allow it to bleed off the page so that it seems to expand the design and make the page seem bigger.

'White space' can often be found within a picture and used to place titles, captions and even body text. This is discussed further in Chapter 14.

The traditional position for the title of a

feature is at the top of the spread and ranged left, but it pays to be adventurous now and again. Titles in unorthodox positions will probably need some help in attracting the reader's eye; this might be achieved by the sheer size and weight of the type chosen, by the strategic use of white space, or perhaps by the movement within a picture.

If the title crosses the fold it should be arranged so that the fold falls between two words. This can be achieved by editing, resizing, blowing up or reducing the title.

If the heading is to be placed in two or more lines, ensure that the line-breaks help, rather than hinder, understanding.

Captions are traditionally placed beneath their pictures (and this is where readers will usually look first to find them). Other positions may be used, provided the reader does not have to search for them and, having found them, is not confused about which caption applies to which picture. This may mean identifying the pictures with 'Left:' 'Below:' and so on, or by some other device.

If captions cannot be placed immediately below the relevant picture, try to ensure they are adjacent. Avoid, if at all possible, having to number pictures and captions because they are so far apart.

Bylines and standfirsts are usually positioned beneath the title but, again, different positions

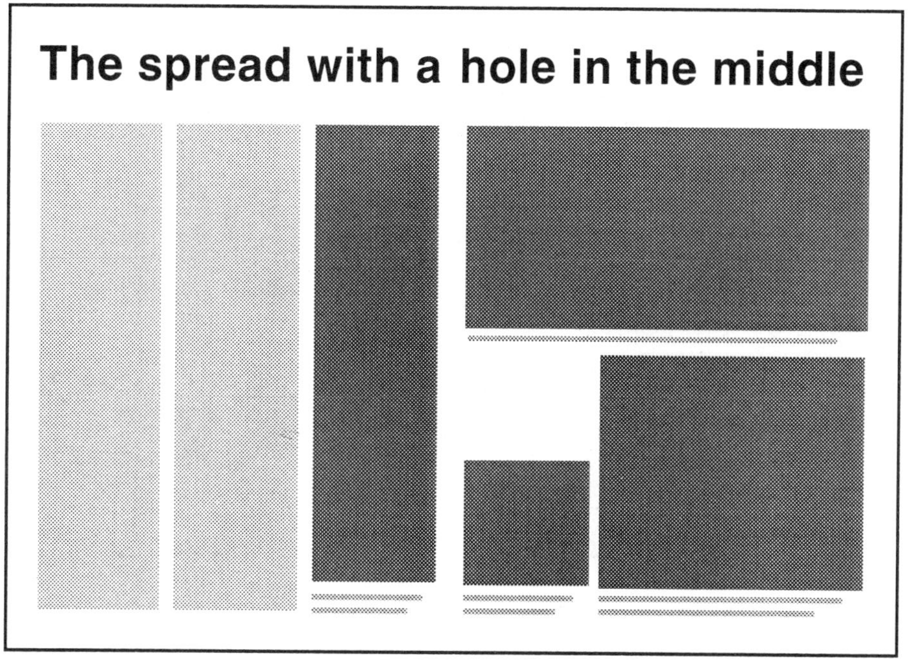

The spread with a hole in the middle

Above: An easy solution to the 'hole' in the middle of this two-page spread would be to increase the depth of the pictures slightly and gather the captions together in the 'hole'. Alternatively the two lower right pictures could be transposed and the single column pic moved up so that its top becomes level with its neighbour's. Note that the fold falls between two words in the title.

Opposite: A typical sheet of roughs for a feature where the main picture is a landscape. Light grey represents text, dark grey pictures. The lower left design shows a full-page bleed picture with title and text set in a night sky.

Man stabbed wife in stomach

Headlines and titles are read line by line, so try to ensure that each line reads as a phrase which makes sense within the overall meaning.

Man stabbed wife in stomach

may be used to make the design more interesting – if they do not also make it confusing.

Do not attempt at this stage to make your layouts too detailed or too exact, but do try out lots of different combinations of the shapes available.

The layout method described in this chapter can, of course, be applied to continuation pages – with minor modifications. You will not need to accommodate a major title, but you might wish to incorporate a smaller continuation heading. You now need to retain attention rather than attract it; design that impacts on the eye could, at this point, prove counter-productive, but visual boredom must be avoided, while ease of reading must be maintained. This, indeed, becomes increasingly important the longer the article.

Full-page advertisements can often be placed facing continuation pages with advantage to both editorial and advertisement. Check through available ads for sympathetic subjects: a feature on fitness, for example, could benefit from a facing page advertising healthy eating, sports clothing, activity holidays etc. – and the advertiser will not be unhappy either. The right advertisement can often seem to have been designed as part of the spread.

If a feature is to continue over four or more pages you might think it appropriate to have identical amounts of text in identical shapes and positions on each spread to provide a unifying theme to those pages.

On the other hand, when a multiple-page feature gives you the freedom to decide how many of the lines of copy will appear on each spread or page, you might decide to use a particularly good picture very big indeed on the opening spread, together with the title and only a short introduction to the main text.

If two features are to appear on the same spread, do not automatically think in terms of one feature to each page. Spreads (or pages) divided neatly in half start out with a design handicap. Asymmetric designs are generally more interesting than symmetric ones, so unequal divisions, either vertically or horizontally, are more interesting than equal divisions – they are also frequently more convenient because the amount of material provided is also, usually, unequal.

If three or more features are to be accommodated, turn to Chapter 11 and follow the advice for news pages.

The reproductions on the following pages illustrate a number of the points made in this chapter but more examples can be found among the other illustrations throughout the book.

The method in brief

1. **Read and cast off the copy.**
2. **Mark off copy shapes and areas on mini-grids.**
3. **Select and crop pictures.**
4. **Mark off picture shapes and areas on your mini-grids.**
5. **Sketch lots of roughs, trying various combinations and positions of the copy and picture shapes while remaining aware of the shape made by the white space.**
6. **On the best of your roughs, sketch in headings, straps and so on.**
7. **Transfer the final design to a full-size grid.**
8. **Mark up the layout, manuscript, pictures, etc. for the printer (see Chapter 8).**

TIMOTHY WHITE

ANDY GARCIA

CALM AND COLLECTED, CUBAN-BORN ANDY GARCIA TAKES ON THE ITALIAN MAFIA IN THE GODFATHER PART III. ELISSA VAN POZNAK MEETS HOLLYWOOD'S LATEST HIT MAN

CUBAN COOL

The morning after the first ever screening of *The Godfather Part III* – or as PR speak would have it, the Movie Event of the Decade – and Andy Garcia is sitting in an LA hotel suite. Clustered around him in a select semi-circle is the world press.

The lady from Norway, who hasn't shut up since passing through immigration, informs the actor that until viewing his spectacular performance in Francis Ford Coppola's hotly anticipated sequel, she had frankly not been remotely interested in talking to him.

'Well I wasn't looking forward to meeting you much either,' guffaws Garcia, eyebrows arched and clearly amused. Andy Garcia – despite the bedroom eyes and smooth double-mattress manner – does not enjoy getting intimate with strangers. Scrutiny, especially in and of the flesh, makes him twitch – even for art's sake he is reluctant to divest too much. Coppola achieved a major coup by getting the actor to reveal not just a previously unseen power but also a luxuriant chest of hair.

'And that's as far as I go,' quips Garcia, who has firm rules about these things. In 1990's *Internal Affairs*, Mike Figgis' smouldering thriller ▷

15

SUPPLIER PROFILE

the FASHION KING WITH THE GOLDEN TOUCH

The Steilmann Group is one of M&S' largest clothing manufacturers, last year supplying £55 million of garments. Alison Young discovers more about the company and the man who created it.

Stepping inside the austere two storey building which forms the front of the head office of Steilmann, anyone would have to admit to being a little shocked.

No glossy reception, no large comfy sofas, no commissionaires or security men. Just a small table surrounded by four upright chairs for visitors, a cool stone floor and one receptionist/telephonist who speaks from inside a glass fronted office of her own.

Can this really be the headquarters of the Steilmann empire? After all, there is not even a sign on the outside of the building saying Steilmann. But as anyone soon finds out, Klaus Steilmann, who founded Steilmann and remains head of the company today, is not interested in projecting a corporate image for its own sake.

He resides on the first floor. The door to his spacious, airy, but strictly functional office is always left open. There's no secretary to bar the way – she has an office down the corridor.

Herr Steilmann, it transpires, does not believe in closed doors – any member of his staff can come and see him, any time.

He turns out to be an approachable man who prefers not to stand on ceremony. He has an air of relaxed confidence, a man who has nothing to prove. Charming, polite, with an easy laugh and razor sharp mind, he's one of those people who would have been a success whatever his chosen field – be it politician or lawyer, adventurer or writer.

Instead, 31 years ago, he chose to start his own retailing company. It is now one of the largest private companies in Germany, with 41 of its own factories in Germany and Austria and contracts with 74 other factories around the world. It manufactured 29 million garments in 1,500 different styles last year and had a turnover of DM 1,520 million. Half of its production was exported – the majority to Britain, followed by the Netherlands, Switzerland and Austria.

Herr Steilmann still retains firm control of the company. As we talk the phone rings perpetually. He answers without fail and when he has finished puts the receiver down and takes up the conversation just where he left off.

He speaks in fluent English. Does he speak any other languages? "French, quite good Italian, I can make myself understood in Spanish. I can understand Portuguese, and I've started to speak Russian again, although I didn't speak it for 35 years and had forgotten most of it."

As he talks, he appears totally unaware of the high speed trains, 232 a day of which hurtle by just 25ft from the windows, some making the room vibrate and the pictures on the wall rattle in their frames. One begins to see that Herr Steilmann is not a man to be easily distracted when there is a business to be run.

Born on June 12, 1929, the son of a middle class Catholic estate manager and a Protestant West Prussian mother, Klaus Steilmann's family was opposed to Hitler's politics. His father died in a Russian concentration camp – believed to be one of 40,000 people whose bodies were found recently buried in mass unmarked graves in woods at Neubrandenburg, East Germany.

In 1944, at the age of 15, Klaus was enlisted into the German army, the same year as his elder brother was killed in action.

After the war he got a menial job with the regional military government being run by the Allies. He was fortunate to meet up with an English lieutenant-colonel, to whom he became a secretary.

Says Herr Steilmann: "We became firm friends and I became an Anglophile."

He later became a court interpreter for the military government, before going to Berlin to join his family.

His original plan to go to university and later become a judge abandoned due to lack of money, he decided to join the clothing trade. He took a job as an assistant in the receiving and despatch department of C&A Brenninkmeyer, and attended nightschool – gaining the British equivalent of A levels at 22.

For a year and a half he went to work for Walter Pape, Berlin's leading overcoat manufacturer at the time. He was immediately convinced of Pape's principles – buying in large quantities, thrifty administration and selling with a minimal sales organisation – all of which have been adopted by the Steilmann group.

From 1952 to mid-1955 he became an assistant buyer of ladies' overcoats and costumes at C&A. He then joined overcoat manufacturer Josef Mayer, and in two years helped to double the company's turnover. "One day we had a row partly because more and more people were going to me and not to him," says Herr Steilmann. "I took my jacket and walked out. I said I just couldn't bear it anymore. I remember walking down hundreds of stairs and thinking what are you going to do now?"

There was only one answer, of course, he had to start his own company. In 1958 he leased his own factory at Wattenscheid. His first customer was C&A.

He has never looked back. There are now ten subsidiaries as well as the Steilmann company itself. Each subsidiary concentrates on a different segment of the market: Neinhaus + Luig manufactures for young women, whereas Hardo Beimdieke caters for the over 45s. DressMaster makes menswear, while KL manufactures a ready to wear collection designed by Karl Lagerfeld, and so on.

Steilmann originally concentrated on manufacturing unbranded merchandise in the belief that it would gain more customers if its garments were not instantly recognisable. It now supplies customers who have 41,000 outlets.

"Then five years ago, we also decided to start manufacturing branded merchandise, because we recognised that the market was becoming segmented. Exclusivity ▷

PHOTOGRAPHS BY TERRY BEASLEY

Klaus Steilmann is a keen football player. He plays twice a week and owns a German first division football team.

Winter coats and jackets being made at a Steilmann production centre.

— 16 —

— 17 —

Opposite: Bold use of white space exemplified in Elle. *Note the unorthodox placing of byline, standfirst and heading, and the contrast in weights of the display faces.*

Above: M&S World *makes use of the 'white space' in a photograph to accommodate title and text .*

Grupo 4 Securitas España's most prestigious guarding contract is the Palacio Real de Madrid, but its services are in demand throughout the country

They're changing guards at the royal palace

TWO-and-a-half centuries after Philip V, King of Spain, began building a new palace for himself in Madrid they decided to change the guards. They now use Grupo 4 Securitas España.

One of the Spanish capital's biggest tourist attractions, the Palacio Real de Madrid is no longer a royal residence. But it is far more than a museum. Its huge banqueting hall is used by the royal family for special occasions when they wish to extend hospitality to visiting dignitaries.

For most days, however, its doors are open to the 410,000 members of the public who visit it every year. And to help control their access and movements, as well as protect the valuable and historic exhibits, a team of 99 guards (we couldn't find out why it wasn't 100!), is employed in the palace and its extensive and beautiful grounds.

A team of 99 guards is employed in the palace and its extensive and beautiful grounds

We were taken on a special guided tour of the splendid building by Eduardo Gonzales Garcia, Group 4's guarding director in Madrid, and his supervisor at the palace, Manuel Morales Alonso.

Security officers in Spain are permitted to carry guns but the palace contract requires only unarmed guards. Those on duty at access points leading to administrative offices do, however, carry truncheons.

The Madrid police guard the perimeter of the palace and Grupo 4 protects the interior. Our access control responsibilities include searching tourists and workers, where necessary, as a precaution against terrorism or theft of its priceless exhibits. And every once in a while these searches prove that such precautions are vitally necessary. The guarding team, a third of whom are female, has, in the past, discovered armaments in a tourist's trunk and our night patrols have intercepted intruders who had gained illicit access. Members of the team are also on duty throughout the palace, in areas of particular importance such as the Throne Room.

For Manuel Alonso and his smartly dressed Grupo 4 men and women, who work as four teams each under a supervisor, their role is a mixture of security deterrent and tourist guide. If a visitor is lost or bewildered, it's only natural that they will turn to someone in uniform for help. And who knows how many tourists take back pleasant memories not only of the royal residence in Madrid but also of Grupo 4, as a result of their visit?

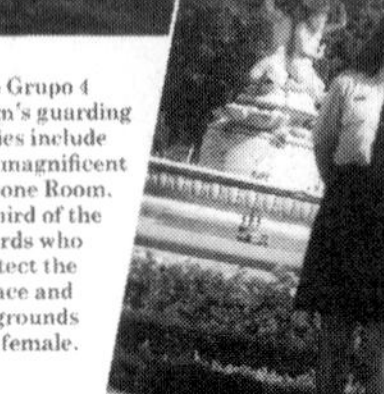

The Grupo 4 team's guarding duties include the magnificent Throne Room. A third of the guards who protect the palace and its grounds are female.

The Palacio Real de Madrid is a glamorous and historic customer but it competes with a number of other customers in the prestige stakes. For example, Grupo 4 has been protecting the United States embassy and consulate in the Spanish capital for the past seven years, the Italian embassy for five years and it also guards the British ambassador.

Armed team for post

Most contracts, of course, are with industrial or commercial customers but their security needs are just as essential and occasionally they throw up surprises that add excitement to the painstaking and methodical security duties that have to be carried out.

Take the Spanish Post Office, for example. It is one of Grupo 4's major customers, requiring a 62-strong team of guards to keep a watchful eye over around 15,000 bags of special mail a day. These, explained Grupo 4 supervisor Emilio José Lopez Jareño, are letters and parcels addressed to government ministers, politicians, prisons and others possible terrorist targets. All members of the team are armed, he added, with the exception of those who work in the scanner and explosive detector area.

On the day we were shown around the Post Office headquarters and main sorting office for Madrid, there had been a letter bomb threat from a terrorist group. Emilio, who began work for Grupo

seventeenth-century façade of the house, but looks more like the best work of the 1920s. Young had read no Ruskin or Morris, and at the time had never heard of the Society for the Protection of Ancient Buildings although he had grown up in the Cotswolds and learnt on his father's farm how to make dry stone walls – a skill he considers fundamental to all building.

Young's next project was an elaborate baroque stone doorcase at Trusley Manor in Derbyshire, followed by the lengthy endurance test of rebuilding Gornal Ground, a farmhouse near Millom in Cumbria. Here he worked with Constantinides and other young craftsmen. The house was interesting because it was typical seventeenth-century vernacular, of a kind that is commonly restored out of recognition or left to fall down. Constantinides and Capps were able to retain its integrity, experimenting in reviving traditional building techniques, often arguing furiously about the correct way of working. For both of them, it was a study-course in the use of lime, once the staple material for mortar, plaster, roughcast and colourwash and now unobtainable through the normal building trade.

Lime is a material they all feel passionate about and use regularly – they slake their own quicklime to make lime putty. It is a material with remarkable properties, and the decline of traditional building can be dated from the 1880s when lime began to be replaced by Portland cement. In using lime, the modern craftsman is using an obsolete, pre-industrial technique, but one which combines beauty of texture with versatility and endurance.

All three building concerns have stonemasonry workshops. Young works as an inscription designer and letter-cutter. St Blaise includes a stonemason, Piers Denny, among its directors. At Capps & Capps, work has been going on for five years on the restoration of Hereford Cathedral's central tower, carving thousands of ball-flower ornaments on the pinnacles, each one copied as far as possible from the damaged medieval stone, and introducing a liveliness and variety visible from several hundred feet below.

Building work of this kind is chiefly in demand for old buildings, but does it have a place in the development of modern crafts? Such skilled and self-aware craftsmen have the ability to create imaginative and successful new work, although it is seldom called on.

Constantinides has however completed some remarkable new work such as his swimming pool at sub-basement level in a mews house near Grosvenor Square, London. It was conceived as an example of fake history, as if a ruined Roman temple had been unearthed. The pool surround is tilted, and the columns chipped and broken, requiring quite the opposite of restoration techniques for its construction.

Working so much with the past requires different priorities to those of most architects whom all three builders find unsympathetic to their outlook. One of the main problems builder-craftsmen face is the lack of proper apprenticeship. New labour has to be trained on the job, and the few middle-class drop-outs who stay the course are likely to set up on their own. In spite of this both Capps & Capps and St Blaise manage to keep a work-force of about 50 each.

In 1911, Philip Webb, William Morris' closest architect friend, called the Society for the Protection of Ancient Buildings 'the best modern school of building we have', meaning that physical contact with old buildings and methods could have a beneficial effect on what otherwise seemed a bleak architectural future. There is surely a rôle for practising building craftsmen of the calibre of Capps, Constantinides and Young to contribute to the improvement of architecture. Those who argue that 'Percent for Art' schemes for new buildings risk diminishing the quality of the building in favour of stuck-on art bits may not be thinking of the buildings themselves as craft objects, but it is an ideal that has existed before. The recognition of intelligent hand-work is desperately needed in modern architecture, whether it presents itself as smoothly polished or machine-made rustic. □

For Stockists, see page 64

LEFT: Mock-Roman swimming pool, by Ian Constantinides

ABOVE: Statue of King Alfred, Stourhead, restored by Constantinides

Introducing a dropped type horizon as in Group 4 International *(opposite) is a useful and frequently employed way of ensuring white space on the page.* Crafts *(above) shows that raising the base of the text area can be equally effective.*

BEE NATURAL
RICETTE NATURALI
PERLIER
BODY CARE RANGE
Now there's a body care range for those who don't mind admitting that Mother Nature knows best. It's Perlier from Italy, made using a unique recipe of honey to cleanse, nourish and moisturise your skin, and virgin beeswax to protect it.
Nothing could be more naturali, as they say in Milan, Florence....
WHAT COULD BE MORE NATURAL?
Available from larger Boots Stores, the John Lewis Partnership, House of Fraser and other leading department stores and chemists

BEAUTY NEWS

Face finish Professionals recommend loose powder as a final touch to "set" your make-up. According to make-up artist Beverley Brooke, the latest loose powders have a finer finish and are less drying. Try her tips to get the most from your powder:

- Apply all over – including lips, lids and lashes – to improve the staying power of all your make-up.
- Blend a little loose powder and lipcolour on the back of your hand using a lipbrush, then apply to your lipline for definition with a softer look.
- If you use blusher, use a powder formula *only* over face powder. Brush off the excess powder following the growth direction of your facial hair.
- If you are confident enough to wear powder alone, don't overdo it. Press on to your skin (don't pat it on) to absorb oil and control shine.
- If you are looking for a shade to suit your skin tone, we recommend Estée Lauder's new Lucidity Translucent Loose Powder (£17), Lancôme's Poudre Majeur Loose (£17) or Swedish Formula's Finishing Powder (£3.65).

Make a fresh start for spring with our gift from Gucci. Parfum No 3 is a rich floral scent which blends top notes of narcissus, rose, jasmine and iris with a warm base of amber, patchouli and vetiver. We have a complete set of the Parfum No 3 bathcare range: shower

gel, deodorant, body lotion and soap, plus a 100ml Eau de Toilette spray of Parfum No 3 (worth £150), to give away to the first name drawn on April 22. Forty-five runners-up will each receive a 50ml Parfum No 3 Eau de Toilette (worth £30). Name and address on a postcard to: SHE/Gucci Offer, 72 Broadwick St, London W1V 2BP.

Photographs: Transworld, Box Office, Foto Theme

Try this simple relaxation technique from the Belle Vue Lodge Clinic, London. It's a quick and simple way to ease tension: Put two tennis balls in a sock and knot the sock to hold the balls together. Lie flat on your back and place the tennis balls under your neck at the base of your skull. (With this method, the balls fall into position on the correct pressure points so you don't struggle to keep them in place.) Close your eyes, lay your hands flat on the floor and then breathe in deeply for a count of seven. Repeat five times. Always stand up slowly afterwards because you'll be in a very relaxed state and will perhaps feel a little unsteady.

BY JO GLANVILLE-BLACKBURN

HOT TIPS

- Don't use different brands of hairspray between shampoos. Some are formulated with acrylic polymers and others with anionic polymers: the combination can be insoluble in water, leaving your hair feeling sticky after washing.
- How stubborn is your cellulite? According to research by experts at Elancyl, the situation could be worse than we feared! They've discovered a new type of cellulite – even more resilient to treatment – which is found in particular areas of the body, such as the backs of the arms, navel, neck and shoulders, knees, lower legs and ankles. Now Elancyl have developed MP24 Specific (£22.50, 75ml), a non-greasy gel which they claim is specially formulated to treat these newly defined cellulite problem areas.
- Last year women in the UK spent over £50m on mascaras, according to market analysts Mintel. It's the item of make-up most women cannot live without. Of the mascaras around, here's our top five: Body Shop's Colourings Mas-

cara (£2.15), Estée Lauder's More Than Mascara (£9), The Mascara by Ultima II 'The Nakeds' (£10.75), Almay's Colour Performance Conditioning Mascara (£6.95), and No 7 Superlash (£2.45).

25

She *magazine has a conscious policy of trying to match ads to the editorial, as exemplified in these two spreads on health and child education respectively.*

"Humpty, I can put you together again and again and again."

Playskool's Humpty Dumpty is as much fun to build up as he is to burst apart. Just one push on the lever will send him on another great fall. Each colourful interlocking piece is designed so small hands can have fun learning to build with simple shapes and bright colours. 'That was a great fall Humpty. How about another one?'

HUMPTY DUMPTY

LEARNING **CURVE**

Why some children underachieve...How you can assess a good primary school teacher...The farmyard fantasies of Dick King-Smith

COULD DO BETTER?

If your child is underachieving at school, she isn't necessarily stupid or lazy. She could just lack confidence, or be afraid. John Mascoll, educational psychologist for Avon County Council, has the following suggestions:

- **Build up your child's self-esteem by showing that you value her. If she feels good about herself, she'll be more likely to want to learn.**
- **Discourage fear of failure. Some children are so afraid of mistakes that they will only do repetitive work with which they feel safe. Try to encourage good work instead of criticising bad.**
- **Don't overpressure her. Vast quantities of homework can cause stress.**
- **Don't do too much for her (she will never learn self-confidence) –** ***or*** **too little. With homework, offer lots of help initially, then phase it out.**
- **Praise, but don't overpraise. If you set very high standards, she may feel she will never again achieve them.**
- **Use bribery (or "positive reinforcement") where appropriate. Self-motivation doesn't always come naturally.**

ANIMAL MAGIC

"Children like to be amused, frightened, excited, saddened and, above all else, interested," believes Dick King-Smith, award-winning author of over 60 children's books in the 12 years since he retired from teaching. Now aged 68, and a grandfather of ten, he has learned not to be a sentimentalist about children – nor about his subject matter. "I suppose I usually – though not exclusively – write farmyard fantasies," he explains. "But I do not blench at nature red in tooth and claw. My animals always reflect the human condition: they get killed off. And much as I love *The Wind in the Willows* and the work of Beatrix Potter, I never dress my animals in clothes."

A self-confessed failed farmer before training as a teacher, Dick came late to the children's book stakes, but he now writes prolifically. His past successes include *The Sheep-Pig, Dodos Are Forever* and *The Fox Busters* (all published by Puffin). His newest publications are *The Cuckoo Child* (Viking, £7.99), and *Sophie's Tom*, published on April 25 (Walker Books, £6.99).

Dick King-Smith likes to file his readers under one of three categories: "First, the younger child of around six or seven years who is not well enough equipped to read himself, but enjoys being read to. Second, the reader of around eight to 11 who does read. And third, the wretched adult who has to do the reading. I occasionally stick in jokes and quotations that go over the child's head, just to give the poor adults a giggle!" (Witness Lucrezia Gorger, the rat with blood lust who attacks the dodos.)

As a young man, Dick wrote romantic and rural poetry with modest success, and still admits to a great love of "word play, puns and the poetical sound of words". His characters are far from prissy, but nor are they ashamed to exhibit the finer qualities of life, "such as moral and physical courage, reliability and kindness to others," says Dick. Except for the unpleasant Lucrezia, of course. Her just desserts are unkindly sweet: she is "pancaked" by a coconut...

Photographs: Box Office, Bill Block/Working Mother

TEACHER TEST

A good primary teacher can make all the difference to a child's performance. But how can you judge if your child has drawn an ace? Ask yourself these questions, advises headteacher Graeme Kent:

- Does she treat the children with respect? Does she foster a spirit of friendliness in the class? Is your child developing his self-confidence? Does she have the ability to develop a positive attitude to learning?
- Is she available to discuss problems? Does she welcome parental help in class? Does she seem genuinely interested in your child?
- Does she display the children's work and change it regularly? Is the classroom attractive and interesting?
- Does she seem to like children – and do they like her? Does the head speak of her in glowing terms? Does she take part in out-of-school activities?
- Does she mark homework conscientiously and write encouraging comments in your child's exercise books?
- Does she move the children around so they can develop their social skills?
- Do you feel respect for her as a person and as a teacher?

159

TRY A NEW ANGLE

The subjects and events in the pictures on these pages are typical of most issues of Naafi News – indeed they have all appeared in past issues. Those printed square to the page are 'square' in every way, those printed at an angle show how imagination can bring the same situations alive.

Photographs submitted for publication in *Naafi News* come in all shapes and sizes and conditions. They are all welcome but some are more welcome than others and the best pictures push the poorer pictures out when space is short.

The criteria used to decide which pictures should be published are: print quality (how well will the photograph reproduce?) and reader interest. Of these, the latter is the more important. There are a number of basic situations and subjects which regularly make up the bulk of the photographs received: they are presentations, groups, new shops, new clubs, sporting or social events, and personalities. It is on the exercise of imagination in the taking and presentation of these photographs that a magazine relies to maintain its interest from one issue to the next.

So, to a large extent, the success of a house magazine depends upon its contributors. Here are a few tips for ensuring that the pictures you submit stand a good chance of appearing – and perhaps winning the editor's award for the best contribution of the month. These tips can be applied equally well to photographs submitted to other publications or to entries for photographic competitions; they raise the humble snapshot to the level of creative photography and lift photograph albums right out of the humdrum into something you can be proud to show, and friends will be interested to see.

14

SUBJECTS should generally be close to the camera, providing as large an image as possible. If the principal subject is large and sharp it does not usually matter that the background is not quite in focus – in fact this can often help the composition by throwing more emphasis on the subject.

TOPICALITY Prints which appear on an editor's desk within days of the event take priority over pictures which are several weeks or perhaps months old.

GROUPS A photograph which is interesting *as a photograph* will catch the attention of those readers who are not in the picture or otherwise concerned with the event.

Large, posed groups gazing into the camera have a low interest rating; smaller, animated groups are better.

ACTION Posed groups can usually be avoided: don't line up the football team in rows with arms folded, shoot them during a match, or at practice; try a shot in the dressing rooms, or show the coach discussing tactics with the team around a blackboard or – even better – a table-soccer set. Avoid lifeless or hackneyed settings.

The same kind of thinking can be applied to any group whether it is a working, sports, or social group. If you can't shoot the subjects unawares – give them something to do.

PRESENTATIONS Much of what was said under the previous heading applies to presentation pictures. Avoid the boring duet of the presenter and the receiver looking into the camera. Change the angle, shoot over the shoulder of the person making the presentation, show the recipient trying out his gift for the first time, doing his job for the last time, packing his bag to go off on a retirement holiday, or in any other appropriate situation your imagination suggests. Above all, make sure that the people being photographed are interested in what they are doing and not in the camera.

PERSONALITIES Avoid the stereotyped portrait. Photograph personalities as naturally as possible against a background which will add to the story or feature in which they are involved. If the subject is a driver, photograph him in a busy transport yard; if he is a local councillor, use a high-street-and-town-hall background.

ESTABLISHMENTS Photographs of empty shops,

15

Occasionally, when appropriate, headings can be set an angle.

8 Preparing for the printer

When you are finally satisfied with one of your rough designs (or when deadlines do not permit further development of your ideas) it must be scaled up to full size.

Turn your master grid over and place it under a clean layout sheet with the full-size grid now uppermost. In the top margin of the layout write the publication's name, the issue and the appropriate page numbers.

With your chosen rough as a guide, mark out the text area or areas, the outline of the photographs, and the position of the title, standfirst, captions, byline, etc. – but this time your measurements and drawings must be accurate.

Because the mini-grids were proportionately reduced from the master, this transcription from miniature to full size should pose no major problems. The line count for text (which you noted on your rough layout sheet) remains exactly the same, so the text area can easily be marked up, in position, using the type-scale or counting off the text line guides on the grid.

If there is to be more than one story or feature on the spread, each manuscript should be given an identifying tagline – which should be repeated on every page and followed immediately by a folio sequence number. If a batch of manuscripts is dropped and the pages scattered it must be possible for anyone to sort them back into order easily and quickly.

The first folio of each story or feature should also identify the publication title, the issue, and the number of the magazine page on which the text will appear.

Write the setting instructions – typeface, style, size, leading and measure – on the layout, in the text area, for each story or feature. Repeat the

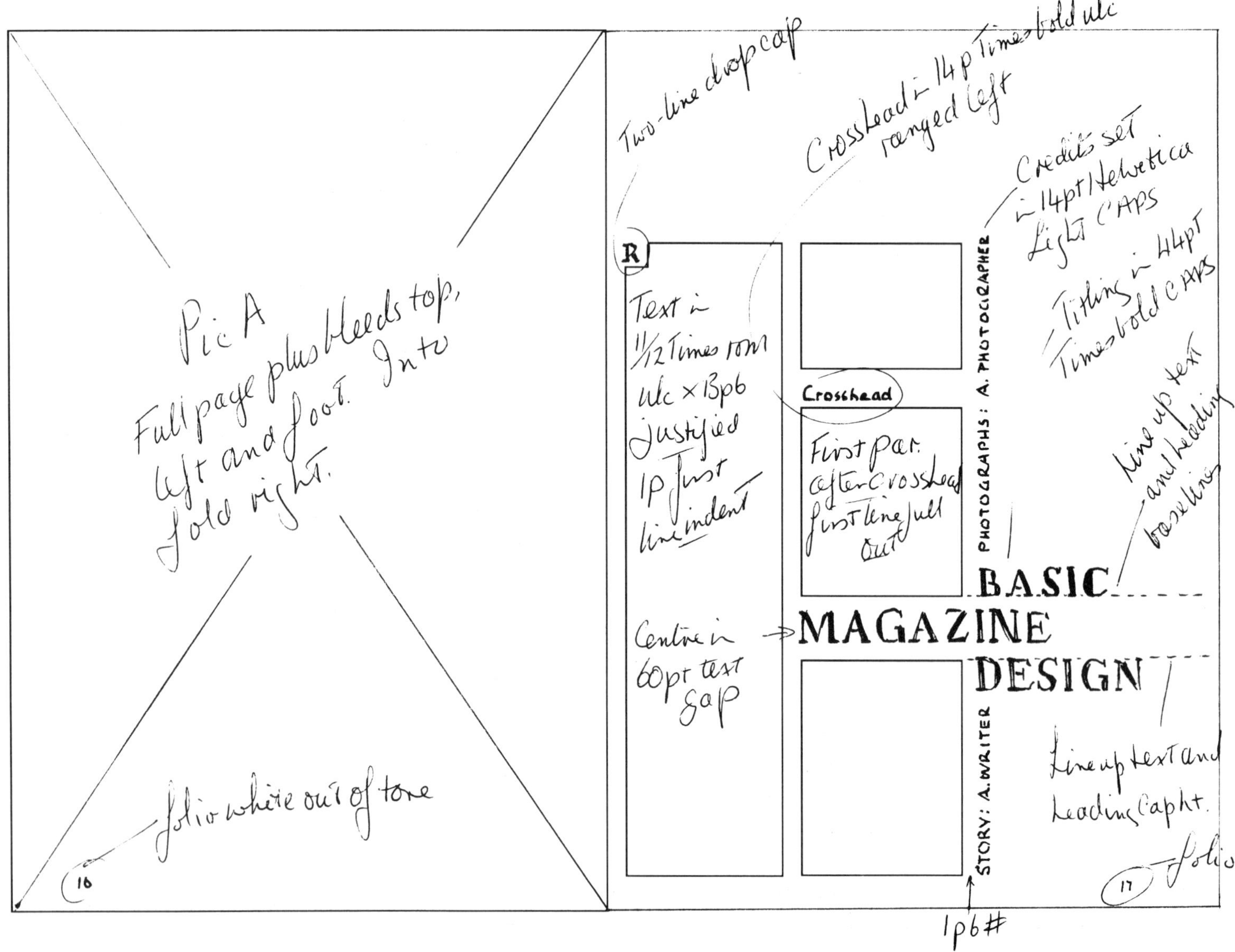

A layout marked up ready for the printer.

Opposite: Typescript marked up for the printer.

appropriate instructions on the the first page of each manuscript.

Read through the manuscript, marking all special instructions (bold setting, italics, indents and so on) with the appropriate proof-readers' marks. Encircle all instructions to the printer so that they are easily distinguished from any additional text to be set.

Instructions to the printer should be written in colour on the layout and on the manuscript. Use blue ink for preference at this stage. (The common convention is that, on the proofs, the printer's proof-reader will use green ink and you will use red to mark printer's errors and blue for author's corrections.) Do remember to replace the cap of your pen and, preferably, pop it in a drawer or pen pot.

PREPARING COPY

All typed copy should be presented double-spaced, on one side only of a standard size of paper, with no inter-paragraph spacing, with paragraph indents of two spaces and with the same number of lines to each page. Ideally, as suggested in Chapter 5, the lines should be typed to give the same character count (or double) as that of a line of printed body text in the magazine. Any handwritten corrections or instructions should be made using the appropriate proof-readers' symbols. If there are pages on which all the copy has been cut, strike

Tagline 1 The Mag/July/P6

Two-line dropcap 12/14pt Helvetica medium x 17p with 1p first line indents First par only in bold

If there is to be more than one story or feature on the spread, each manuscript should be given an identifying tagline - which should be repeated on every page and followed immediately by a folios sequence number. if a batch of manuscripts is dropped and the pages scattered it must be possible for anyone to sort them back into order easily and quickly.

The first folio of each storyor feature should also identify the Publication title, the issue, and the number of the magazine pag on which the text will appear.

Write the setting instructions - typeface, stlye, size, leading and measure - on the layout, in the text area, for each story or feature. Repeat the appropriate instructions on the the first page of each manuscript. Read through the manuscript, marking all special instructions (bold setti ng, italics, indents and so on) with the appropriate proof-readers marks. Encircle all instructions so that they are easily distinguished from any additional text to be set.

A galley proof of copy set by the printer according to the instructions given in the example on the previous page.

If there is to be more than one story or feature on the spread, each manuscript should be given an identifying tagline – which should be repeated on every page and followed immediately by a folio sequence number. If a batch of manuscripts is dropped and the pages scattered it must be possible for *anyone* to sort them back into order easily and quickly.

The first folio of each story or feature should also identify the publication title, the issue, and the number of the magazine page on which the text will appear.

Write the setting instructions – typeface, style, size, leading and measure – on the layout, in the text area, for each story or feature. Repeat the appropriate instructions on the the first page of each manuscript.

Read through the manuscript, marking all special instructions (bold setting, italics, indents and so on) with the appropriate proof-reader's marks. Encircle all instructions to the printer so that they are easily distinguished from any additional text to be set.

through the copy but leave the pages, in sequence, with the manuscript.

If new copy is being provided on additional pages, give these new pages the same page number as the page on which the copy is to be taken in and add 'A' (if more than one page is being added mark subsequent pages with the page number and 'B', etc.). Mark the insertion point on the original page and write 'Take in new copy from page…'.

If the manuscript has been heavily edited and corrected you should think out the relative economics of having it re-typed by a copy typist or letting it go to the typesetter. There are not only the different hourly rates of the keyboard time to consider: you will be on hand to settle quickly any queries from a company typist, but the typesetter may be forced to guess or, at the very least, break off to check with his supervisor and then, perhaps, telephone you. There is also the question of the psychological effect on a typesetter of receiving 'dirty' copy; if the thought arises that this is a client who does not have high standards, the job may be treated accordingly.

HANDLING HEADINGS

To position the heading on the layout, begin by laying a sheet of tracing paper over the appropriate type specimen sheet and trace out the heading in the selected size. Use the same phrasing and positioning as on the rough, but

Tracing headings from a type-sheet.

Opposite: Marking up tracing paper overlays to indicate precise crops.

check once again that line-breaks do not make nonsense of the heading. Place the tracing paper under the layout paper, adjust it until the heading is correctly positioned, and then trace the heading on to the layout. (Pasting the original tracing on to the layout never gives a true impression of how the spread will look.) If the heading does not fit, you can edit it, change its position, select a different size or style, or have it enlarged or reduced photographically or electronically depending upon the setting method being used. Provide setting instructions on the layout and, in addition, write or type the heading and the instructions on a sheet of paper (marked up with the magazine name, issue and page number) to accompany the main manuscript. (Any other display text which is to be set in the same typeface, regardless of size, should be included on the same sheet with the appropriate instructions.)

Do not forget to indicate positions of, and provide instructions for, captions, straps, standfirsts, bylines, crossheads, and any other items. Any text which appears on the layout must also be sent to the printer in manuscript; writing these on the layout alone is not good enough because manuscripts and layouts go to different people when they reach the printer. Any text items being set in the same typeface should be grouped together so that, for example, all captions could be typed on one A4 sheet with instructions at the head for the typeface, size and style, and each caption marked individually for variations in setting width.

PHOTOGRAPHS AND ARTWORK

Illustrations which are to be cropped should have a sheet of tracing paper attached with masking tape to the back of the print and then folded over to cover the front. The crop marks can then be drawn on the tracing paper using a soft pencil. (Check that any enlargement or reduction works accurately.) Write on the tracing paper or on a post-it note which can be stuck to the back of the print (never attach notes to pictures with paper clips) the name and issue of the publication, the page number, an identifying letter or number, and the width and height of the picture as it is to appear on the printed page. If the picture is to bleed, state whether the bleeds have been included in your crop marks and measurements or must be added (simply write 'includes bleeds' or 'add bleeds', remembering to say whether the bleeds will be at the top, left, right or foot). Draw an accurate keyline on the layout in the correct position and repeat the identifying letter or number inside it.

Half-tones should be kept together and separate from line artwork. Wherever possible provide artwork or photographs the same size or slightly larger than the final image. Any blemishes will be magnified if the original has to

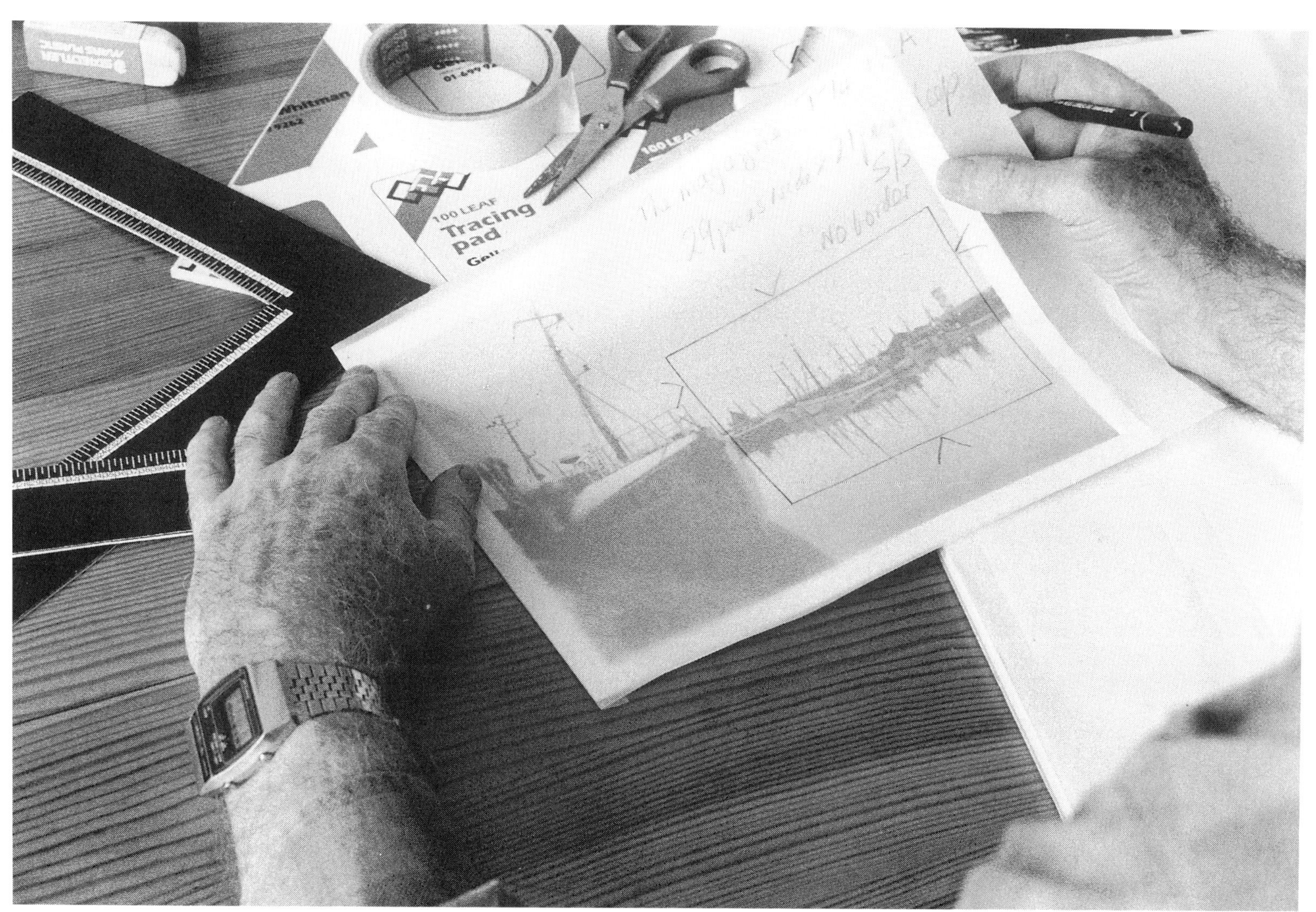
Whitman
100 LEAF
Tracing
pad
No border

be blown up, but minimized if the original is to be reduced in size.

By grouping any photographs or artwork which are to be reduced or enlarged in the same proportions you will reduce camera or scanner time and costs. Glossy unglazed bromides are generally preferable to matt finishes. Textured prints should be avoided.

Do not write on the backs of photographs – you are liable to ridge the photographic surface and this could show up in the reproduction. If you allow photographs to get out of control on a disorganized desktop, they have a perverse habit of, sooner or later, finding their way under a piece of paper on which you are writing and so are likely to be damaged. To lessen the chances of accidental damage to photographs and artwork, do not allow coffee cups, felt-tip pens and the like to float about on your working surface; use soft (e.g. 2B) or chinagraph pencils as your main drawing and writing tools. Never write on the backs of photographs in any wet medium – it is sure to transfer to the image surface of another picture or piece of artwork as soon as you put it aside. All wet-writing instruments such as fountain pens and markers are a source of danger and should be kept in pots (jam jars, coffee jars or cocoa tins will do nicely) or drawers. Ensure that artwork and bromides (the common term for photographic prints) are not allowed to come into contact with writing

which is still wet, and always check that pen and marker caps are firmly replaced.

CHECK AND DOUBLE CHECK

When you believe you have covered everything, check it all again. Have you marked the layout with the publication name, dateline and page numbers? Are you sure you have collected together and identified all photographs, artwork and manuscripts? Are the manuscript pages numbered and in the correct sequence? Have you given instructions for any spot colours, wobs (white text out of black panels), tints, rules, borders, drop letters, crossheads, pulled quotes? Every object on your layout should be covered by an instruction to the printer.

When you and the printer have been working together for some time on a particular publication some of this detail can, with the printer's agreement, be covered by the words 'follow style' but, if in doubt, spell it out. With a printer who is new to you, leave nothing to chance.

When you receive the page proofs back from the printer check everything again, marking and correcting errors and any areas where your instructions have not been carried out. You may even change your instructions at this point – but that extra work will be charged to you. Learn and use the proof-readers' marks (pages 67-68).

Designers using DTP have a different final routine which is covered in Chapter 15.

British Standard BS 5261: Part 2 1976 proof correction marks

Instruction	Textual Mark	Marginal Mark
Delete and close up	through character or through character e.g. charaácter charaácter	
Substitute character or substitute part of one or more word(s)	/ through character or through word(s)	New character or new word(s)
Wrong fount. Replace by character(s) of correct fount	Encircle character(s) to be changed	
Change damaged character(s)	Encircle character(s) to be changed	
Set in or change to italic	under character(s) to be set or changed	
Set in or change to capital letters	under character(s) to be set or changed	
Set in or change to small capital letters	under character(s) to be set or changed	
Set in or change to capital letters for initial letters and small capital letters for the rest of the words	under initial letters and under rest of word(s)	
Set in or change to bold type	under character(s) to be set or changed	

Instruction	Textual Mark	Marginal Mark
Take over character(s), word(s) or line to next line, column or page		
Take back character(s), word(s) or line to previous line, column or page		
Raise matter	over matter to be raised; under matter to be raised	
Lower matter	over matter to be lowered; under matter to be lowered	
Correct horizontal alignment	Single line above and below misaligned matter e.g. misaligned	
Close up. Delete space between characters or words	linking characters	
Insert space between characters	between characters affected	
Insert space between words	between words affected	
Reduce space between characters	between characters affected	

British Standard BS 5261: Part 2 1976 proof correction marks (continued overleaf).

Instruction	Textual Mark	Marginal Mark
Invert type	Encircle character to be inverted	
Substitute or insert full stop or decimal point	/ through character or ⅄ where required	⊙
Substitute or insert semi-colon	/ through character or ⅄ where required	;
Substitute or insert comma	/ through character or ⅄ where required	,
Start new paragraph		
Run on (no new paragraph)		
Centre	[enclosing matter to be centred]	[ ]
Indent		
Cancel indent		

Instruction	Textual Mark	Marginal Mark
Correction is concluded	None	/
Leave unchanged	------ under character to remain	
Push down risen spacing material	Encircle blemish	⊥
Insert in text the matter indicated in the margin	⅄	New matter followed by ⅄
Move matter specified distance to the right	enclosing matter to be moved to the right	
Delete	/ through character(s) or ⊢—⊣ through word(s) to be deleted	
Change capital letters to lower case letters	Encircle character(s) to be changed	
Change italic to upright type	Encircle character(s) to be changed	
Reduce space between words	between words affected	
Make space appear equal between characters or words	between characters or words affected	

British Standard BS 5261: Part 2 1976 proof correction marks (continued from overleaf).

9 Covers

The influence of the readership profile naturally extends to cover design; but if the magazine is to be displayed and sold through the bookstalls, that fact in itself imposes some conventions and restraints. Its title must be visible in the bookstall display. It must display its cover price and will probably also need to carry messages ('teasers') about the principal contents and, perhaps, information about competitions or giveaways. A comparatively recent arrival on the cover scene is the abominable bar code.

The most important of these demands is that the title must be visible when the magazine is on display. This once meant that (because of the then ubiquitous vertical display system) the title had to appear at the top of the cover design. This no longer holds true, but comparatively few designers or publishers seem to have grasped the fact that the marketing of magazines has undergone radical change. Most shops have changed to a horizontal racking system which should allow the whole cover to be visible, but the number of titles commonly stocked, and the display space available, rarely match up. The result is that most magazines – even in the larger branches of the popular chains – overlap, leaving only some two inches or less of the left side of the cover showing. This means that many magazine titles never catch the customer's eye. Even when a regular reader is searching for a particular title, it is easily missed. This gives the advantage to magazines with short titles like *Q*, or with tight logo-style titles like that of *TV Times*, provided they position their titles in the top left corner of the cover with their teasers or other text beneath. Publications with longer titles will

Comparatively few titles are instantly identifiable when magazines are racked horizontally and overlapped – which is how the majority of magazines are now displayed. Q had no problem, BBC World *magazine has a repeat logo which can be seen in such displays, and* Nursing Times *produced a neat solution.*

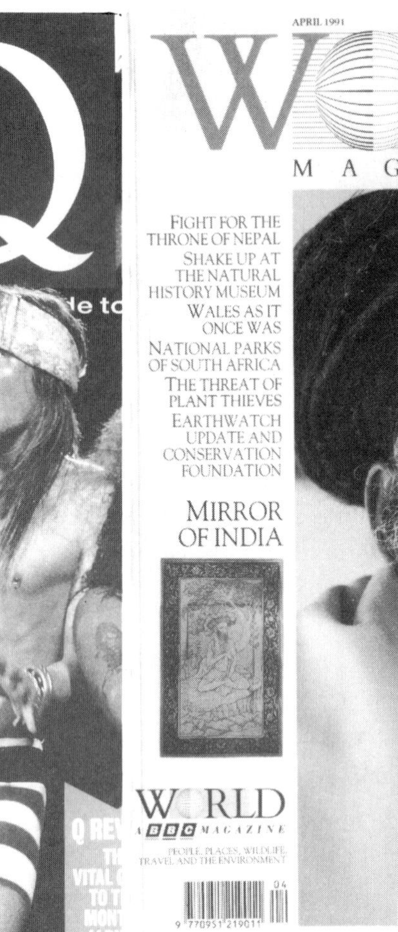

need to produce different solutions such as that produced by *Nursing Times* which, at the time of writing, was one the handful of magazines to have spotted the problem and reacted to it.

The more text the cover must carry the more difficult it becomes to produce a design which will attract the prospective buyer's eye away from the competition. Typographic skill and discipline, combined with sensitive placement, can still achieve a great deal, as a browse around the magazine racks will demonstrate.

Subscription-only magazines, internal and external house journals and the like escape many of these problems and should be designed accordingly. They need not, for example, stick to a top-of-the-page or left-of-the-page position for the title. They still have to compete, but in a different arena. Their competition is the ever-increasing flood of ephemera fighting for our attention: the free magazines thrust into our hands at railway stations, the colourful catalogues and other direct mail in our post, and that inexhaustible, talking, moving picture magazine in our living-rooms.

PICK-UP APPEAL

The successful magazine cover must persuade the intended reader to pick up the magazine from the display stand, the coffee table, the office desk or the canteen counter, and open its pages.

Many magazines rely almost entirely on the title to distinguish them from their competitors. Certainly the title is one area where some originality in the name and in the typography can be helpful in claiming attention, but while the degree of oddity should be enough to halt the passing glance it should not be so far over the top that it confuses the readers to the point that they reject the problem of sorting it out.

If the money is available in the budget, a drawn title can add considerable distinction.

There must be (with very few exceptions) a direct connection between cover and content or the reader will feel cheated and will not be inclined to repeat the experience. This requirement accounts for, but does not necessarily excuse, the similarity of the covers of a range of magazines competing for the same readers, and from issue to issue of the same magazine. Unfortunately, there are publishers who are nervous of allowing designers the freedom to express that essential cover-to-content connection in any but conventional and hackneyed ways. How many hundreds of anonymous, female faces have stared at us from the racks devoted to women's interest magazines?

The humble house journal, which at first sight would appear to have much less scope for cover variety than a general interest bookstall magazine, must achieve variety to maintain its appeal from one issue to the next. A tea company which used a pack shot (a 'dead' photograph of the packaging as used in many advertisements) on the cover of every issue of its house magazine would soon find that its staff were leaving the magazine untouched at the pick-up points. But a tea company has not only products but also plant, processes, workers, growers, supply lines, auctions, wholesale customers, retail customers, and more, from which it can draw inspiration. It can also take advantage of company innovations and developments, and any industrial, fiscal, political or other news which will affect the company or industry, to provide topical cover material.

It is difficult to imagine any magazine in which the subject matter, its market, or events, could not provide subjects of interest for thousands of covers.

WHEN THE CUPBOARD IS BARE

But when a good cover picture is proving hard to find, it is sometimes possible to combine two or more mediocre photographs, perhaps with graphics, to produce something more exciting. Occasionally, printing the photograph through a textured screen, or using other darkroom techniques as suggested in Chapter 13, can give an average picture added value.

For those who like to plan well ahead, theme covers can provide a challenge and satisfaction. A year's issues can be researched and shot (or drawn or painted) in advance if an appropriate theme can be found. Seasonal themes are usually the first to spring to mind and these can be developed to include diary events, anniversaries, or anything else which links to the issue dates. Once the thought process is channelled in this direction – particularly in a 'think tank' environment – a surprising flow of ideas can be produced.

OUT OF THE STRAITJACKET

Although non-bookstall magazines have no compelling reason to place their titles at the top of the page, few take advantage of this additional freedom. Nor do they have to clutter their covers with teasers and offers (although a cover caption pointing to the main feature is often useful).

Typographical covers are now somewhat rare but they, too, can be attractive and eye-catching for some specialized markets.

Covers are sometimes printed separately from the rest of the magazine. This may be done to allow the covers to be printed on a heavier weight or a better quality of paper, or so that colours can be run which are not available in the rest of the magazine, without breaking the budget. If two colours are available, this provides the designer with further opportunities.

By choosing appropriate colours in transparent inks and overprinting, three colours can be had for the price of two. A simple example would be the use of yellow and blue which, overprinted, would produce green. More variation can be achieved by printing tints of various weights on white, on solid second colour, and on tints of the second colour.

Back covers of bookstall magazines are usually given over to advertisements, but those magazines which do not accept advertising can take advantage of that fact to make the magazine look interesting whether face up or face down. The editor who leaves an outside back cover blank wastes an opportunity. It is the ideal place for the strong picture that demands big display but has few words to accompany it. It can be used to expand the front cover picture to provide a wrap-around cover. Suitable pictures for wrap-around treatment do not arrive on the designer's desk very often. They must contain three pictures in one and be cropped so that the front and back covers each display a complete, stand-alone picture and, when the magazine is open, the front and back covers together must display a third well-composed picture.

When a magazine deadline approaches and the chosen cover picture is ruled out for one reason or another, quick solutions must be sought. Above: Photographs from a series of in-house sporting events provide a wrap-around. The panels were printed in orange and blue – which combined to produce brown on the overlap. Left: Cut-outs from two stage performance pictures (each of which had distracting background clutter) combined to produce this cover printed in black on yellow.

Theme covers for Naafi News *began with a year in which a series of wrap-around artwork covers were linked to the month of issue.*

In the following year all twelve issues had photographic covers featuring the same model in different situations again linked to the month.

In the next year the covers had drawings illustrating anniversaries and diary events for the coming month.

A strong text theme, supported sometimes by photographs, sometimes by artwork, give Director *covers a distinctive look.*

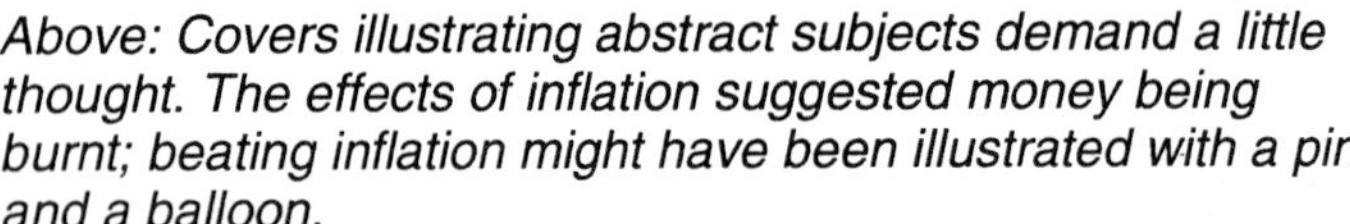

Above: Covers illustrating abstract subjects demand a little thought. The effects of inflation suggested money being burnt; beating inflation might have been illustrated with a pin and a balloon.

Right: Examples of the wrap-around cover. The identical twins were obvious candidates for this treatment, the naval subject less so – but the repetition of the titling helped meet the three-pictures criterion. The twins were printed as a black/orange duotone, the ships black on blue with the title and date reversed out of both plates and the repeats reversed out of the black only.

For centuries the British have celebrated their great spring festivals in the merrie month of May.
May, the herald of summer, the month for crowning May Queens, for raising Maypoles, and for Morris dancing, festivities which may still be seen today in villages up and down the country – even London has its May Queen festival. And in Minehead, at least, the famous hobby-horse (see below) still makes its annual appearance to dance through the town escorted by musicians

Back covers can benefit from the application of a theme just as front covers can. On the left the theme is traditions (the maypole), on the right it is star signs (Sagittarius).

Below: Strong pictures, bleeding all round, are a favourite for back covers – but not always available. Interesting but brief stories with less interesting pictures can sometimes be made to work with the addition of some related artwork and a little imagination.

SAGITTARIUS
The archer
23 November – 20 December
Planet: Jupiter
Vitality is the key to the Sagittarian charact
They enjoy sports, travel, action of any kind
They are frank, sincere people of good judgement. Room to breathe and expand is
essential for them. They are ambitious and have a strong sense of duty. They are given
occasional exaggeration and their restlessn
can be wearing on their companions.

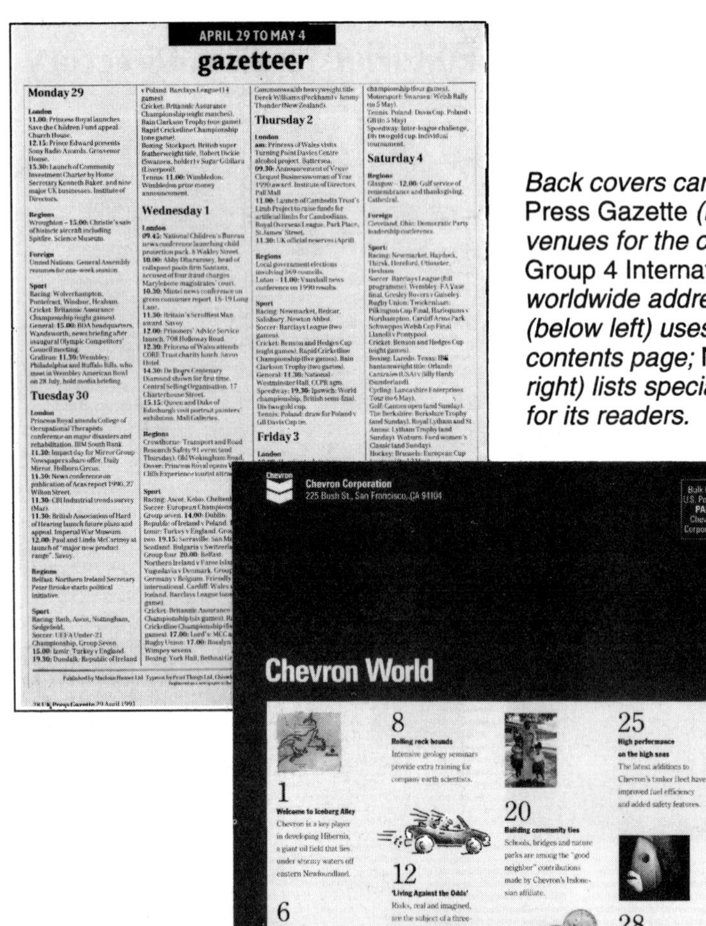

APRIL 29 TO MAY 4

gazetteer

Monday 29

London
11.00: Princess Royal launches Save the Children Fund appeal. Church House.
12.15: Prince Edward presents Sony Radio Awards. Grosvenor House.
15.30: Launch of Community Investment Charter by Home Secretary Kenneth Baker, and nine major UK businesses. Institute of Directors.

Regions
Wroughton – **15.00:** Christie's sale of historic aircraft including Spitfire. Science Museum.

Foreign
United Nations: General Assembly resumes for one-week session.

Sport
Racing: Wolverhampton, Pontefract, Windsor, Hexham.
Cricket: Britannic Assurance Championship (eight games).
General: **15.00:** BOA headquarters, Wandsworth, news briefing after inaugural Olympic Competitors' Council meeting.
Gridiron: **11.30:** Wembley: Philadelphia and Buffalo Bills, who meet in Wembley American Bowl on 28 July, hold media briefing.

Tuesday 30

London
Princess Royal attends College of Occupational Therapists conference on major disasters and rehabilitation. IBM South Bank.
11.30: Impact day for Mirror Group Newspapers share offer. Daily Mirror, Holborn Circus.
11.30: News conference on publication of Acas report 1990. 27 Wilton Street.
11.30: CBI Industrial trends survey (Mar).
11.30: British Association of Hard of Hearing ...

... v Poland. Barclays League (14 games).
Cricket: Britannic Assurance Championship (eight matches). Bain Clarkson Trophy (one game). Rapid Cricketline Championship (one game).
Boxing: Stockport: British super featherweight title. Robert Dickie (Swansea, holder) v Sugar Gibiliru (Liverpool).
Tennis: **11.00:** Wimbledon: Wimbledon prize money announcement.

Wednesday 1

London
09.45: National Children's Bureau news conference launching child protection pack. 8 Wakley Street.
10.00: Abby Dharamsey, head of collapsed pools firm Santans, accused of four fraud charges. Marylebone magistrates' court.
10.30: Mintel news conference on green consumer report. 18-19 Long Lane.
11.30: Britain's Scruffiest Man award. Savoy.
12.00: Prisoners' Advice Service launch. 708 Holloway Road.
12.30: Princess of Wales attends CORE Trust charity lunch. Savoy Hotel.
14.30: De Beers Centenary Diamond shown for first time. Central Selling Organisation. 17 Charterhouse Street.
15.15: Queen and Duke of Edinburgh visit portrait painters' exhibition. Mall Galleries.

Regions
Crowthorne: Transport and Road Research Safety 91 event (and Thursday). Old Wokingham Road.
Dover: Princess Royal opens ... Cliffs Experience tourist attra...

Sport
Racing: Ascot, Kelso, Chelten...
Soccer: European Champions... Group seven. **14.00:** Dublin ...

... Commonwealth heavyweight title: Derek Williams (Peckham) v Jimmy Thunder (New Zealand).

Thursday 2

London
am: Princess of Wales visits Turning Point Davies Centre alcohol project. Battersea.
09.30: Announcement of Veuve Clicquot Businesswoman of Year 1990 award. Institute of Directors, Pall Mall.
11.00: Launch of Cambodia Trust's Limb Project to raise funds for artificial limbs for Cambodians. Royal Overseas League, Park Place, St James' Street.
11.30: UK official reserves (April).

Regions
Local government elections involving 369 councils.
Luton – **11.00:** Vauxhall news conference on 1990 results.

Sport
Racing: Newmarket, Redcar, Salisbury, Newton Abbot.
Soccer: Barclays League (two games).
Cricket: Benson and Hedges Cup (eight games). Rapid Cricketline Championship (five games). Bain Clarkson Trophy (two games).
General: **11.30:** National Westminster Hall, CCPR agm.
Speedway: **19.30:** Ipswich: World championship, British semi-final. Div two gold cup.
Tennis: Poland: draw for Poland v GB Davis Cup tie.

Friday 3

London

... championship (four games).
Motorsport: Swansea: Welsh Rally (to 5 May).
Tennis: Poland: Davis Cup, Poland v GB (to 5 May).
Speedway: Inter-league challenge, Div two gold cup, individual tournament.

Saturday 4

Regions
Glasgow – **12.00:** Gulf service of remembrance and thanksgiving. Cathedral.

Foreign
Cleveland, Ohio: Democratic Party leadership conference.

Sport
Racing: Newmarket, Haydock, Thirsk, Hereford, Uttoxeter, Hexham.
Soccer: Barclays League (full programme). Wembley: FA Vase final, Gresley Rovers v Guiseley.
Rugby Union: Twickenham: Pilkington Cup Final, Harlequins v Northampton. Cardiff Arms Park: Schweppes Welsh Cup Final: Llanelli v Pontypool.
Cricket: Benson and Hedges Cup (eight games).
Boxing: Laredo, Texas: IBF bantamweight title: Orlando Canizales (USA) v Billy Hardy (Sunderland).
Cycling: Lancashire Enterprises Tour (to 6 May).
Golf: Cannes open (and Sunday). The Berkshire: Berkshire Trophy (and Sunday). Royal Lytham and St Annes: Lytham Trophy (and Sunday). Woburn: Ford women's Classic (and Sunday).
Hockey: Brussels: European Cup ...

Chevron Corporation
225 Bush St., San Francisco, CA 94104

Bulk Rate
U.S. Postage
PAID
Chevron
Corporation

Chevron World

Back covers can also be utilitarian. UK Press Gazette *(left) gives dates and venues for the coming week's events;* Group 4 International *(right) lists its worldwide addresses;* Chevron World *(below left) uses the back cover as its contents page;* NatWest Magazine *(below right) lists special offers it has obtained for its readers.*

GROUP 4 WORLDWIDE

group4

Where to find us –
Group 4 Securitas (International)

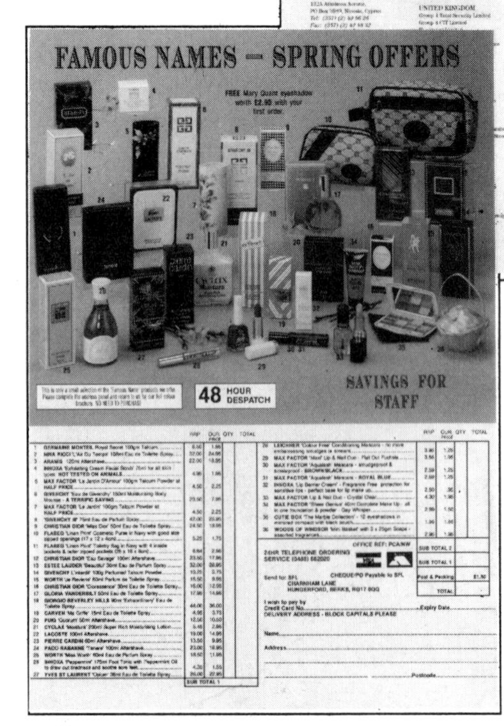

FAMOUS NAMES – SPRING OFFERS

FREE Mary Quant eyeshadow worth £2.95 with your first order.

48 HOUR DESPATCH

SAVINGS FOR STAFF

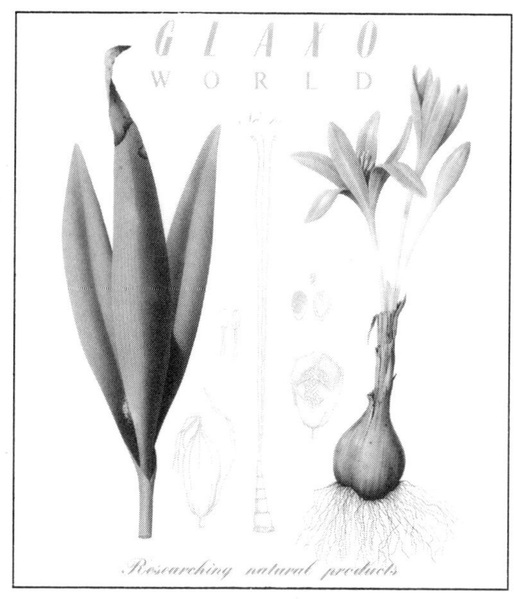

Four markedly different styles of art for the covers of BAT Industries' Outlook *(above left),* Glaxo World *(above right), Prudential's* Envoy *(left) and Data Logic's* Datalog *(right).*

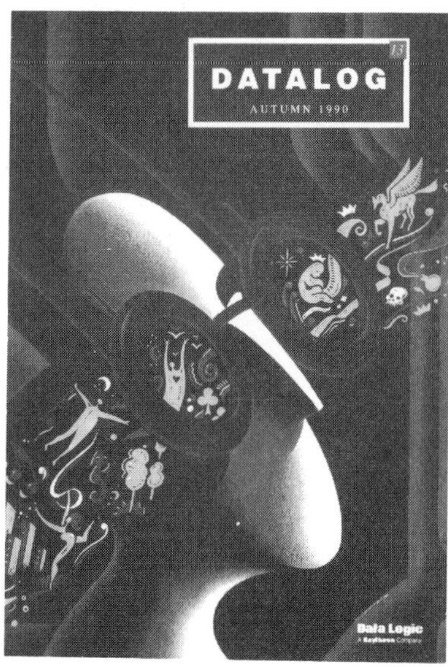

News (or a news picture) can provide a suitable cover for a news magazine. The modular, news-oriented cover of UK Press Gazette *targets British journalists.*

UK PRESS

gazette

JOURNALISM'S INDEPENDENT NEWSPAPER

29 APRIL 1991 £1

INSIDE THIS WEEK

He enjoys surprising people, especially critics. He hates to be categorised. He is ready to take on any opposition. He enjoys being the underdog – for now. Who? The new editor of *Today*, Martin Dunn. Page 5

6 Bolton hits back at new claims against the truth of "Death On The Rock"

7 BBC fund for independents may kick-start sector into sustainable orbit

8 Haymarket looks likely to be hit by industrial action in the near future

News contacts	17
Editorial services	27
Appointments	23

Sacked Mirror man finds place in Sun

By Jean Morgan

Tony Frost, the former deputy editor of the *Sunday Mirror* who left the paper in controversial circumstances five months ago, joins the *Sunday Sun*, Newcastle, tomorrow, as the new deputy editor.

Frost, 40, has been working as an editorial consultant in Washington. He flew home at the weekend.

His appointment was announced to the *Sun*'s journalists at a dinner last Wednesday celebrating the title's award as North-East Newspaper of the Year.

The *Sun* is claiming that it is currently the fastest-growing newspaper in the country – 21% up in the past year – and recently appointed editor Chris Rushton said: "We are giving the *Sunday Mirror*, *People* and the *News of the World* a bloody nose in the region. Tony will help us land the knock-out blows."

Frost will help the 20-odd journalists expand their investigative work. A new investigative reporter, Nigel Green, 27, joins the paper on the same day as Frost, from the *Sunderland Echo* where he was crime reporter. Frost's priority will be news.

Frost told *UK Press Gazette* from the USA: "There's enormous potential at the *Sunday Sun*. I went over at Easter to see Chris Rushton and I was very impressed by his positive ideas for increasing circulation. He is backed by a forward-thinking management and there's a good job to be done there."

Rushton said the appointment would show rivals just how serious Thomson Regional Newspapers was about increasing circulation – "taking on our rivals head-to-head and winning".

Frost, more than 20 years in journalism, met Rushton at the Mirror Group's training school. Frost went on to spend 12 years with the *Sunday Mirror*, except for a year in the USA on the *National Enquirier*. He filled most executive roles from chief reporter to his last as deputy editor.

His career with the *Mirror* came to an abrupt end last November when he was sacked by publisher Robert Maxwell after an internal inquiry revealed professional irregularities.

Unlike assistant editor Peter Miller, who was sacked at the same time, Frost did not appeal against dismissal.

News editor Yvonne Ridley said her staff were all delighted at the news. "He's a very lucky man," she said.

Frost gets a second chance on the award-winning NE daily.

Plea for BBC three missing in Iraq

The BBC and the NUJ are appealing for the safe return of three British reporters missing in northern Iraq for the past four weeks.

Husband-and-wife team Nicholas and Rosanna Della Casa and colleague Charles Maxwell were working for the BBC. They were last seen crossing the border from Turkey into Iraq on 23 March. Nothing has been heard of them since. It is believed they may have been detained and held by the Iraqi authorities.

BBC director general Michael Checkland has written to the Iraqi Minister of Information about the three journalists. In his letter he said: "I can assure you that the three concerned are *bona fide* journalists concerned only with reporting the events taking place during the conflict and after."

The NUJ, the International Federation of Journalists and the anti-censorship group Article 19 have released a joint statement calling on the relief agencies, the UN and the Turkish and Iraqi governments to make a special effort to find the journalists.

NUJ deputy general secretary Jake Ecclestone said: "The safety of journalists must become an international issue and must be supported by the international community to ensure that journalists are not easily mistreated."

Checkland: letter to Iraq.

PRESSPACK

10 Contents pages

The contents page provides some designers with the opportunity to indulge their personal tastes, particularly in typography, to a degree not possible elsewhere. Here we can expect to see lots of white space, a graceful use of type, a variety of rules. Here design does not have to follow the conventions applied to other pages: there are no long stretches of continuous text; if several pictures are used they may well be of equal importance and given equal prominence; subtle variation of the weight or style of type is needed to create order which the reader can follow.

But such elegant pages are becoming rare as, in more and more publications, contents are expected to share a page with advertisements, editorial, letters, credit boxes or whatever. Such congestion, I am sure, is counter-productive. The contents page is second only to the cover as the page most likely to sell a magazine to the bookstall browser. It is, in a sense, the menu where we should be able to get not only a foretaste of what's in store, but also a whiff of the quality we may expect.

The designer needs to collaborate with the editor on the contents page because, while the presentation of the information is important, it is also necessary to strike the right balance. The information should not be so sparse that it fails to intrigue (a bare list of titles, authors and page numbers would simply represent a lost opportunity to sell), but there should not be so much that it cannot be scanned in a few minutes.

Ideally the contents page should face the inside cover, but in more and more publications advertising is allowed to push the contents back. This can be a real irritation to the browser who wants to discover, quickly, whether this magazine would be entertaining, or informative, or would fulfil some other requirement. And opening immediately on to pages of advertisements can also give the impression that there will be more ads than editorial, or that the publishers consider advertising to be more important than editorial and, by implication, regard their advertisers more highly than their readers.

Another frequent irritation with contents pages is the difficulty of relating the cover picture, which tempted us to pick up the magazine in the first place, with any of the contents as listed. Those magazines which provide us with a miniature of the cover picture (or an obviously related picture, or clearly list 'Cover story') with a few words about the piece and the page number do their readers a service.

Subscription magazines, company magazines, parish magazines and the like do not have to sell themselves by means of a contents page and, consequently, many provide no contents list at all. Certainly, news magazines do not require them (unless, perhaps, they have a number of clearly defined departments) but features magazines do benefit from a contents page or at the very least (if they carry very few features per issue) a contents panel.

Listings, like contents pages, are information and reference pages rather than editorial but the design objectives are usually quite different. These pages may carry programmes, reviews, names and addresses of suppliers, advertisers, the dates and venues of events and so on. More often than not, there will be a great deal of information and comparatively little space available for it. Readers, nevertheless, will expect to be able to find the information they want quickly and easily, so organization and clear flagging will be priorities. Rules, boxes, bold and light faces, all caps and lower case – anything which helps readers find their way (not forgetting white space if it is available) is legitimate.

The following pages offer some examples of contents pages and listings pages.

Director is one of comparatively few magazines to devote two pages to contents. Finding one's way is simplicity itself and descriptive paragraphs following the titles are the norm.

M&S World's fewer pages require only one elegant page (below) to list the contents but it, too, is easy to follow and informative.

MARCH 1990 VOLUME 43 NUMBER 8

Director

For decision-makers in business

Tales of the unexpected
See page 52

The axeman cometh
See page 85

Art: portraits for the working man
See page 78

Editor Stuart Rock Executive Editor Carol Kennedy Associate Editors Tom Nash, Sara Jackson Consultant Editor George Bickerstaffe
Chief Sub-editor Caroline Proud Assistant Sub-editor Sarah Bain Editorial Assistant Louise Phillipson Editorial department 01-730 6060
Art Editor Stephen Devane Assistant Art Editor David Eccles Picture Researcher Ruth Wilkinson Design 01-823 6657
Production Manager Kate Brockenbury Production Assistants Jenny Harknett, Jennifer Doughty Production 01-823 6657 Fax: 01-235 5627

Advertisement Director Peter Mokbjr Special Projects Manager Elizabeth Lewis-Slade Advertisement Executives Kate Pennington, Jeni Wilcox, Ed Hicks
Classified Sales Executive Angus Metcalfe Advertisement Assistant Magda Hartoch Advertisement Department 01-235 1303
Market Research Manager Derek Levy Circulation Executive Daviola Hindley Accountant Kate Holmes Assistant Matt Wilks
Chairman John Nicholas Managing Director Mike Bokaie

Published for the Institute of Directors by The Director Publications Ltd, Mountbarrow House, Elizabeth Street, London SW1W 9RB
Telephone 01-235 1303 Fax: 01-235 5627 Telex: 918802 DPG
Printed by Passmore International Maidstone England

M&S WORLD

CONTENTS

20/20
E·U·R·O·P·E
VOL.3 NO. 4 • MAY 1991

CONTENTS
SOMMAIRE
INHALT
SOMMARIO
SUMARIO

2 • 20/20 EUROPE MAY 1991

HAWKER SIDDELEY
WORLD
2ND QUARTER 1991

ELLE
APRIL 1991

500
FORTUNE
INTERNATIONAL
JUNE 3, 1991

"Intellectual capital is useless unless it moves. It's no good having some guy who is very wise and sits alone in a room." PAGE 42

"The Pope will welcome investment in Eastern Europe, as long as we don't invest Western values along with it." PAGE 8

"I believe we are going to see national banking in the United States, probably within the next five years." PAGE 71

"Computers have been so dumb compared to their users. Now the computer and the human have fused." PAGE 100

"An ethic is not an ethic, and a value not a value, without some sacrifice for it. Something given up, something not gained." PAGE 111

"The way the ball bounces has a huge amount to do with what happens." PAGE 121

"America stands to become the biggest casualty in the 21st-century battle of the capitalisms." PAGE 123

ABOVE: Polaroid CEO Mac Booth, photographed by John Abbott with the output of the Helios medical imaging system his company developed in record time.

COVER: Abbott also shot this picture of Vagelos, at Merck's corporate headquarters in Rahway, New Jersey.

2 FORTUNE JUNE 3, 1991 — JUNE 3, 1991 FORTUNE 3

20/20 Europe *copes remarkably well with its five languages (on its other pages too).* Fortune *uses white out of red panels to flag subject areas; titles and page numbers are bold and three- or four-line descriptions are the norm.* Elle *relies more – and equally effectively – on subtlety.* Hawker Siddely World *illustrates lavishly to catch the eye. All have organization and clarity in common.*

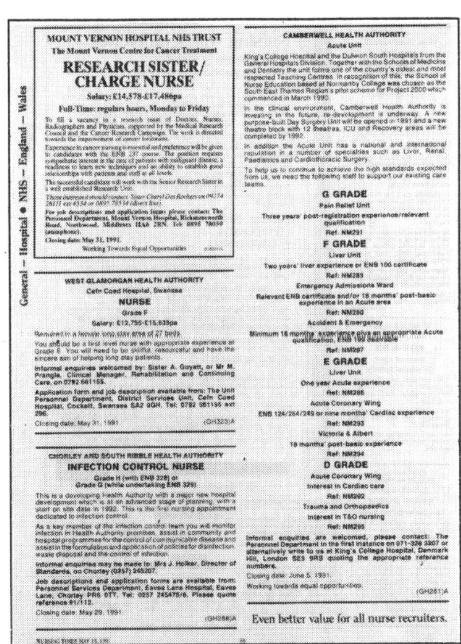

General — Hospital • NHS — England — Wales

MOUNT VERNON HOSPITAL NHS TRUST
The Mount Vernon Centre for Cancer Treatment

RESEARCH SISTER/ CHARGE NURSE

Salary: £14,578-£17,486pa

Full-Time: regular hours, Monday to Friday

To fill a vacancy in a research team of Doctors, Nurses, Radiographers and Physicists, supported by the Medical Research Council and the Cancer Research Campaign. The work is directed towards the improvement of cancer treatment.

Experience in cancer nursing is essential and preference will be given to candidates with the ENB 237 course. The position requires sympathetic interest in the care of patients with malignant disease, a readiness to learn new techniques and an ability to establish good relationships with patients and staff at all levels.

The successful candidate will work with the Senior Research Sister in a well established Research Unit.

Those interested should contact Sister Cheryl Des Rochers on 09274 28111 ext 4334 or 0895 78534 (direct line).

For job descriptions and application forms please contact: The Personnel Department, Mount Vernon Hospital, Rickmansworth Road, Northwood, Middlesex HA6 2RN. Tel: 0895 78039 (answerphone).

Closing date: May 31, 1991.

Working Towards Equal Opportunities

WEST GLAMORGAN HEALTH AUTHORITY
Cefn Coed Hospital, Swansea

NURSE

Grade F

Salary: £12,755-£15,833pa

Required in a female long stay area of 27 beds.

You should be a first level nurse with appropriate experience at Grade E. You will need to be skilful, resourceful and have the sincere aim of helping long stay patients.

Informal enquiries welcomed by: Sister A. Guyatt, or Mr M. Prangle, Clinical Manager, Rehabilitation and Continuing Care, on 0792 561155.

Application form and job description available from: The Unit Personnel Department, District Services Unit, Cefn Coed Hospital, Cockett, Swansea SA2 0GH. Tel: 0792 561155 ext 296.

Closing date: May 31, 1991. (GH323)A

CHORLEY AND SOUTH RIBBLE HEALTH AUTHORITY

INFECTION CONTROL NURSE

Grade H (with ENB 329) or
Grade G (while undertaking ENB 329)

This is a developing Health Authority with a major new hospital development which is at an advanced stage of planning, with a start on site date in 1992. This is the first nursing appointment dedicated to infection control.

As a key member of the infection control team you will monitor infection in Health Authority premises, assist in community and hospital programmes for the control of communicable disease and assist in the formulation and application of policies for disinfection, waste disposal and the control of infection.

Informal enquiries may be made to: Mrs J. Holker, Director of Standards, on Chorley (0257) 245207.

Job descriptions and application forms are available from: Personnel Services Department, Eaves Lane Hospital, Eaves Lane, Chorley PR6 0TT. Tel: 0257 245475/6. Please quote reference 91/112.

Closing date: May 29, 1991. (GH288)A

CAMBERWELL HEALTH AUTHORITY
Acute Unit

King's College Hospital and the Dulwich South Hospitals form the General Hospitals Division. Together with the Schools of Medicine and Dentistry the unit forms one of the country's oldest and most respected Teaching Centres. In recognition of this, the School of Nurse Education based at Normanby College was chosen as the South East Thames Region's pilot scheme for Project 2000 which commenced in March 1990.

In the clinical environment, Camberwell Health Authority is investing in the future, re-development is underway. A new purpose-built Day Surgery Unit will be opened in 1991 and a new theatre block with 12 theatres, ICU and Recovery areas will be completed by 1992.

In addition the Acute Unit has a national and international reputation in a number of specialties such as Liver, Renal, Paediatrics and Cardiothoracic Surgery.

To help us to continue to achieve the high standards expected from us, we need the following staff to support our existing care teams.

G GRADE
Pain Relief Unit
Three years' post-registration experience/relevant qualification
Ref: NM291

F GRADE
Liver Unit
Two years' liver experience or ENB 100 certificate
Ref: NM289
Emergency Admissions Ward
Relevant ENB certificate and/or 18 months' post-basic experience in an Acute area
Ref: NM280
Accident & Emergency
Minimum 18 months' experience plus an appropriate Acute qualification, ENB 199 desirable
Ref: NM297

E GRADE
Liver Unit
One year Acute experience
Ref: NM286
Acute Coronary Wing
ENB 124/254/249 or nine months' Cardiac experience
Ref: NM293
Victoria & Albert
18 months' post-basic experience
Ref: NM294

D GRADE
Acute Coronary Wing
Interest in Cardiac care
Ref: NM292
Trauma and Orthopaedics
Interest in T&O nursing
Ref: NM295

Informal enquiries are welcomed, please contact: The Personnel Department in the first instance on 071-326 3207 or alternatively write to us at King's College Hospital, Denmark Hill, London SE5 9RS quoting the appropriate reference numbers.

Closing date: June 5, 1991.

Working towards equal opportunities. (GH281)A

Even better value for all nurse recruiters.

081-975 9759

News Contacts

THE JOURNALISTS' GUIDE TO MAJOR NEWS SOURCES

ACCOUNTANTS · ADVISORY SERVICES · AIR CONDITIONING · AEROSPACE INDUSTRY · AIRLINES · AIRPORTS · ANIMALS · ARMED FORCES · ASSOCIATION FOOTBALL · ATOMIC ENERGY · BANKING & BUILDING SOCIETIES

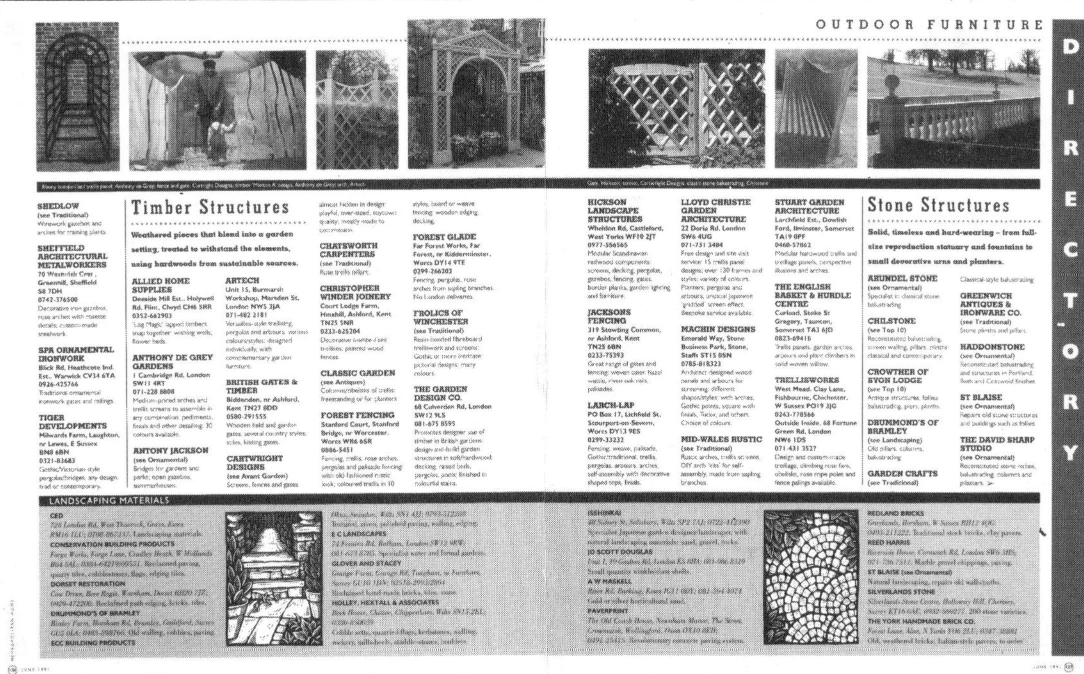

OUTDOOR FURNITURE

DIRECTORY

SHEDLOW
(see Traditional)
Wirework gazebos and arches for training plants.

SHEFFIELD ARCHITECTURAL METALWORKERS
70 Westwick Cres., Greenhill, Sheffield S8 7DH
0742-376500
Decorative iron gazebos, rose arches with rosette details; custom-made steelwork.

SPA ORNAMENTAL IRONWORK
Blick Rd, Heathcote Ind. Est., Warwick CV34 6TA
0926-425766
Traditional ornamental ironwork gates and railings.

TIGER DEVELOPMENTS
Milwards Farm, Laughton, nr Lewes, E Sussex BN8 6BN
0321-83683
Gothic/Victorian-style pergolas/bridges, any design, trad or contemporary.

Timber Structures

Weathered pieces that blend into a garden setting, treated to withstand the elements, using hardwoods from sustainable sources.

ALLIED HOME SUPPLIES
Deeside Mill Est., Holywell Rd, Flint, Clwyd CH6 5RR
0352-662903
'Log Magic' lapped timbers snap together: wishing wells, flower beds.

ANTHONY DE GREY GARDENS
1 Cambridge Rd, London SW11 4RT
071-228 8808
Medium-priced arches and trellis screens to assemble in any combination: pediments, finials and other detailing; 30 colours available.

ANTONY JACKSON
(see Ornamental)
Bridges for gardens and parks; open gazebos, summerhouses.

ARTECH
Unit 15, Burmarsh Workshop, Marsden St, London NW5 3JA
071-482 2181
Versailles-style treillage, pergolas and arbours: various colours/styles; designed individually, with complementary garden furniture.

BRITISH GATES & TIMBER
Biddenden, nr Ashford, Kent TN27 8DD
0580-291555
Wooden field and garden gates: several country styles; stiles, kissing gates.

CARTWRIGHT DESIGNS
(see Avant Garden)
Screens, fences and gates almost hidden in design: playful, over-sized, toytown quality; mostly made to commission.

CHATSWORTH CARPENTERS
(see Traditional)
Rose trellis pillars.

CHRISTOPHER WINDER JOINERY
Court Lodge Farm, Hinxhill, Ashford, Kent TN25 5NR
0233-625204
Decorative trompe-l'oeil treillises; painted wood fences.

CLASSIC GARDEN
(see Antiques)
Columns/obelisks of trellis: freestanding or for planters.

FOREST FENCING
Stanford Court, Stanford Bridge, nr Worcester, Worcs WR6 6SR
0886-5451
Fencing, trellis, rose arches, pergolas and palisade fencing with old-fashioned rustic look; coloured trellis in 10 styles; board or weave fencing; wooden edging, decking.

FOREST GLADE
Far Forest Works, Far Forest, nr Kidderminster, Worcs DY14 9TE
0299-266203
Fencing, pergolas, rose arches from sapling branches. No London deliveries.

FROLICS OF WINCHESTER
(see Traditional)
Resin-bonded fibreboard trelliswork and screens: Gothic or more intricate pictorial designs; many colours.

THE GARDEN DESIGN CO.
68 Culverden Rd, London SW12 9LS
081-675 8595
Promotes designer use of timber in British gardens: design-and-build garden structures in soft/hardwood; decking, raised beds, pergolas, pools; finished in colourful stains.

HICKSON LANDSCAPE STRUCTURES
Wheldon Rd, Castleford, West Yorks WF10 2JT
0977-556565
Modular Scandinavian redwood components: screens, decking, pergolas, gazebos, fencing, gates, border planks, garden lighting and furniture.

JACKSONS FENCING
319 Stowting Common, nr Ashford, Kent TN25 6BN
0233-75393
Great range of gates and fencing: woven osier, hazel wattle, riven oak rails, palisades.

LARCH-LAP
PO Box 17, Lichfield St, Stourport-on-Severn, Worcs DY13 9ES
0299-33232
Fencing: weave, palisade, Gothic/traditional, trellis, pergolas, arbours, arches, self-assembly with decorative shaped tops, finials.

LLOYD CHRISTIE GARDEN ARCHITECTURE
22 Doria Rd, London SW6 4UG
071-731 3484
Free design and site visit service: 15 trellis panel designs; over 130 frames and styles: variety of colours. Planters, pergolas and arbours, unusual Japanese 'gridded' screen effect. Bespoke service available.

MACHIN DESIGNS
Emerald Way, Stone Business Park, Stone, Staffs ST15 0SN
0785-818323
Architect-designed wood panels and arbours for screening: different shapes/styles: with arches, Gothic points, square with finials, Tudor, and others. Choice of colours.

MID-WALES RUSTIC
(see Traditional)
Rustic arches, trellis screens, DIY arch 'kits' for self-assembly, made from sapling branches.

STUART GARDEN ARCHITECTURE
Larchfield Est., Dowlish Ford, Ilminster, Somerset TA19 0PF
0460-57862
Modular hardwood trellis and treillage panels, perspective illusions and arches.

THE ENGLISH BASKET & HURDLE CENTRE
Curload, Stoke St Gregory, Taunton, Somerset TA3 6JD
0823-69418
Trellis panels, garden arches, arbours and plant climbers in solid woven willow.

TRELLISWORKS
West Mead, Clay Lane, Fishbourne, Chichester, W Sussex PO19 3JG
0243-778566
Outside Inside, 68 Fortune Green Rd, London NW6 1DS
071-431 3527
Design and custom-made treillage, climbing rose fans, obelisks, rose rope poles and fence palings available.

Stone Structures

Solid, timeless and hard-wearing – from full-size reproduction statuary and fountains to small decorative urns and planters.

ARUNDEL STONE
(see Ornamental)
Specialist in classical stone balustrading.

CHILSTONE
(see Top 10)
Reconstituted balustrading, screen walling, pillars, plinths: classical and contemporary.

CROWTHER OF SYON LODGE
(see Top 10)
Antique structures, follies balustrading, piers, plinths.

DRUMMOND'S OF BRAMLEY
(see Landscaping)
Old pillars, columns, balustrading.

GARDEN CRAFTS
(see Traditional)
Classical-style balustrading.

GREENWICH ANTIQUES & IRONWARE CO.
(see Traditional)
Stone plinths and pillars.

HADDONSTONE
(see Ornamental)
Reconstituted balustrading and structures in Portland, Bath and Cotswold finishes.

ST BLAISE
(see Ornamental)
Repairs old stone structures and buildings such as follies.

THE DAVID SHARP STUDIO
(see Ornamental)
Reconstituted stone arches, balustrading, columns and pilasters. ➤

LANDSCAPING MATERIALS

CED · CONSERVATION BUILDING PRODUCTS · DORSET RESTORATION · DRUMMOND'S OF BRAMLEY · ECC BUILDING PRODUCTS · E C LANDSCAPES · GLOVER AND STACEY · HOLLEY, HEXTALL & ASSOCIATES · ISSHINKAI · JO SCOTT DOUGLAS · A W MASKELL · PAVERPRINT · REDLAND BRICKS · REED HARRIS · ST BLAISE (see Ornamental) · SILVERLANDS STONE · THE YORK HANDMADE BRICK CO.

Metropolitan Home's easy-to-follow directory of suppliers (above) is divided into product areas. The appointments pages in Nursing Times *(above left) have marginal guides to geographic and occupational areas. The contacts pages of* UK Press Gazette *(left) are also flagged with subject headings.*

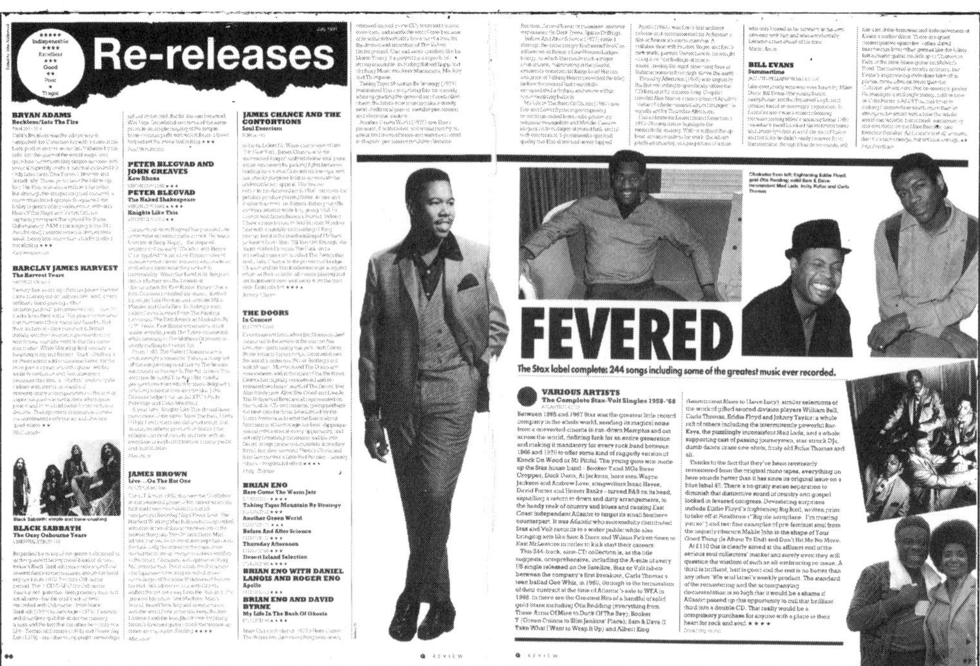

Q (above left) packs in a great many reviews (films, videos, books, concerts, LPs, re-releases, equipment). It does so simply and effectively by running them on through the columns but enlivens what could be dull pages by expanding on selected items.

Rules divide off geographical areas in Crafts' directory of shops and galleries.

11 News in magazines

The problem the designer faces in fitting several news stories and pictures into a magazine format is simply that posed by the small page area.

As so often happens, the seed of the solution is to be found in the problem itself. The magazine page is too small to accommodate a number of news stories and pictures (or other short pieces such as new products) in an interesting and yet ordered way. The answer is to treat the two facing pages as one landscape page so that, for example, two A4 pages are treated as an A3 landscape. For most magazines this means an adjustment to the grid to reduce the inside margins (see the illustration on page 88).

Centre spreads in magazines (and in the tabloids) have been treated in this way for many years and gradually the idea was carried over to other magazine feature-page spreads. A few designers recognized that this idea could also be applied to the treatment of news pages and have used it with considerable success. But acceptance of the two-page news spread, despite its obvious benefits, has been much slower than that of features and is still comparatively rare. In many instances, where it has been used, the designers have failed to adjust the margins and the resulting wide, central river of white defeats the objective.

Viewing the spread as a single entity for news requires the designer to adopt a disciplined, modular approach – in effect, a modification of the method already described for dealing with features in Chapter 7. The modular approach can, of course, also be used while treating left and right pages as single entities.

On feature pages, the elements are formed into simple shapes of differing sizes, ratios, and

The news pages of many magazines are designed with equal margins on the left and right of each A4 page – this produces a double width margin as a central gutter. In this grid the central gutter is equal to the outer margins which helps tie the two facing pages together.

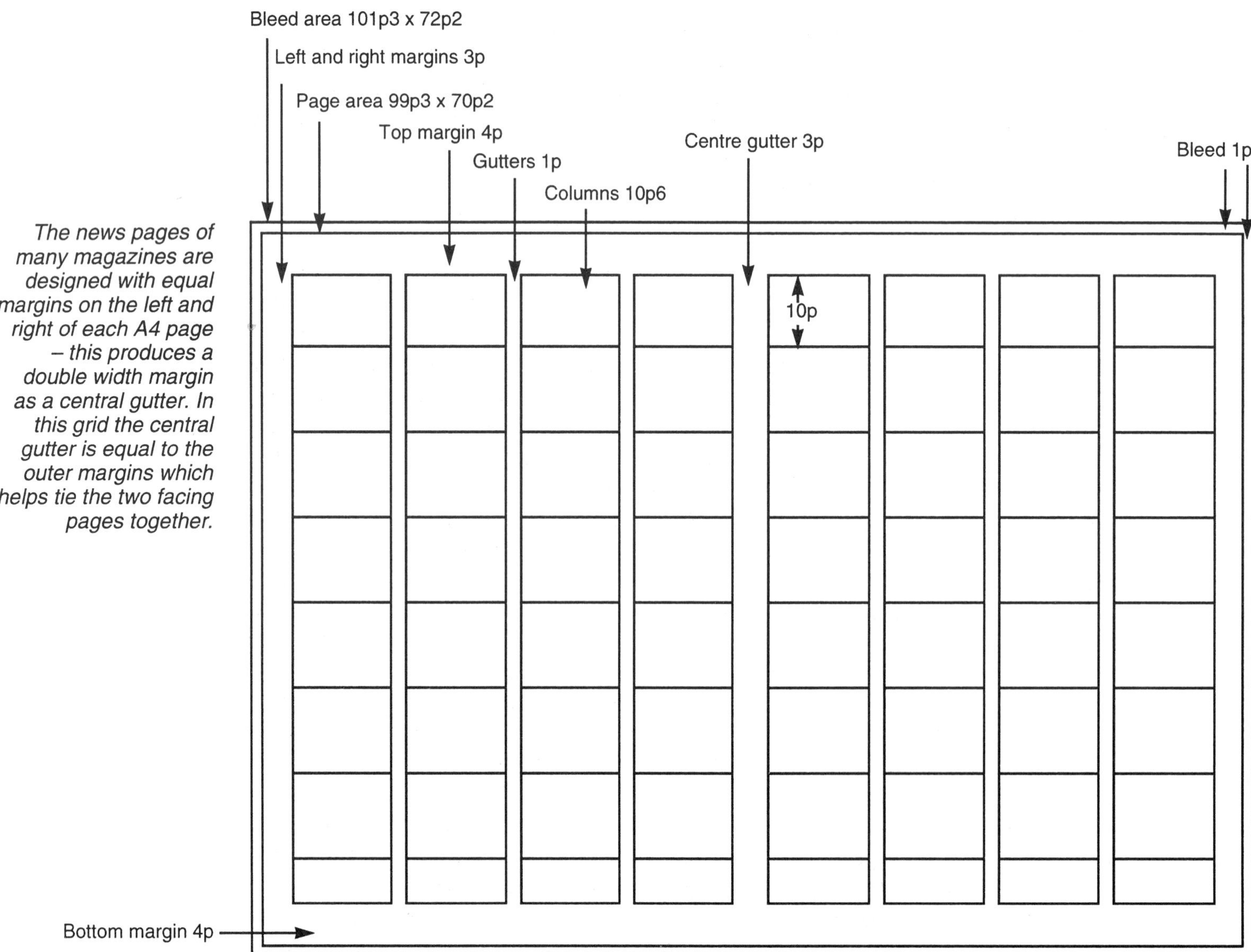

stress, to create contrasts and balance across the spread. The same approach is adopted on news pages, but each story or story-and-picture is treated as a separate rectangular module.

As with feature pages, one of these modules should be made to dominate the spread. Which story, picture, or combination, should fill this role is, generally, an editorial decision basd on interest values.

A DIFFERENT GRID

The mini-grids described in Chapter 7 would probably prove too small for sketching the more complex roughs of news layouts and, indeed, the grids for features and news may well be different in the number and width of columns, text size and so on. Four quarter-size spreads (as illustrated on page 91) or even two half-size spreads produced from the master grid will probably prove more convenient than the eight-up used for feature spreads. And you may find that you need to produce many more roughs before you are satisfied with a layout.

As an exercise, draw up a new grid with four columns (as illustrated) and reduce it to half-size. Cut out several news stories and pictures from a newspaper or magazine and try out some roughs as you did for the feature pages. If you cannot find text set to the width of your columns, simply trim wider columns down to fit.

Your lead story, its headline, and any accompanying picture should be placed on the spread as a single module. The position and shape are likely to be influenced by the direction of any movement in the picture and by the layout of other pages in the magazine (avoid repetition from spread to spread). Bear in mind, however, that the outer, upper corners of the page are what most readers see first. This is particularly significant where regular departments such as 'New products' or 'Overseas news' are important features of a publication. These generic headings usually appear as comparatively small wobs or tint panels. They should be positioned on the outer edges of the pages.

Within its allotted space, each module is treated as if it were a small feature: the text is cast off and the number of lines tried across differing numbers of columns to see which text shape, in combination with picture (if used) and headline, produces the most dynamic overall shape. A two-deck headline over two columns, placed above text divided evenly between the two columns, above a two-column picture, would provide vertical stress; the same material could provide horizontal stress if the text and picture shapes were placed side by side with a single-deck four-column headline above them.

Each item is added to the spread in turn, but not necessarily in order of importance – indeed, it is as well to position one fairly strong item at the foot of the spread to provide balance. As each module is added, try to vary the size, ratio and thrust of the shapes they make.

CROSSING THE GREAT DIVIDE

Taking at least one module across the fold, often the major one, helps to unify the spread. When a headline crosses from one page to the other arrange it so that the fold falls between two words. This might require some adjustment to the wording, but it can frequently be achieved simply by sizing the headline up or down, using a condensed or expanded version of the typeface, or making minor adjustments to the word-spacing. These adjustments are invariably easier if the fold comes nearer the end of the headline than the beginning – the more words to the left of the fold, the more flexibility you have. Headlines with short words will usually prove easier to accommodate than those with long words.

Designing across the fold gives the news pages a horizontal look which is quite different from the usual vertical look of a newspaper page. This look can be reinforced by ensuring that the horizontal white spaces between items line up across the spread whenever possible, and by breaking up some of the vertical ones.

Rules, headlines and even pictures can also be taken across the fold. If a picture is to print across the fold, ensure that the fold runs through an unimportant area and not, for example through a face.

You will find that the demand for rules, boxes, tint panels, hoods and other devices (discussed in Chapter 13) is greater in news pages than in feature pages, because of the need to separate the stories and make it easy for readers to find their way.

Although designing across the fold in news pages is far from being the general practice (it does require more time and effort), the modular approach is fast becoming the standard in both magazines and newspapers. Other approaches to designing news pages in magazines have been tried (indeed still are) without notable success: the 'jigsaw' approach of old-fashioned tabloids, the squared-up look of the Sunday 'qualities', and what might best be described as the 'pop' approach.

Many news magazines simply run stories from column to column allowing headlines, usually identically set, to fall as they will. The formula for this type of magazine usually requires department headings to be placed in a coloured strap at the page head. For some reason, in British and American magazines, the strap is almost invariably red but continental Europeans often favour yellow. This formula certainly places no obstacles in the path of the readers, who know exactly where they are and

Opposite: Four mini-grids can be mounted up on an A3 sheet (in a similar way to the eight-page features grids) as a master for roughing out news pages.

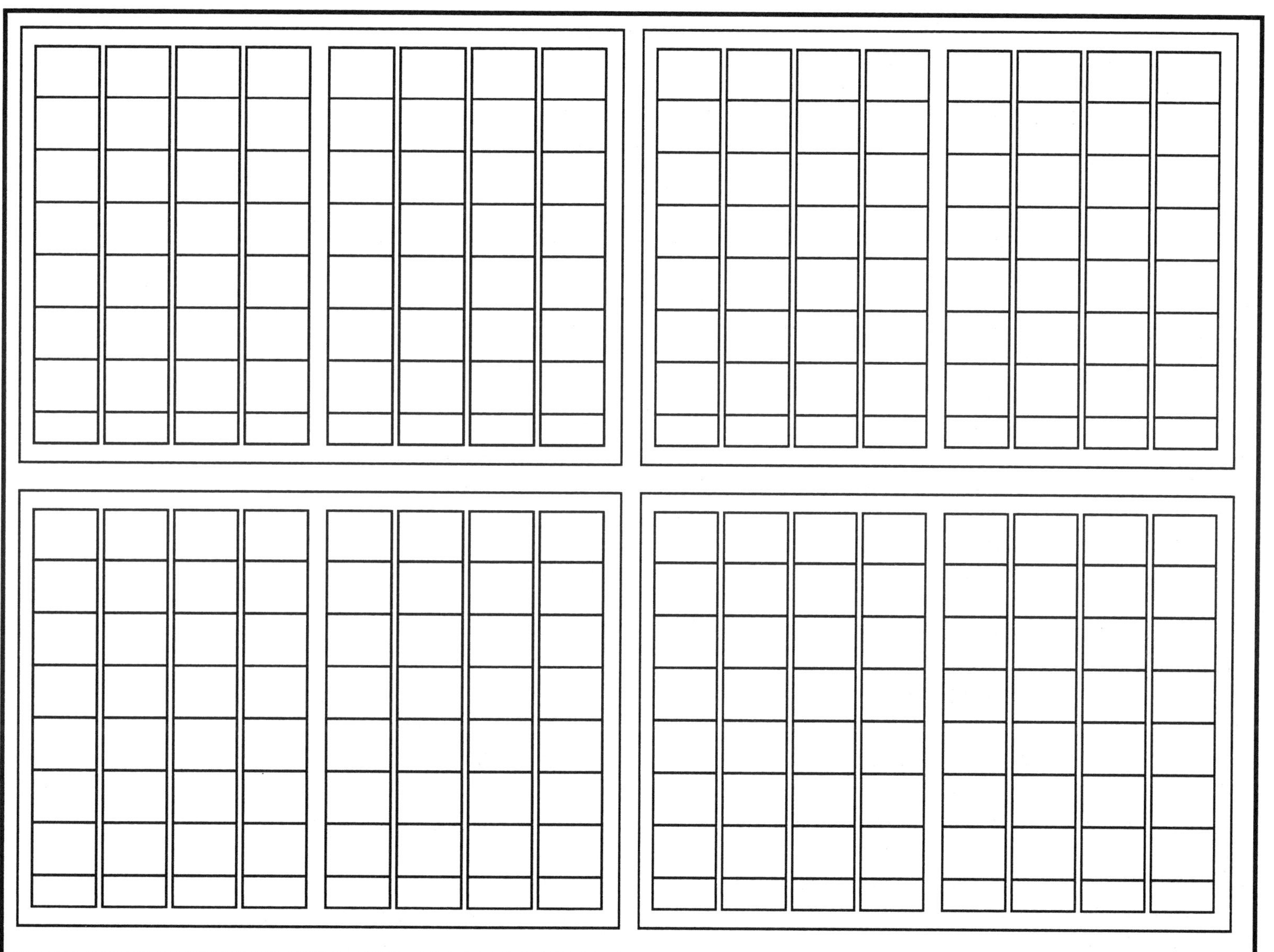

where they are going, but it is a suitable approach only for those magazines which are regarded as required reading by committed readers, or where topicality is important but schedules tight.

Although newspaper design imposes a number of different constraints and conventions, magazine designers who familiarize themselves with the methods of designing news and feature pages described here will find no great difficulty in adapting if they move over to the design of newspapers.

UK Press Gazette *(right) uses a modular layout and contrasts vertical and horizontal shapes. It employs single column rules broken by the double horizontal rules.*

MAGAZINES

Realm revamp

IPC is to revamp *Woman's Realm* as "the definitive mid market weekly for women 40-49". A new logo and editorial design will be introduced from 5 June. A number of new features will be added and *WR*'s advice columns will be grouped together in a four-page 'Advice file'. The revamp will be backed by advertising in sister titles.

Out to tender

RM Publications is understood to be seeking buyers for its two trade titles, the 9,000-circulation monthly *Food Production* and the bi-monthly *National Security International*. The titles closed at Easter with the loss of around six jobs when RM closed.

Quick increase

H Bauer is expected to increase the price of *TV Quick* to between 35p and 45p this week, six weeks after the weekly title launched with a 10p starter price. The company is also planning to acquire a UK printing operation capable of handling the 2m circulation magazine, according to a *Printing World* report.

Peskett buys DMI

Peter Peskett, the former md at Emap Response, has returned to magazine publishing by acquiring *Direct Marketing International* from Charterhouse Communications.

Peskett is to publish the 13,000-circulation monthly with partner David Cowles, formerly a publisher at Response. DMI's staff transfer with the magazine.

Emap switch

Emap National is switching *Yours*, its over-60s monthly, from tabloid to A4 format. The change has been made to increase the title's exposure in retail outlets by raising it from the plinth to news-stand level.

The magazine has an ABC of 117,792, 30% up in two years.

Pain reliever

Rita Carter has won the first Medical Journalists' Pain Relief Award for a feature published by *She* magazine last year. The £1,000 award will be made again this year by sponsor Nurofen.

Union action imminent at Haymarket

By Mike Dash

Haymarket Magazines looks certain to be hit by industrial action. NUJ staff balloted on Monday voted 86% in favour of action up to and including a strike as management and the chapel exhausted the disputes procedure laid down in their house agreement.

Last week's ballot showed a hardening in the chapel's support for action since the dispute began. Three weeks ago, 79% had voted in favour of taking a stand against management attempts to introduce what the NUJ alleges is a system of personal contracts.

MoC Hashi Syedain said the chapel was considering options including working to contract, one-day stoppages and an all-out strike.

"Action will begin sooner rather than later," she told *UK Press Gazette*. "We have got a very strong mandate to do whatever is necessary to achieve our aims."

Haymarket has denied it is attempting to derecognise the NUJ. It has said it will no longer conduct collective bargaining over pay but will continue to consult the union on health, new technology, dismissals and training.

A pay rise of "at least" 7.5% appears in all April pay packets.

Personnel director Martin Hover said: "We are determined to continue to produce our magazines regardless.

"We hope this small minority, 14% of our total staff, will recognise that a system of settling pay that works perfectly well for the other 86% will also work perfectly well for them."

Syedain said focus on the derecognition dispute had limited the chapel's protest over the recent announcement of a package of eight redundancies (*UKPG*, 22 April).

Most of the eight staff affected, including Syedain and fellow chapel committee member Dan Butler, have been offered alternative jobs with the company. One has already left Haymarket.

Accountancy Age pays out in audit libel case

AccountancyAge

The VNU weekly *Accountancy Age* has paid undisclosed libel damages to three chartered accountants.

The magazine published a story last July alleging that David Rose, David Kappel and Irving Zackheim of David A Rose & Co had failed to hand over audit papers relating to Dunsdale Securities to either the Serious Fraud Office or Dunsdale's liquidator.

VNU paid an "acceptable sum" into court to settle the action and apologised for the story.

The men said they had brought the action not for financial gain but to vindicate their professional reputations.

Sales near completion

Petersons Publishing is at an "advanced stage" in negotiations that should see all five of the company's titles continue production under the existing management.

The company went into receivership a month ago along with its parent, Worcestershire Web Offset, after being hit by bad debts.

Managing director Bruce Ayling said: "The deal can't come quickly enough for us."

Watch Out! suspended

Apple Communications has suspended publication of its Watch Out! Group, three crime prevention quarterlies published in Kent.

Two of the titles launched this month. The magazines had circulations of between 50,000 and 70,000.

Publisher Anthony Williams said: "I still believe in the concept, but my faith was not supported by the advertising revenues."

Now to join Star in track battle for speed readers

A weekly magazine aimed at speedway enthusiasts launches on 15 May.

Speedway Now, which will run to 48 pages and sell at 95p, has an initial print-run of 35,000 and is backed by Dave Lanning, the head of forward planning at *TVTimes*. He has been involved with the sport as a commentator and promoter since the 1970s.

The magazine will be edited by Lanning's son, Russell, with the assistance of another son, Philip, who has been poached from his job as news editor of the market-leading weekly competitor *Speedway Star*.

"We will major on the riders, not the managers and the tracks. We're optimistic and believe we can do better than the existing titles," Russell Lanning said.

Speedway Star editor Philip Rising said there could be room for a new title in the sector but described Lanning's circulation target as "the heights of ambition".

The *Star*, published since 1953, sells 25,000 copies a week. Rising claimed: "I would doubt they will sell five figures."

Wood steps down

John Wood, the FoC at Morgan-Grampian, stood down from office at the chapel's AGM on Thursday.

Last year Wood led the chapel in an eight-week work to contract, which ended in December when journalists accepted a 7.5% pay offer plus improved benefits.

8 UK Press Gazette 29 April 1991

MAGAZINES

Craver quits Reed for top Ziff-Davis post

By Mike Dash

Ziff-Davis, the US computer publishing giant, has appointed David Craver managing director of the UK operation it plans to establish this year.

Craver, currently publishing director and editor-in-chief of Reed Business Publishing's 112,000 circulation *Computer Weekly*, leaves Reed at the end of the month to take up the post. He is currently recruiting staff for a possible autumn magazine launch.

Ziff, a market leader in the USA, has publishing interests in Germany and France and already licences two of its titles to UK-based publishers. VNU produces *PC Week* and Reed publishes *PC Magazine*.

Last week Craver said Ziff wanted to "keep its good relations" with Reed and VNU but wanted "a fairly substantial operation in the UK".

He declined to elaborate on the company's launch plans or give a date for its first UK launch. Industry speculation suggests an edition of *PC Professional*, launched in Germany this March, may appear in the autumn, to be followed next year by a title such as *PC Sources*, aimed at direct buyers.

Renegotiation of the company's contracts with Reed and VNU also appears to remain a possibility.

"Ziff believe in high quality and high circulations," Craver said. "They are a little aghast at the pruning that is going on in the UK market at present. They want to be a major player internationally."

● Craver was one of at least five UK computer magazine publishers approached by Ziff.

One of the four who rejected the company's approaches said: "Ziff is an excellent publisher, but like all American companies it can be very demanding to work for."

Craver: to head UK arm of US computer giant.

And in this corner…

A new title has stepped up to challenge for Britain's monthly boxing magazine crown. The current champion, *Boxing Monthly*, reeled from an early blow but is now eager to slug it out on the news-stands.

First the contender: *Boxing Outlook* is the product of a breakaway team from the *Boxing Monthly* camp. It is led by Barry Hugman, former chairman and partner in Boxing Monthly Limited, and made up of a number of his employees including former *BM* editor George Zellaney.

According to Hugman, the decision to quit had been forced on the team by a financial crisis so severe that word has since spread that the magazine was out for the count.

But a last-minute takeover by Greenflex Associates got *Boxing Monthly* up off the canvas.

A new team led by Graham Houston, former editor of the venerable weekly *Boxing News*, has been recruited under the banner of British Sports Magazines. Two issues of *Boxing Monthly* will appear in May, and it looks as if *Boxing Outlook* has a fight on its hands after all.

The combatants are evenly matched. Chris Ashton of Seymour, which distributes *Boxing Monthly*, said: "Side by side they look like they were done by the same people."

Barry Hugman concedes that the magazines have a similar design but adds: "*Boxing Outlook* is going back to the original coffee-table idea, with more variety and colour."

Having recovered from its knock-down, *Boxing Monthly* is keen to continue the bout. Nigel Baker, managing director of British Sports Magazines, said: "We feel we have the best boxing magazine in the world. If they want to do another in competition then let the best man win. We want a good clean fight."

Pay bargaining dispute erupts at FT Mags

NUJ staff at Financial Times Magazines are to go into dispute with management over what the chapel sees as an attempt to abandon collective bargaining on pay.

The dispute arose after journalists claimed a 13.5% pay rise plus additional benefits on 28 March. Management responded by saying it could not afford an across-the-board rise for the 55 NUJ-eligible staff, who produce titles including *Investors Chronicle*, *Pensions Management* and *The Banker*.

Instead, journalists were offered merit rises which vary from 1-2% to 10.5%. Around three-quarters of FT Magazines' staff have received an offer.

After requesting a further meeting journalists attempted to involve *Financial Times* chief executive David Palmer, who replied that he was not prepared to meet the chapel as he never participated in pay negotiations.

Around 20 NUJ members have since written letters of protest to Palmer. Joint FoC Adrian Bowden said: "We now consider negotiations have reached a stalemate and intend to put the matter into dispute.

"We believe that if applied generally the sums offered would mean a rise of 3.5-4%. We believe this undermines the claim that the company has no resources to make an across-the-board offer."

FT Magazines publisher Mark van de Weyer said: "The full value of the claim was over 15%, perhaps as high as 17%. We will talk to the union at any time, but there is no point in talking further about such a ridiculous claim."

Van de Weyer said the offer of merit rises was not intended to set a precedent and added that the company would bring forward the start of 1992's pay round.

McLeavy closures bring sackings and leave freelances unpaid

Flamboyant publisher Terry McLeavy has shut down his West Country-based group of glossy county magazines, dismissing more than a dozen staff and leaving an army of freelances owed thousands of pounds.

County Publications ceased trading on 17 April. Its three titles, *Gloucestershire – the County Magazine* and sister monthlies covering Worcestershire & Herefordshire and Warwickshire, have closed.

Staff were asked to return the keys to company cars and leave. McLeavy's son had to ferry some stranded employees home.

Journalists had been producing the magazines from barns in the grounds of McLeavy's Regency mansion, putting out buckets to catch water from a leaky ceiling when it rained.

Kettles were filled at an outside tap also used to wash down McLeavy's polo ponies.

Former editor-in-chief Viv Hargreaves resigned last year because of a six-month backlog of unpaid bills. "I had about 60 contributors on my books, about half of them professional journalists," she said. "By the end of August there was a bill of about £10,000."

David Green, the freelance editor of the Worcestershire and Warwickshire magazines, said he was owed £1,600.

McLeavy told the local Press: "We are simply ceasing to trade. In the current economic climate it is not worth continuing."

A member of McLeavy's family answered with a terse "no comment" when *UK Press Gazette* telephoned him at Grove Court, his mansion near Bristol.

29 April 1991 UK Press Gazette 9

Fortune makes use of the typical news magazine approach (right) with text running on through the columns but switches to a modular layout (below) for product news.

NEWS/TRENDS

WHAT COMPANIES MUST SELL TO PAY FOR AN APPENDECTOMY

COMPANY	PRODUCT
Dayton Hudson	39,000 Ninja Turtle action figures
Atlantic Richfield	192,000 gallons of gas
Southern California Edison	1 year's electricity for 330 households
Anheuser-Busch	11,627 6-packs of 12 oz. Bud
Goodyear Tire & Rubber	461 radial tires for passenger cars

CEO Macke: One appendectomy adds up to a lot of turtles.

CEOs SEEK HELP ON HEALTH COSTS

■ How many Ninja Turtle action toys does it take to pay for an appendectomy? Answer: 39,000, at least if you're Dayton Hudson. ... Kenneth Macke, CEO ... retailer, ... to say it. the problem is beyond our control. We need the government to get involved."

In 1990, 35 corporations, including AT&T, Chrysler, Eastman Kodak, 3M, and Wal-Mart Stores, got together with ... groups to ... vs. $85 million of $162 million in 1989.

Prognosis? Says Kenneth Thorpe, associate professor at the University of North Carolina's school of public health: "We've had national health care insurance debate for 80 years. But now you've got big corporate players at the table who have a lot of influence in Republican circles. That hasn't happened before." –Rick Tetzeli

... doesn't breathe life into the health club industry, which has plateaued after the boom decade of the 1980s, what does? Judging by statistics provided by Bally Manufacturing's Health & Tennis subsidiary, operator of 317 clubs, Americans get most serious about their regimen three times a year. New Year's resolutions spark the first effort, and early-summer fears of looking flabby on the beach the second. The third comes in the fall when colder weather drives some back to the clubs. Mothers in particular, having packed the kids off to school, return to the pleasure of the treadmill and exercise bike. –R.T.

INVESTMENT ADVICE FROM THE POPE

■ Westerners eyeing business opportunities in Eastern Europe will find encouragement in Pope John Paul II's new 114-page encyclical. The Pope, once thought to have a slightly leftish political tilt, makes clear that the Roman Catholic Church will not play an obstructionist role in the econom-

... Ferrari in Fiorano, Italy: giving capitalism its due

INNOVATION

PRODUCTS TO WATCH

By Stephanie Losee

FLYING BOAT

■ Now you can *really* fly over the water—if you can spare $60,000. The speedy Flarecraft, made by Flarecraft Corp. of Westport, Connecticut, becomes airborne at about 42 mph. It takes advantage of the ground effect—the increase in lift that acts on aircraft and birds when their outstretched wings are close to the ground or water—to rise above the surface. As the Flarecraft's speed approaches 70 mph, the boat rises until it's skimming along about a yard over the waves. The 30-foot-long speedster holds three adults and gear weighing up to a total of 550 pounds. Controlled with a steering wheel, it's no harder to operate than a regular powerboat. Nor is any pilot's license required. It can easily handle swells up to three feet, and its BMW motorcycle engine burns just three gallons per hour at the cruising speed of 72 mph. The Flarecraft lands in boat dealerships at the end of July.

JOGGER'S COMPANION

■ This personal stereo not only entertains you as you run but also keeps track of your progress. Sanyo's SPT1000 Sportable has a built-in pedometer to calculate distance and lap speed. Choose among three exercise modes: walking, speed walking, and jogging. Then punch in your stride and pace, or use the preset defaults. The Sportable records each strike of your foot to calculate distance, and beeps when you've completed your trek. If you suspect you're slowing down, press a button—the pedometer will beep each step until you synchronize. The Sportable, with cassette player and AM/FM radio, will appear in stores in July for $54.99.

ONE VERSATILE PERFUME

■ This liquid does the work of four toiletries to save space in a suitcase. One Unlimited Perfume, from La Parfumerie of New York City, changes forms to act as a fragrance, moisturizer, bath oil, and body oil. Placed on pulse points such as wrists, it is a perfume. Mixed in your palm with water, it thickens into a whitish lotion. It can be added to a bath or rubbed on damp skin as a body oil. One Unlimited comes in six alcohol-free fragrances named for exotic locales such as Indochine, Malaga, and Provence. A 3.4-ounce bottle is available at department stores for $30.

SMART WINDOWS

■ Let the sun shine in—or not. Taliq Corp., a subsidiary of Raychem Corp. in Sunnyvale, California, has developed windows that turn from clear to frosted with the flick of a switch. In Varilite Vision Panels, a thin polyester film coated with liquid crystal droplets is bonded with polyvinyl butyral interlayers and laminated between two panes of glass. When the panel is switched on, voltage causes the liquid crystals to align, making the glass transparent, as in the window on the left in the picture. With power off, the liquid crystals realign randomly to scatter light, as with the right window. Taliq has been selling panels for interior windows for 18 months, and now it offers insulated exterior windows, too. Vision Panels cost about $80 per square foot installed for interior panels, $90 for the exterior windows.

Sure, curtains would be cheaper. But, says Stephen Selkowitz, a fan who is program leader of the windows and lighting program at Lawrence Berkeley Laboratory, "there are situations where you want something more dynamic and readily controllable than shades and shutters."

110 FORTUNE JUNE 3, 1991

The Bagleys at home. Colgate-Palmolive helped them buy this house.

ic—read capitalist—development of these predominantly Catholic countries.

To help prepare his message, the Polish-born pontiff sought the views of a dozen respected economists, including Stanford University professor Kenneth Arrow, winner of a 1972 Nobel Prize, and Harvard professors Hendrik Houthakker and Jeffrey D. Sachs.

Their free-market opinions are reflected in the papal letter to the faithful. John Paul's concern for the poor in the former Eastern bloc, along with those in the Third World, is tempered by a recognition of the hard economic realities. He acknowledges wealth creation as a precursor to wealth distribution. Says Father Francis McHugh, director of the Von Hugel Institute, an ethics research center at Cambridge University: "You can safely say the Pope will welcome investment in Eastern Europe, as long as we don't invest our whole system of Western values along with it." –Christopher Knowlton

MORTGAGE HELP AS JOB BENEFIT

■ Medical and dental coverage, a good pension . . . and help financing a house? At many corporations, generous assistance with home purchases and interest-free loans have long been a perk for top executives. But a few companies extend similar benefits to employees at all levels. Colgate-Palmolive, for example, helps its workers buy homes by paying points and origination fees on mortgages of up to $191,250, and a portion of such costs on bigger ones. The New York City company does this to keep aboard workers who might otherwise leave to take jobs in areas where housing is less expensive.

Among the beneficiaries of Colgate's program: toxicologist Daniel Bagley, 32. He and his wife, Laurie, a Johnson & Johnson chemist, bought a $215,000 house in Somerset, New Jersey. Bagley estimates Colgate's program saved them about $2,000 up front. He also figures he'll save at least $5,000 in interest payments over the 15-year period of his mortgage because Fleet Mortgage Services, the lender, gives Colgate employees favorable rates.

According to Martin Levine, a senior vice president at the Federal National Mortgage Association, or Fannie Mae, other companies find housing costs "a serious issue" and have asked for help in developing programs that aid lower-paid employees in buying homes. Fannie Mae has put together several. In one, workers who don't have the down-payment money to qualify for a bank loan could borrow the difference from their employer. Then Fannie Mae would guarantee the mortgage as a way of encouraging banks to lend the balance to the borrower. –Jennifer Reese

KOREA'S GORILLAS WIN AGAIN

■ Government policymakers in South Korea have long wanted to pare down the size and influence of Korea's three-dozen largest conglomerates, corporate gorillas whose sales equal a monstrous 91% of the country's GNP. Samsung Group, the largest with annual sales of $35 billion, sells just about everything imaginable, from excavators to X-ray machines.

Most recently the government floated a policy aimed at forcing the *chaebol*, as the conglomerates are known, to limit the scope of their widely diversified businesses to just three industries per company. But two days before the *chaebol* were to announce their "chosen" areas of concentration, the government diluted its proposal, an insider at one conglomerate told FORTUNE. Under a revised plan, the conglomerates will find it far easier to hang on to any business they particularly want to keep. That further confirms the suspicion of foreign companies that might have wanted to buy valuable pieces spun off: It will be a long time before the *chaebol* are cut down to size. –Ford S. Worthy

WOMEN'S WORK IS ON THE LINKS

■ More women are confirming what they've suspected for years: Golf is good for business. Janet Thompson, vice president of marketing at Mazda Motor of America in Irvine, California, says she's built strong contacts with many important car and truck dealers she first met on the links. "Dealers always have golf outings," she says. "If I wasn't there too, I'd be standing on the sideline missing out."

Thompson is a member of the Newport Beach Country Club. It has always had women members. Now some former men-only clubs are changing their minds, thanks in part to pressure from the U.S. Golf Association. It has decreed that its prestigious championship tournaments can be hosted only by clubs with nondiscriminatory policies. (For a sampling of holdouts, see table.)

While only about 20 of the

Janet Thompson is waiting for her club's opening time for women.

MEN ONLY
Adios, Coconut Creek, Fla.
Burning Tree, Bethesda, Md.
Butler National, Oak Brook, Ill.
Oak Tree Golf, Edmond, Okla.
Pine Valley, Pine Valley, N.J.
Preston Trail, Dallas

JUNE 3, 1991 FORTUNE 9

Q targets its youth/rock market with cut-outs and run-arounds. It does not use headlines but employs drop caps to identify stories (with bold intros on lead stories). It also picks out personalities and other key words in bold type.

Stories

Ralf Hutter, one half of the Hutter-Schneider mainspring at the heart of Kraftwerk, is as neat

KRAFTWERK

"Studio problems, man, studio problems." Andrew Roachford is accounting for the three and a half

ROACHFORD

Remember this sultry vision in Play-Do?

Glaxo World (right) uses one type style and size for all its news headlines and a dropped type horizon which is occasionally flouted to good effect. Rules are used only to divide the modules.

World view

Finland's family affair

Shining light

Investors' updates

Historic print

Pioneer retires

Technology for tablets

Eminent councillor

News

ENSA's effort recalled by stars

Staff praised by Army director

New site sales soar

Weekend won by Guard wife

Sweet smell of success

Best-of-three bags prize

Branch hives in on cash award

Naafi News is one of the few magazines to design news pages across the fold. Note the narrow centre gutter. Bold horizontal rules accentuate the horizontal look to make the two pages look like one.

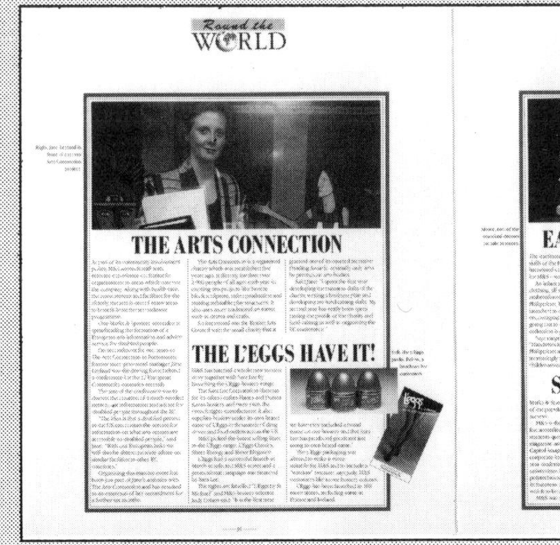

Round the WORLD

THE ARTS CONNECTION

THE L'EGGS HAVE IT!

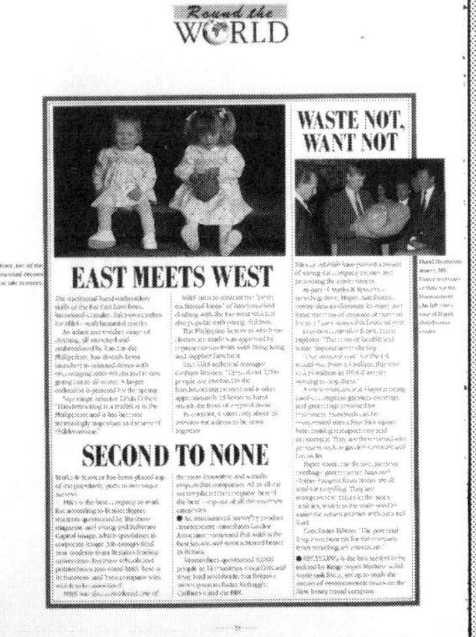

Round the WORLD

EAST MEETS WEST

WASTE NOT, WANT NOT

SECOND TO NONE

M&S World is largely a features magazine with only two or three back pages given to news. On these pages it tries to maintain the features look by the use of borders and generous white space.

Group 4 International's *news stories are run on but the magazine retains a featurish look to the page through the use of white space.*

Director's *highly individual news pages have four narrow columns and an even narrower fifth which is frequently used for head and shoulder portraits and occasionally gives added width to other pics by allowing expansion from adjacent columns.*

Nursing Times *adopts a modular approach with the addition of column rules and a hood over the text area. Headlines are in capitals throughout.*

The narrow fourth column is a regular feature of *Crafts magazine's* news pages. The text in the narrow column is in bold caps in a tint of black with key words printed solid – and it always fits the column.

High
society
Alfred Wainwright
Twin Peaks
...and on Ama Dablam
Editorial
Spate of fatalities on Scottish ice

High Magazine runs on news stories from column to column. The same typeface and size is used on all headlines.

NEWS
ALUMAR LINE III COMES ON STREAM
Bogosu pours first gold
BMT makes moves Eastwards
Research shares transferred

Billiton Magazine mixes the modular approach with run-on. The reversed out 'NEWS', the heavy rules and folio are all in red. A thin red rule runs around the type area. Note the folio style.

Garden notes

The Chelsea Flower Show (21-24 May) is the unmissable event of the horticultural year, with over 700 exhibitors displaying everything from garden designs to artful arrays of fruit and veg. This year's coups include the launch of a new National Trust garden in Staffordshire. James Bateman's Biddulph Grange is a horticultural *tour du monde* with an Egyptian court and Cheshire cottage packed into 15 acres.

Gardeners' note: The Conran Shop sells a generously proportioned handmade willow basket to store and carry garden tools and seedlings, price £44.90.

Child's view

American art critic Philip Isaacson has written a children's architecture book in simple terms of how a building feels. *Round Buildings, Square Buildings and Buildings that Wiggle like a Fish* (Walker, £14.95) moves fluidly between the TWA terminal, left, the Taj Mahal and a Shaker barn, and still elicits from Richard Rogers the accolade: "This is a truly wonderful book."

Spirit houses

In a design world full of Holly Golightlys all trying to be top banana in the shock department, Richard Snyder's totem-like 'Spirit Houses' have a quietude and intensity of feeling which London gallery owner David Gill applauds: "They are unlike anything we have seen before. The finishes are very beautiful." Snyder, an industrial designer from New York, is holding his first London exhibition at David Gill's gallery in May.

Glass fights back

Last summer's Milan lighting fair rescued Murano glass from the souvenir circuit and made it desirable again. Months later, Romeo Gigli opened his Manhattan shop – complete with a spangly vineyard of Murano Pinot Noir. At last month's Milan furniture fair, the glass revival spread to furniture. Flam's new glass pieces include this Cobra umbrella stand by Elio Vigna, £495, and a sinuous side-table by Makio Hasuike.

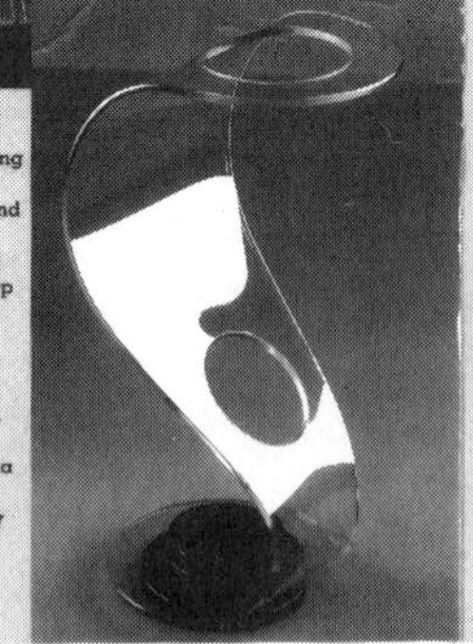

Editor: **LUCIE YOUNG** *Researcher:* **HILARY ROBERTSON** *Photographs:* **CRISPIN THOMAS**
For further information see Resources

Hot prints

Geoffrey Bennison, king of the much-copied faded-splendour look, died in 1984. His collections are now edited by Gillian Newberry, who this season has sprung a set of brightly coloured Moroccan furnishing fabrics on the market. Bennison won't be turning in his grave – they are his own creation. He drew them in 1982 for the Baroness Rothschild's house in Marrakesh. The originals were considered particularly daring in minty greens, turquoise and pinks.

It's a wrap

Papier Phantastique are packaging designers of the most imaginative kind. They use recycled paper to mould soft, tactile forms onto everyday objects: clocks, TVs, telephones – whatever you choose. The bright, rich colouring of their pieces is a by-product of designer Gus Tun's childhood in Burma. Gus's wife Sandra, a school-teacher, helps out with "the smelly bit" – mulching old shredded newspapers in an industrial food processor.

Hands-on art

After years of genteel print-making at the RCA, Simon Packard wanted to break into a more passionate method of painting. The imagery on his new ceramics is drawn with a nail in wet clay. The decision to do ceramics evolved out of the need to furnish his cottage in Stroud. Malmesbury Abbey in Wiltshire is holding an exhibition of his work, past and present, in July, including the gold-slipped piece, below.

Odd eats

A guide to the incredible edible. Sophie Grigson's *Ingredients Book* (Pyramid, £20) takes the armchair eater to the wilder shores of food. Their names alone make some of the ingredients seem aphrodisiac or emetic. But we just have to trust Grigson – and she has amply earned this – through the culinary minefield of *horchata de chufas, quinoa, pounti* and *frumenty* et al.

Another highly individualistic treatment of news and product news with panels in a variety of colours – from Metropolitan Home.

12 Ornamentation

Nothing in design distinguishes the amateur from the professional so quickly as over-ornamentation – with the possible exception of an over-indulgence in different typefaces. Both are symptoms of the same urge to throw everything at the page in the mistaken belief that design and decoration are synonymous.

Successful page design stems from organization of the elements, and the contrast and balance of the shapes and colours. Embellishment can often be helpful and appropriate, but its successful application is one of the most difficult aspects of page design to master. The safest guide when considering adding any embellishment to a page is to ask yourself why you are doing it. Will it help readers find their way? Will it draw the eye to some important element? Will it separate elements which should be separated? If it has a worthwhile function, ask yourself if it is the best way of achieving the objective.

Perhaps the most obvious and useful embellishment is the rule. It can be used to separate sections of a feature, to allow the eye a moment's respite, to provide horizontal or vertical stress, or to organize information.

The rule's once almost universal use in newspapers to separate columns led to a fashion for using it similarly in magazines. But magazines generally have wider gutters (the white space separating columns) than newspapers. Does one really need two devices to perform one function? Might it not be better to save these reinforcements for use where they will do most good? Rules are almost essential, for example, in the presentation of tabular matter, listings, or classified advertisement pages, where the use of different weights and

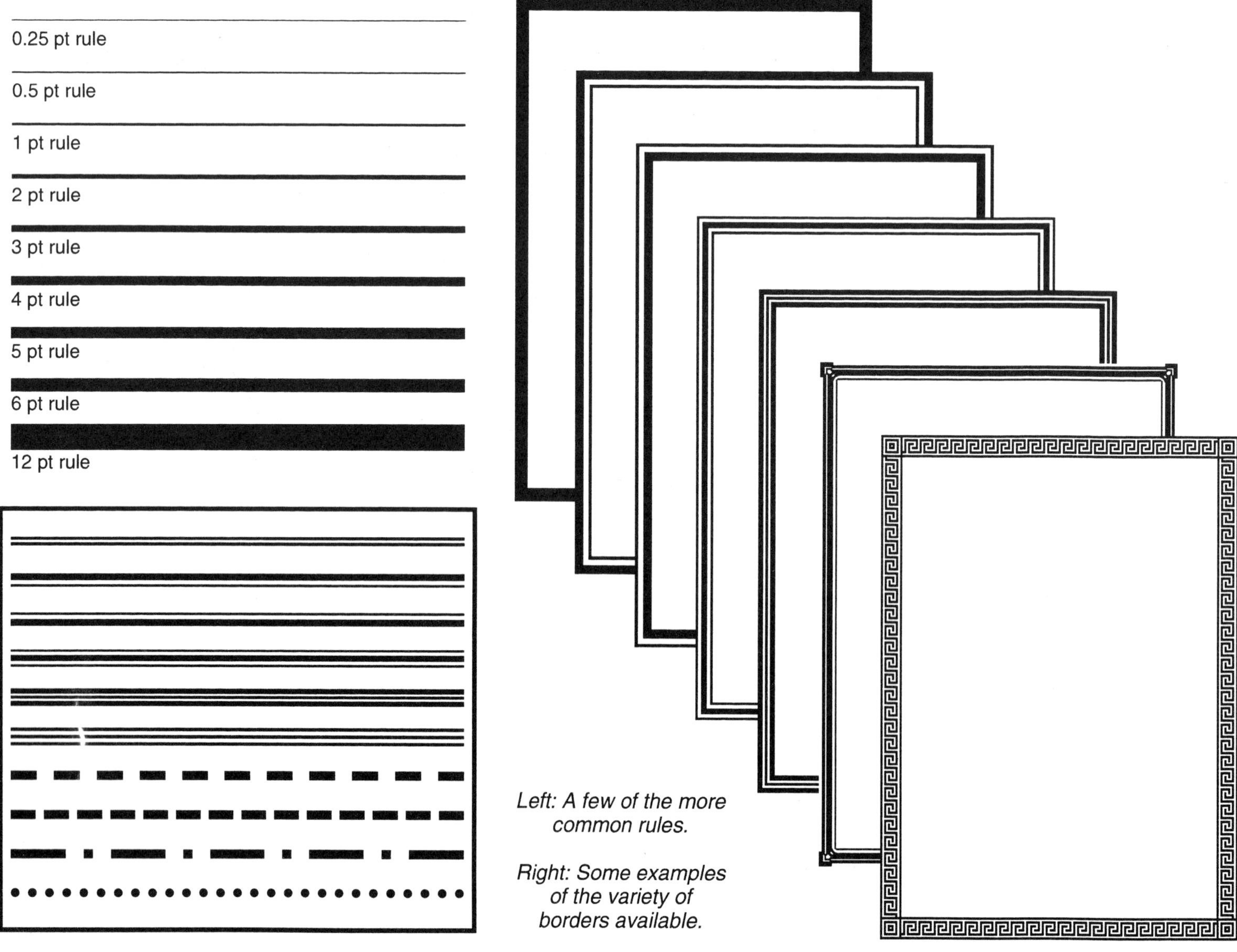

Left: A few of the more common rules.

Right: Some examples of the variety of borders available.

styles can help organize and enliven the page.

Rules, like typefaces, are specified in point sizes. You should find many styles displayed in your type specimen book, but the general typographical caveat about the use of too many variations on one page applies.

PANEL GAMES

A first cousin to the rule is the border (a rule joined up to make a box), a device for containing and perhaps highlighting text, table or illustration.

Boxes and panels can have black type on white backgrounds, or white text out of black (a wob). They can be filled with tints with the text either black on the tint, or white out of the tint, or in a contrasting tint. Whenever text appears as a tint, or on a tint, ensure there is sufficient differential between the text and the background for comfortable reading.

Boxes need not always be rectangles. A polygon, for example, can be used to 'point' a heading to a story or a caption to its picture. A hood (three sides of a box) can also be used to link headline to story, caption to picture and so on.

Text itself can be used as an embellishment, obvious examples being the enlarged initial capital letter, the crosshead and the pulled quote.

Oversize initial capital letters are older than

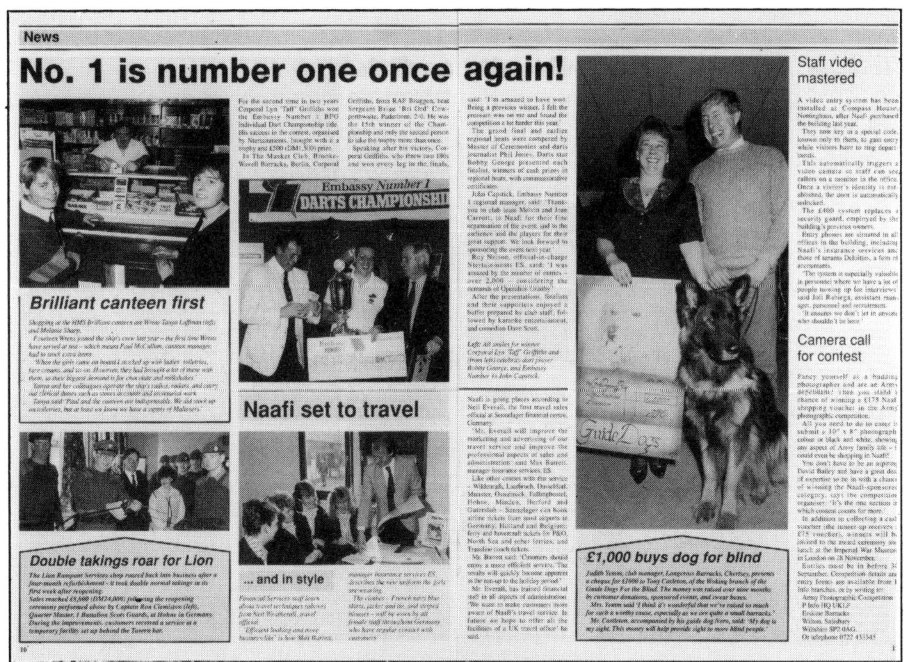

News

No. 1 is number one once again!

Brilliant canteen first

Embassy Number 1 DARTS CHAMPIONSHI

Naafi set to travel

Double takings roar for Lion

... and in style

£1,000 buys dog for blind

Staff video mastered

Camera call for contest

A hood ties the caption story 'Brilliant canteen first' to its picture. Tinted polygons do the same for 'Double takings roar for Lion' and '£1,000 buys dog for blind'.

printing and many beautiful examples can be seen in early monastery manuscripts. Drop caps are the most common current form, but raised caps and hanging caps all have their uses. Illustrated and decorated caps are still used today, particularly by calligraphers. Although they appear more often in specialist and art books than in the general run of magazines, the opportunity to use them on an appropriate feature is worth taking.

In a long feature article, crossheads provide a simple rest stop for the eye, but they should also be informative signposts. The size, weight and spacing of crossheads need careful attention. The lines of body text across the spread should line up from column to column and should not be thrown out by badly judged crosshead spacing. This means that the crosshead, regardless of size, should always sit in a space which is a multiple of the text leading. The available white space (after allowing for the crosshead itself) should normally be divided so that two thirds is placed above the crosshead and one third below. For example the text you are reading is 12/14 pt., the crossheads are set 10/10 pt. with 14 pt. of space above and 4 pt. below. If you add 10 pt. (the crosshead), 14 pt. (space above) and 4 pt. (space below) you get 28 pt. which is equal to the space taken up by two lines of text. (Note that the space between the crosshead and the text below it is actually 6 pt. because the 2 pt. leading in the text appears above the line in this computer setting.)

This principle of avoiding disruption of the line-up of text from column to column should be applied whenever the text flow is interrupted, whether by rule, box, picture, white space or any other element.

Numerals are often used to itemize points or paragraphs but, unless the numbers are to be referred to elsewhere, there are many graphic symbols more suitable. The most common – but not necessarily the best – being the bullet (a circle) and the quad (a square). Such symbols are available in a variety of styles so that solid, outline, shadow and so on can be chosen as appropriate.

Pulled quotes are particularly useful when illustrations are lacking. They consist of selected pieces of text set in larger and, usually, heavier type to provide a change of tone. They will often be set within oversize quotation marks. Place them in the middle of paragraphs rather than between, so that there is a full line of text above and below to define the space.

ADDING COLOUR

We must not leave the subject of embellishment without referring to spot colour – which is frequently misused or squandered. Too often we see it used simply to highlight other embellishments and, even worse, we see drop

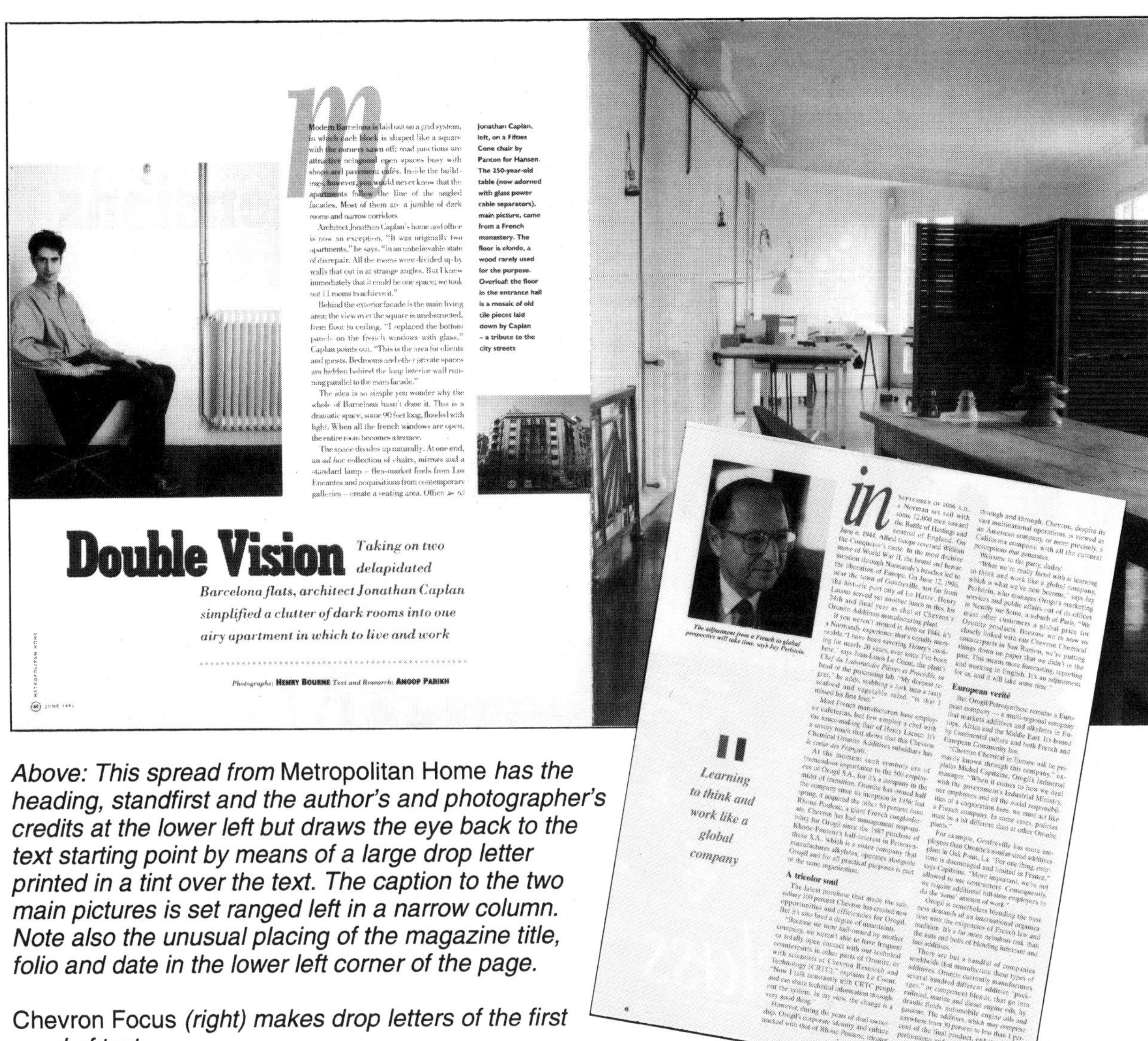

Modern Barcelona is laid out on a grid system, in which each block is shaped like a square with the corners sawn off; road junctions are attractive octagonal open spaces busy with shops and pavement cafés. Inside the buildings, however, you would never know that the apartments follow the line of the angled facades. Most of them are a jumble of dark rooms and narrow corridors.

Architect Jonathan Caplan's home and office is now an exception. "It was originally two apartments," he says, "in an unbelievable state of disrepair. All the rooms were divided up by walls that cut in at strange angles. But I knew immediately that it could be one space; we took out 11 rooms to achieve it."

Behind the exterior facade is the main living area; the view over the square is unobstructed, from floor to ceiling. "I replaced the bottom panels on the french windows with glass," Caplan points out. "This is the area for clients and guests. Bedrooms and other private spaces are hidden behind the long interior wall running parallel to the main facade."

The idea is so simple you wonder why the whole of Barcelona hasn't done it. This is a dramatic space, some 90 feet long, flooded with light. When all the french windows are open, the entire room becomes a terrace.

The space divides up naturally. At one end, an *ad hoc* collection of chairs, mirrors and a standard lamp – flea-market finds from Los Encantes and acquisitions from contemporary galleries – create a seating area. Office ➢ 63

Jonathan Caplan, left, on a Fifties Cone chair by Pancon for Hansen. The 250-year-old table (now adorned with glass power cable separators), main picture, came from a French monastery. The floor is elondo, a wood rarely used for the purpose. Overleaf: the floor in the entrance hall is a mosaic of old tile pieces laid down by Caplan – a tribute to the city streets

Double Vision

Taking on two delapidated Barcelona flats, architect Jonathan Caplan simplified a clutter of dark rooms into one airy apartment in which to live and work

Photographs: **HENRY BOURNE** Text and Research: **ANOOP PARIKH**

METROPOLITAN HOME

60 JUNE 1991

The adjustment from a French to global perspective will take time, says Jay Perlstein.

European verité

A tricolor soul

Learning to think and work like a global company

Above: This spread from Metropolitan Home has the heading, standfirst and the author's and photographer's credits at the lower left but draws the eye back to the text starting point by means of a large drop letter printed in a tint over the text. The caption to the two main pictures is set ranged left in a narrow column. Note also the unusual placing of the magazine title, folio and date in the lower left corner of the page.

Chevron Focus (right) makes drop letters of the first word of text.

Somebody Up There Likes Us

"Appalling" videos. Hopeless interviews. A disappearing bass player. Despite them all, The Wonder Stuff's career has been miraculously revived . . . So what are they doing busking in Birmingham city centre? And has Peter Kane got 10p?

"There must have been a hefty baby boom about 14 years ago. We're selling twice as many singles as we used to."

Pulled quotes are often placed within oversize quotation marks to draw the eye. The Q style is to use a single bold side rule (top right). Drop caps are usually used only at the beginning of a feature but Q has them standing in for crossheads. Note the placing of the caption as a wob at the lower right corner of the picture.

caps in one colour, rules in another, crossheads in yet another. Too many colours on a page can confuse the eye and distract it from the critical path it should follow and which should be designed into the page.

Treat spot colour as another basic element of the design. Mass it and shape it as you would any other element to contrast or harmonize with the other shapes on the page.

Spot colour can be used as background to text or pictures. In appropriate circumstances it can be used to produce a duotone (in which a picture is printed in one colour over the same picture printed in another colour). Picture density and screen angle must be carefully chosen, and the inexperienced would be well advised to consult the printer on this.

If setting type in colour remember that to achieve a similarity of weight with text printed in black the coloured type will need to be set in a bolder face. This is particularly important if you propose to print body text in colour.

When type is printed in colour against a background of a different colour, its apparent weight will be greatly affected by the choice of colours. Red, for example, will recede if printed against purple but will appear to leap out from a yellow background.

When used in conjunction with colour illustrations, spot colour requires particularly sensitive handling. A colour which tones with the overall cast of the illustration generally works better than a contrast. But colour illustrations can also look good when they are set against a black background.

Take particular care when reversing type out of four-colour half-tones. The slightest registration problems will show up on the thin strokes and fine serifs of old style typefaces. Sans would be safer, but if a serif face is essential choose a slab serif or a bold old face which offers less variation between thin and thick strokes.

Some colours have particular connotations; the problem is that they frequently have more than one. Green, for example, is symbolic of freshness, but also of jealousy. Blue is associated with Mediterranean sea and sky – but also with freezing cold. But take heart, when you choose a colour to reinforce an idea which is already apparent on the page – for example, green used with black in a duotone reproduction of a country scene – it is unlikely to have the wrong effect. The moral is, do not rely on colour alone. Do obtain a good colour reference book or chart to keep by you.

There is one use of spot colour where the general rule of massing the elements can often be broken to good effect and that is where it is used to aid the clear presentation of complex information. Typical would be its use in tables, graphs, maps, diagrams, charts and listings.

Where budgets are tight and full colour or spot colour is only available on a restricted number of pages, the designer will need to obtain of a copy of the flat plan showing the imposition of the magazine pages. This can be obtained from the printer or the production manager and will show on which pages colour can be employed.

Some medical research suggests that as many as one in ten males of European origin has colour-defective vision. The problem colours are, most frequently, red and green. It is a point worth bearing in mind if you work on a publication with a largely, or perhaps totally, male readership. Editors and publishers will not thank you for losing ten per cent of the readers.

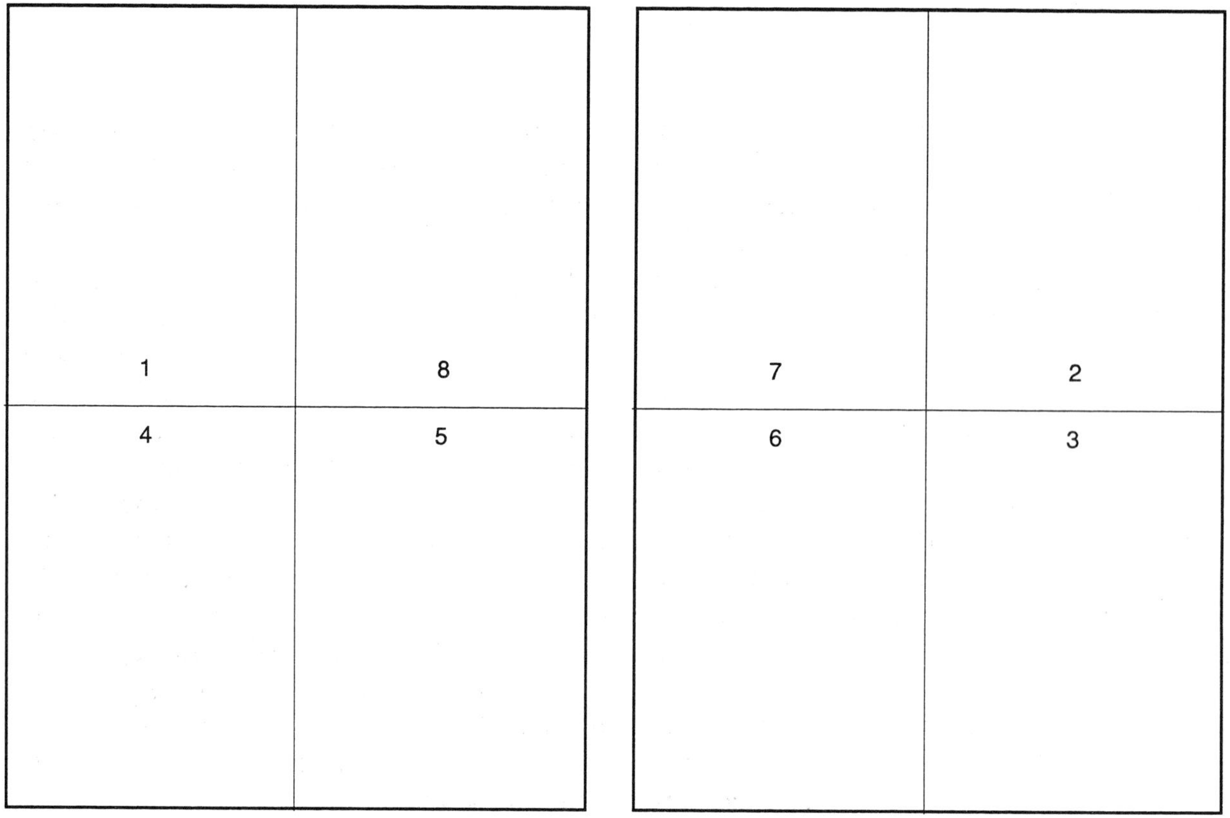

A simple flat plan for an eight-page magazine. The right-hand sheet represents the left-hand sheet turned over so that page 2 prints on the reverse of page 1, 7 on the reverse of 8 etc.

1	8
4	5

7	2
6	3

13 About illustration

The designer who is invited to read the copy and then brief (or join in the briefing of) the photographer or artist chosen to illustrate the piece is fortunate – but, unfortunately, rare. The right illustration can almost design the page for you, and is as near as you are likely to get to a guarantee of the reader's attention.

By far the most common scenario is one in which the designer is presented with the copy, a bundle of photographs and an allotted number of pages. This inevitably calls for the operation of the selection process described in Chapter 7.

It is important, when using the elimination method mentioned in that chapter, not to discard a good picture prematurely simply because it is not the shape you are looking for, or because it contains extraneous detail. Cropping (masking out the unwanted parts of the picture) may produce exactly the shape you require. For this reason it is important that photographers are briefed to print the whole negative; they should not be allowed to frame the picture to their own taste.

Use your L-shapes (described in Chapter 5) to choose the precise area of the print you wish to use, cutting out unwanted detail and, where possible, creating a dynamic shape. Often you will find pictures within pictures, with one print yielding two or more pictures. Sometimes a mediocre picture can be transformed by cropping it hard and printing it big. But cropping demands care and sensitivity. Study cropping techniques in newspapers and magazines. The national daily newspapers can be particularly instructive as the same picture is often used by several of them with each giving it a different treatment. Analyse which treatment works best.

Cropping photographs with the aid of L-shapes. The shadow effect used here is a popular method of enhancing photographs.

As you study the cropping of portraits you will discover that, whereas head and shoulder pictures tend to be dull, cropping in hard from all four sides so that attention is concentrated on the features that matter (eyes, nose, mouth) can add dramatic impact. But beware of cutting through the top of the head only; it can look like a trepanning.

Similarly, whereas a horizontal cut between shoulder and hip is usually acceptable (even lower on skirts and kilts), a cut through trousered or bare legs tends to look like a double amputation. A vertical cut through the shoulder is fine, but not through an extended arm.

Conversely, do not allow disembodied hands or other appendages to creep into your pictures. Ensure, too, that verticals (e.g. telegraph poles) and horizontals (e.g. horizons) are appropriately vertical or horizontal. If they are out of true on the bromide, correct them in the cropping.

Tight cropping to get down to the essentials, the meat of the picture, will generally work well with news and action pictures but could be totally inappropriate for a mood or atmosphere photograph.

GO WITH THE FLOW

Where there is movement in a picture, leave space on the print for the moving object to move into. 'Movement' should be understood

Two different landscape shapes cropped from the same picture – which also produced the shapes on the next pages.

GY 412

GY 412

GY 412

to include any kind of directional thrust in the subject matter so that, for example, a head looking to the right should have space on the right to look into. An athlete must have space to run into. Crop the picture just in front of the nose and the runner will appear to be running into a wall.

A picture which shows movement should usually be placed so that the movement leads the eye into the story. Although this is not always essential it provides a safe bet for the inexperienced. If the subject of the picture is moving the 'wrong' way, it may be possible to reverse the picture left to right so that the movement is also reversed – but beware of such tell-tales as clocks, buttonholes and, of course, lettering. Even such giveaways can sometimes be removed by retouching.

The art of photographic retouching has reached new heights with the aid of electronics: complicated or unsuitable backgrounds can be changed or removed, objects can be taken from one picture and placed in another, the colour of a dress transformed, a skyline altered.

Such 'doctoring' is not cheap, but there are other ways in which photographs may be manipulated (in the darkroom or during the printing processes) which can add to their pulling power without draining the budget. One of the simplest is the burn-out, in which a suitable photograph has its mid-tones (greys) removed and takes on the appearance of a pen-and-ink sketch. A variety of screens can be introduced between negative and print to produce various textural effects from shot silk to tree bark. Pictures may be printed in a spot colour, in black on (or reversed out of) a colour panel, or printed as a duotone (the same picture printed in two different colours in perfect register but in different weights and with different screen angles). These and other techniques, such as reticulation (producing a pattern in the emulsion) and solarization (a darkroom process which produces an outline effect), are all worthy of study by the designer. Of course, designers do not need to be able to produce such effects but they can considerably expand their armoury by knowing what effects are possible.

Interesting shapes and careful positioning can occasionally come to the designer's rescue when the only available pictures fall considerably short of sparkling. Pictures may be printed as circles or other shapes, or overlapped, or tilted. They may be printed with borders, with round corners, or made to look like snapshots in an album, or as a strip of film or contact prints. Vignettes can occasionally prove useful, perhaps combined with sepia printing to give a period look to a feature. Partial or full 'cut-outs' can provide impact, exaggerate movement, add a touch of humour or a 3D effect to the right picture. (Partial cut-outs are often more effective than complete cut-outs and can give the impression that the subject is emerging from the picture.) Don't take a pair of scissors to the print, but indicate the cut-out with pencil on the overlay and explain your requirements to the studio or printer.

There are occasions when you can take a scalpel to a photograph if you have a good eye and a steady hand. Typical of this kind of surgery would be the need to bring two people closer together in a picture and so reduce the width required on the page. Planning where to make the cut and how to rejoin needs considerable care to avoid leaving an obvious scar, and there are some backgrounds where such crude surgery would be impossible.

SHUN THE UNNECESSARY

Bear in mind that good pictures rarely need (or deserve) any of the more drastic treatments. They should only come into play if they add to the effectiveness of the photograph or the layout as a piece of communication. They should not be used to create a fake photograph of a situation which never occurred. Of course, if they are over-employed they will lose their effectiveness as rescue techniques but, on the other hand, when faced with a poor selection of pictures, the use of cut-outs, circles, overlaps, borders, drop shadows (not all at once!) may prove to be the saving of a spread or cover. Thus, the photographer can sometimes benefit from the designer's skill in a way the writer never can.

If artwork or photographs are to be used to illustrate the work of an artist or photographer then cropping should normally be forgone. If for some reason such an illustration must be cropped then a note of explanation (e.g. 'a detail from . . .') should be included in the caption.

When a picture is cropped, the area to be printed should be clearly marked on a tracing paper overlay and, for all further purposes, the marked area becomes 'the picture'.

Scaling can be done as described in Chapter 5, but many designers prefer to use slide-rules to calculate the measurements and others lean to the purpose-made circular calculator. The manual method is a fail-safe every designer should be familiar with.

MARK THE SPOT

Sooner or later you will need to know how to transfer a specific position – perhaps the horizon, or the top of a telegraph pole – from the original to the scaled-up (or scaled-down) keyline on your layout so that you can, for example, accurately place a title or caption on the picture in a clear portion of sky.

Visualize a photograph, a simple seascape

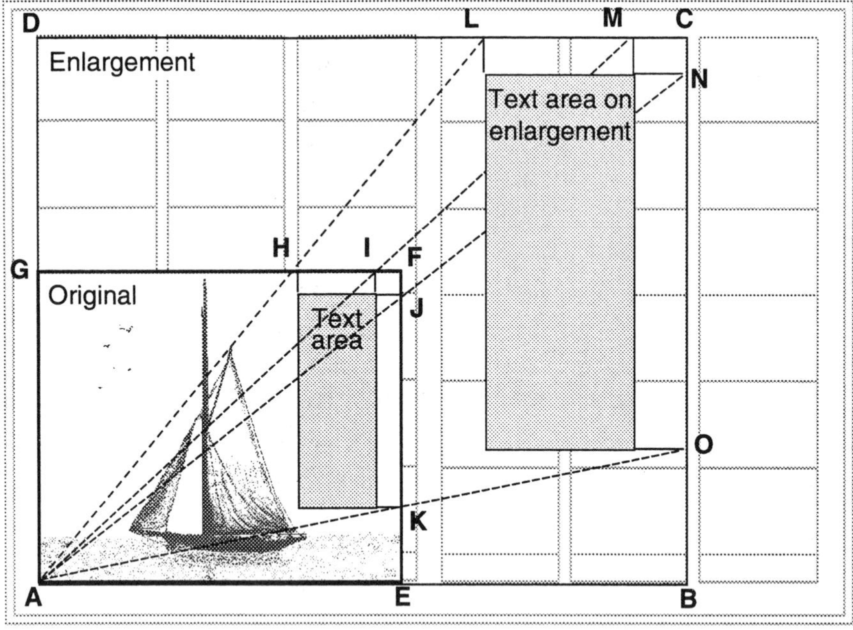

To discover where any point on the original will appear on the page when the picture is scaled up (or down), draw horizontal and vertical lines from that point, on the overlay, to the right and top edges of the original. Draw through these points from the lower left corner to the side and top of the enlargement area. Horizontals and verticals drawn from those points will meet to mark the spot you wish to find. The example above shows an enlargement, from the original, up to five columns wide but the principle is the same for any enlargement or reduction.

with a sailing boat. You wish to place some text in the sky to the right of the sail.

On your layout, draw a keyline for the picture in the size and position you want it to appear on the page (ABCD in the illustration left). Place the picture itself under the layout sheet (which is semi-transparent) and position it in the lower left corner of the text area. Draw an outline (AEFG) of the picture on the layout. On this picture area mark the area in which you wish to place the text. Extend the verticals of the text area to the upper edge of the picture area (H and I) and the horizontals to the right edge (J and K). From A draw lines through H, I, J and K to the edges of the enlargement area (L, M, N and O). Lines drawn at right angles from these points will define the size and position of the type area after the picture has been enlarged.

It will be obvious that this method can be used to transfer any point on the original to its proper position on the enlarged or reduced version and can therefore be used, for example, to scale a cut-out.

If text is to be used within a picture, ensure that there is sufficient contrast between the text and the tone on which it will appear. Avoid placing text on areas of confused tones: a smooth sea will be fine, a ruffled one with mid-tones, dark shadow areas and white-caps will make reading difficult if not impossible.

'Ghosting' (fading) part of a photograph may make it possible to place text in an area which might otherwise have been unsuitable. The reverse, making an area of the print darker, might allow text to be reversed white out of dark tone. Piercing a picture (in effect cutting a hole in it) to place text should, in my opinion, be avoided at all costs.

MAKE IT FIT

Occasionally you will be faced with a situation where you must fit a picture into a predefined space. In these circumstances the basic diagonal-line method can be used, as it were, in reverse.

Begin by accurately drawing the allotted shape in the lower left corner of a sheet of tracing paper (ABCD on the illustration on the next page) and extend the left side (AB) to the top of the sheet (E) and the foot (AD) to the right-hand edge of the paper (F).

Draw a diagonal from the lower left corner (A) of the picture space, through the upper right corner (C) and on to the edge of the paper (G). Place the tracing paper over the picture. The rightangle formed by the lines AE and AF can now be used as one of your L-shapes and a real L-shape placed with its inside corner on the diagonal line (AG).

Sliding the real L-shape up and down the diagonal and adjusting the position of the tracing paper will vary the crop while maintaining the ratio required to fit the desired space. When the appropriate crop has been selected in this way, draw in the top and right side of the crop on the tracing paper. Tape the tracing paper as an overlay, in position, on the print.

In the illustration overleaf the full depth of the original is being retained but the width must be reduced by cropping at the line HI so that the reduced version fits the required space.

Much of what has been said above about photographs applies also to artwork illustrations, but there are some important differences.

Cropping illustrative artwork is inherently more difficult, particularly because it will often be obvious that the illustration has been cropped. Whenever possible, determine in advance the shape to be filled and commission the artwork to fit the space.

Artwork can sometimes be more telling than photographs – because the artist can select, simplify, and distil the material down to its essentials. It can sometimes be produced when photographs are unobtainable. It can often present or explain information (particularly financial or statistical information) more effectively than either words or photographs.

There are many circumstances in which artwork and photographs can be combined,

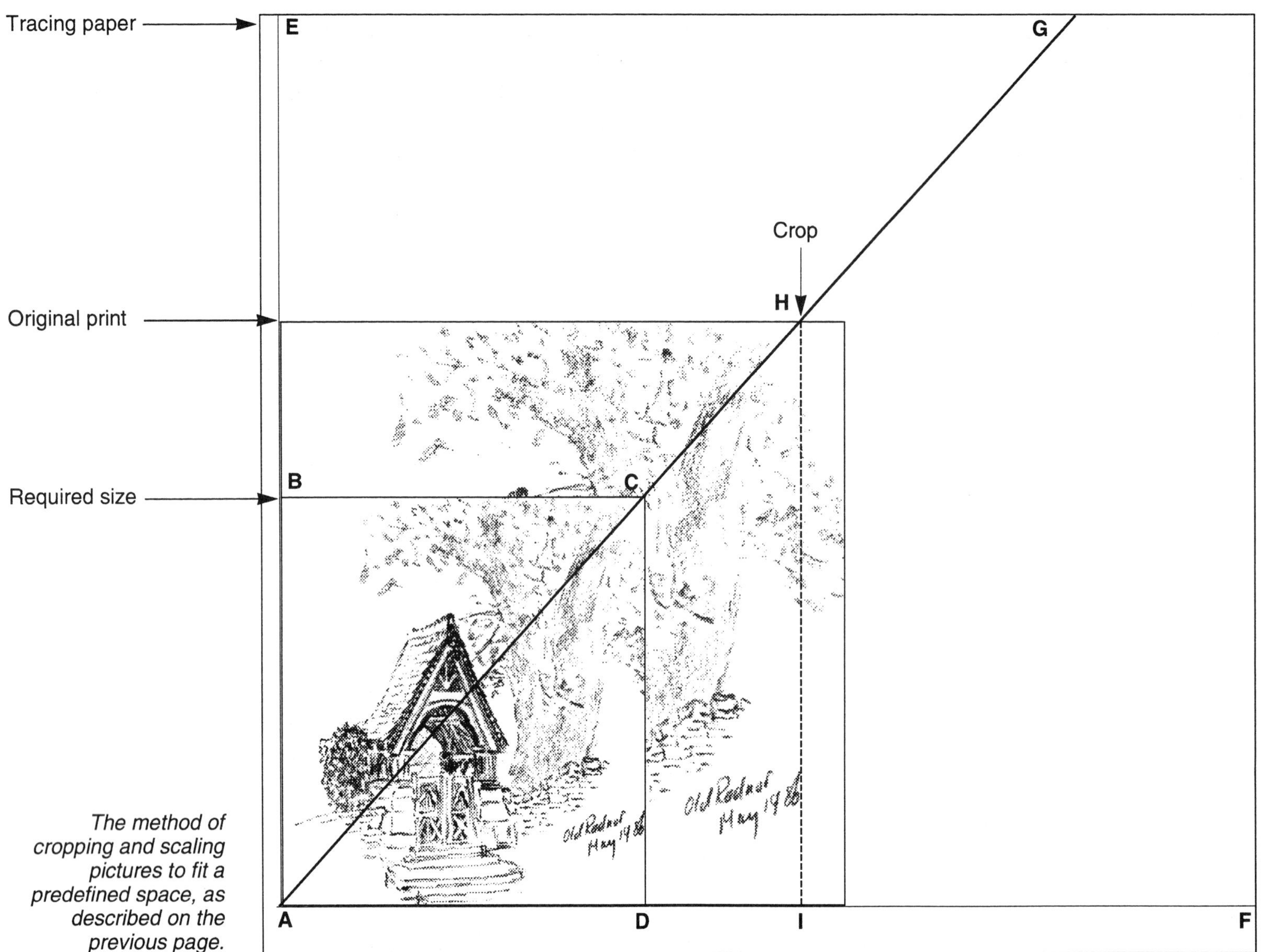

The method of cropping and scaling pictures to fit a predefined space, as described on the previous page.

each adding its own strengths, to produce powerful communication.

LOOK FOR ALTERNATIVES

Unfortunately, artwork is not cheap – or at least, cheap artwork is likely to look just that. For the designer of a non-commercial publication on a tight budget there is a possible source which should not cost an arm and a leg and that is the local art college. If you wish to explore this possibility, do approach the college authorities and not the students direct. The authorities may be able to point you to the appropriate student for the work, or perhaps make a group project of your request. If successful, such a venture can produce artwork at reasonable cost and at the same time provide stimulus, experience and useful funds for hard-pressed students.

More and more magazines, newspapers and television programs are turning to the computer for illustrations and every day they provide stunning examples of what can be achieved. Many budget publications are tempted into DIY computer art but, just as page layout programs do not turn computer operators into designers, the acquisition of a drawing or painting program does not transform the average operator into an artist. A wide range of ready-made clip art is available on disk (and in book form for cut and paste technology) at comparatively low cost. Its appeal and usage is limited but it can be a boon to low-budget productions. In both old and new technologies individual touches can be added by those with a little talent for it.

When no illustrations come with the copy, and there are no funds, or no time, to employ a photographer or artist, there are still a few avenues for you to explore.

You can try to find suitable stock (existing) illustrations. There are many agencies, libraries and galleries offering art and photographs, ancient and modern. Some specialize, and some have more general catalogues. Between them they cover almost every subject imaginable. They will, of course, charge a fee. Some museums provide a similar service within their specialities and they tend to be cheaper than the commercial sources – but, understandably, they also tend to be slower in their responses, so approach them in good time. The *Picture Researcher's Handbook* (Blueprint) lists most of these sources and is well worth a place on your bookshelf.

Freelance cartoonists can often save the day. They are usually quicker and cheaper than illustrators but, like them, can draw to fill a predetermined space, perhaps incorporating the title to the feature.

There are also many sources of free illustrations, including the PR or marketing arms of companies, trade associations, and charities.

PRUDENTIAL ARCHIVES

PRESERVING THE PAST

For years Prudential has been a household name. It's an organisation which has influence at an international level as well as being a major force in the lives of millions of policyholders. Yet how is the story of Prudential being preserved? Fiona FitzGibbon reports on the work of Peter Traynor, Corporation archivist (pictured left), and a project to mark the 150th anniversary with a history of the Corporation

Photograph by Nigel Parry

Personality pictures do not have to be head-and-shoulders passport shots. A high quality relevant study, such as this excellent one in Envoy, *demands to be used big.*

You can also make use of white space and typographic devices to avoid the monotony of unrelieved text. If there is a self-contained section within a feature (career details about the subject of an interview, for example) this may be set separately, in a different weight or style, in a box, or on a coloured or tinted panel. As an element, distinct from the body of the copy, such an item becomes a substitute illustration. Use it to make a shape of a different 'colour' to contrast with the shape and tone of the text.

Standfirsts, pulled quotes, rules, oversize initial letters, white-out-of-blacks, all these and more are devices which can be used to provide interest, but they should be used sensitively, sparingly, and with purpose.

In a slow recovery, buy companies that can increase earnings, says Moltz. Among his picks: CSX and Union Pacific.

JAMES MOLTZ
C.J. LAWRENCE

As the Dow rises, Greene finds less and less worth buying. Among the remaining bargains: IBM and United Technologies.

ALAN GREENE
DAVID J. GREENE

DIRECTOR MARCH 1990

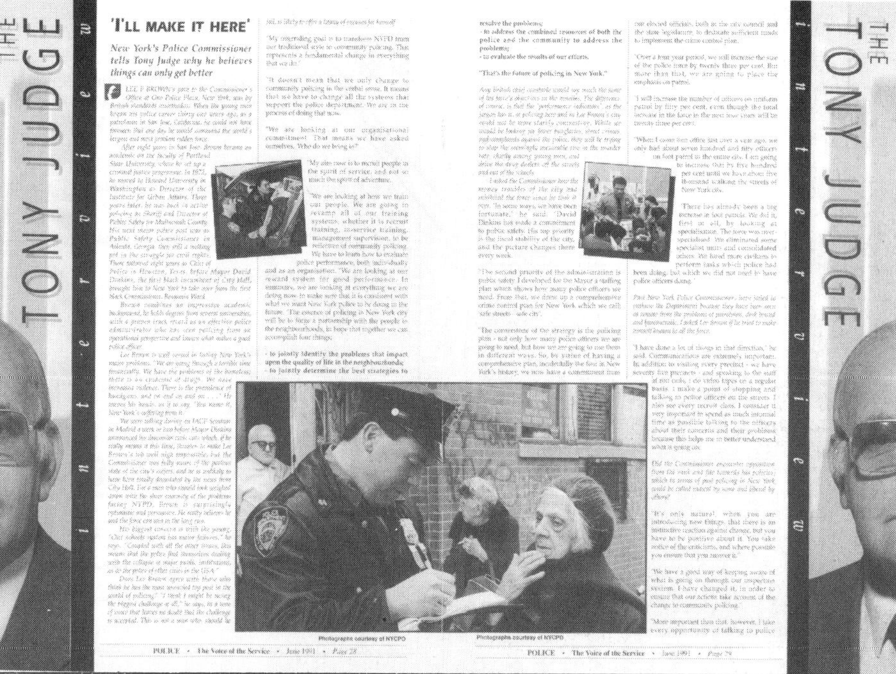

THE TONY JUDGE interview

'I'LL MAKE IT HERE'

New York's Police Commissioner tells Tony Judge why he believes things can only get better

Photographs courtesy of NYCPO

POLICE • The Voice of the Service • June 1991

Head and shoulders pictures, especially if there are several of them, can be boring in the extreme, so designers often need to 'add value'. Faced with a series of six, Fortune *combined the portraits with interesting artwork and a relevant quote.*
For its feature on Norman Tebbit, Director *used a tight crop of a hard print and a touch of second colour. (See also the vignette treatment on the cover of the same issue – page 75.)*
The eye-catching treatment employed by Police, *published by the Police Federation, might upset many subjects, but this portrait happens to be of the editor. Watch for other unusual treatments and add them to your tear-file for reference.*

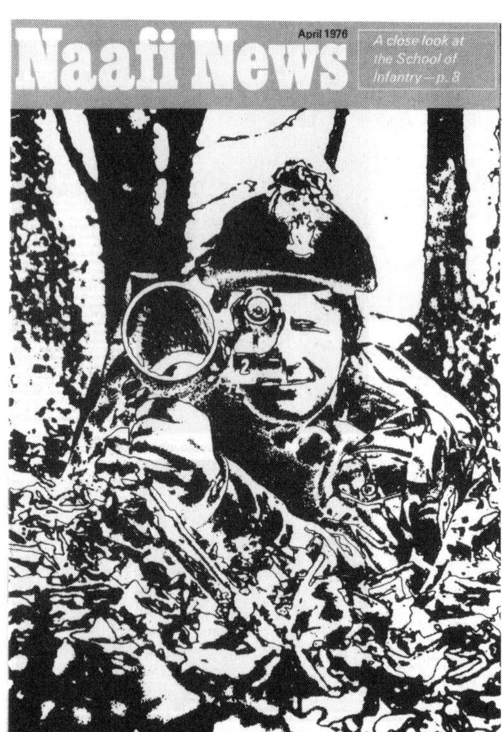

From left to right: Examples of burn-out, solarization and reticulation used to enhance the effect of cover pictures.

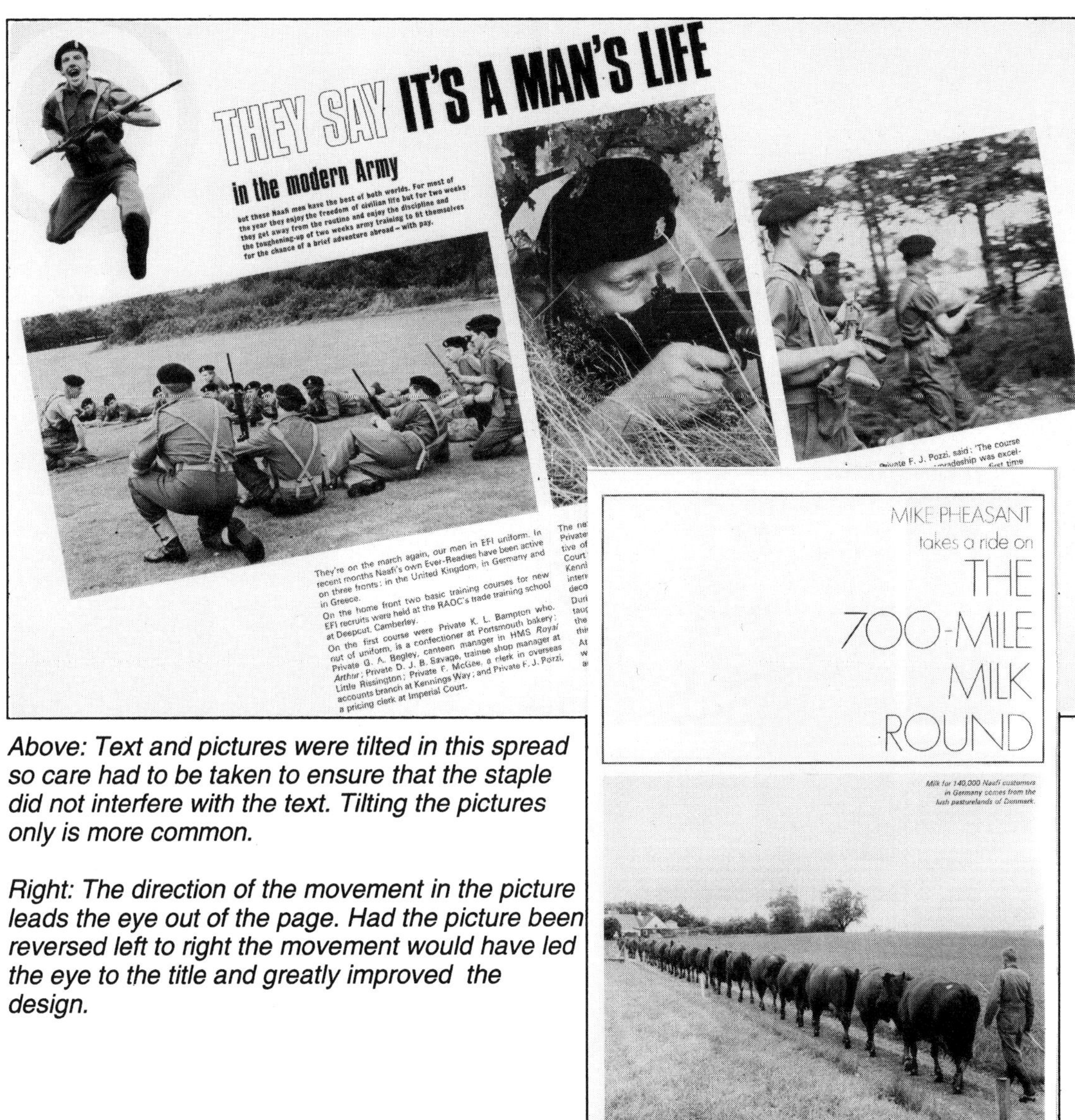

THEY SAY IT'S A MAN'S LIFE

in the modern Army

but these Naafi men have the best of both worlds. For most of the year they enjoy the freedom of civilian life but for two weeks they get away from the routine and enjoy the discipline and the toughening-up of two weeks army training to fit themselves for the chance of a brief adventure abroad – with pay.

They're on the march again, our men in EFI uniform. In recent months Naafi's own Ever-Readies have been active on three fronts: in the United Kingdom, in Germany and in Greece.

On the home front two basic training courses for new EFI recruits were held at the RAOC's trade training school at Deepcut, Camberley.

On the first course were Private K. L. Bampton who, out of uniform, is a confectioner at Portsmouth bakery; Private G. A. Begley, canteen manager in HMS *Royal Arthur*; Private D. J. B. Savage, trainee shop manager at Little Rissington; Private F. McGee, a clerk in overseas accounts branch at Kennings Way; and Private F. J. Porzi, a pricing clerk at Imperial Court.

MIKE PHEASANT takes a ride on

THE 700-MILE MILK ROUND

Milk for 140,000 Naafi customers in Germany comes from the lush pasturelands of Denmark.

Above: Text and pictures were tilted in this spread so care had to be taken to ensure that the staple did not interfere with the text. Tilting the pictures only is more common.

Right: The direction of the movement in the picture leads the eye out of the page. Had the picture been reversed left to right the movement would have led the eye to the title and greatly improved the design.

These three examples of picture handling from Police *show (left to right) photographic distortion, a combination of photographic distortion and artwork, and a film strip.*

KNOW YOUR NEIGHBOUR

David Wickham, a prison governor turned police constable, believes the best race relations training must be based on practical problem solving and living and working with ethnic minorities

The Police Federation intends to compile a guide to race relations for its members. This is a particularly welcome initiative as the Federation is often more potent and credible in representing the practical attitudes of the service, than in the training field. It may therefore have greater impact on attitudes and general behaviour within the service.

Newly joined officers are always anxious to absorb and adopt good practices, but in the field of race relations it is often only bad practices that are well documented.

It is ironic that the police forces with the greatest experience of ethnic communities should be facing the most difficulties with ethnic minorities. Other forces, without any sizeable ethnic communities tend to be even less motivated to learn about the practical problems of policing such neighbourhoods, and developing positive attitudes. Their reluctance stems from a rationalisation about the extent of such problems, ie "race relations training is a low priority because we do not experience inner city riots and do not have any ethnic minority concentrations."

The trouble with this "head in the sand" approach is that the attitudes of newly recruited officers will be largely unaffected if the problem is ignored. One only has to look at national police recruitment figures to see how under-represented are officers drawn from ethnic minority groups. For example, in Surrey there are only ...

"It is ironic that the police forces with the greatest experience of ethnic communities should be facing the most difficulties with ethnic minorities"

POLICE • The Voice of the Service • June 1991 • Page 38

MONSTERS OR NUISANCES?

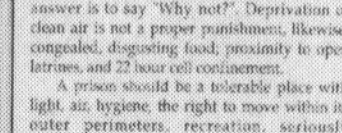

Edward Pearce says our gaols should at least be better than holiday camps

"If the Home Office isn't shamed to its ear tips about the spate of prison suicides, mostly of redeemable young men, it should be."

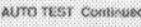

POLICE • The Voice of the Service • Page 20

AUTO TEST Continued

... saloon car of all time.

BRIEF SPECIFICATION

Max power DIN	73ps @ 5 500 rpm
Max torque DIN	108nm @ 4000 rpm
Kerb Weight	5dr 1425kg
	3dr 1400kg
Max speed	103mph
0-60mph	12.8 sec
Fuel Consumption	
56 mph	49.6 mpg
75 mph	38.2 mpg
Urban	31.7 mpg
Price	5dr £9,470
Price	3dr £9,140

My experience of the big selling 1.4LX version (£9,140 with three doors, £9,470 with five) is disappointing but the car is not completely devoid of merit.

... 1.4 guise or high specification 1.6 Ghia trim - just lacks the flair and spirit offered by cars like the Rover 200 and Fiat Tipo, let alone Peugeot's excellent new range of 309s.

... are not searching for ultimate cornering balance, or dynamics. They want something quiet on a motorway, practical around town and reasonably cheap to run. The new Escort is all ...

The New Ford Escort 1.4LX 5DR

... the Service • April 1991 • Page 30

Newcomers to Naafi, husband-and-wife team Denis and Marie Mead (above), with some of their Royal Observer Corps customers

14

Life comes back to Brawdy

The Royal Observer Corps is alive and well and living in RAF Brawdy – at least, temporarily.

The men and women who came to fame during the second world war by spotting enemy planes are still an active force with an up-to-date role. Two thousand of the current strength of 11,000 Observers have attended a series of one-week camps at RAF Brawdy in Pembrokeshire this summer. For the Station itself this has been a rejuvenation. Brawdy closed down as a Royal Naval Air Station 18 months ago and has only recently been taken over by the RAF. With 450 members of the ROC invading the Station each week, life has come back to a station that once seemed doomed.

The Royal Observer Corps, like Naafi, has been trying to throw off its out-of-date, wartime image. Gone are the days when Observers confined themselves to spotting aircraft with powerful binoculars. Though aircraft recognition is still a part of their work, the Corps is now de
event of a
equipment
of nuclear
of radioact

Nuclear w

Today the
Warning a
responsibl
United Ki
fallout dov
Working i
Corps ma
landline a
In the inf
that Home
and issue
public.

The Corps
and every
Scotland a
are from al
65. They s
evening a
taking par
out the ye

ted week's practice of the skills they have developed during training sessions, and the opportunity to renew their special relationship with the RAF. In the past, camps have been held at such places as RAF Coningsby, Watton, Tangmere, Binbrook, and Weeton near Blackpool. This is the first time that the Corps have held their camp at Brawdy.

Naafi has played its part in ensuring the success of these camps, and the establishment at Brawdy is a fine example of how first-class service can be arranged at comparatively short notice.

The buildings at Brawdy had been empty for 18 months before the first ROC members arrived on 26 June. Recruiting staff for the Services shop and club was the first problem that faced Emrys Parry, district manager, St. Athan. Fortunately he speaks a little Welsh so, with his restaurant and welfare superintendent Miss Sandra Davies, he toured the local villages knocking on doors seeking recruits. 'It was rather an unusual way of getting staff, but it got results,' he said. Some of the people he spoke to had been employed at the base when the Navy were in occupation and they were only too pleased to come back. One such was Mrs. Betty Thomas, a former canteen assistant from the nearby village of Trefgarnowen. Mrs. Thomas had spent eight years at Brawdy serving the Navy. 'I was surprised when Mr. Parry asked me to come back' she said 'but it is very nice to be working for Naafi again.'

The Naafi team

Working in the Services shop, near the now disused Naafi petrol station, is Mrs. Ivy Jones another former employee who used to drive the Naafi mobile. Looking after the shop with her is Miss Merion Hayes who came over from the camp at Penally to help out. The two club assistants, Pat Williams and Diane Shackleton, are also on loan from Penally.

The staff at Brawdy occasionally have the benefit of the fine tenor voice of Arthur John, the furnishing fitter for their part of the world. He finds that exercising his vocal chords helps him work and keeps him in practice for his role as a tenor with the Haverfordwest

Above: Somewhat mundane photographs are treated as circles to give this spread a lift – but the injunction about varying sizes still applies.

Right: One simple picture used big transforms a spread.

Two famous landmarks in the area of Lincoln are looked upon with particular affection by the locals. One is the magnificent hilltop cathedral; the other is a well-preserved RAF Lancaster, which stands at the entrance to RAF Scampton.

Thousands of passing motorists stop by the roadside every year to take a closer look at this old veteran from Bomber Command.

RAF Scampton—home of 617 Squadron, the Dam Busters—is the rightful resting place for the aircraft which made that world-famous attack. Even today, the Squadron receives three or four letters every week (mainly from British schools but sometimes from researchers abroad) requesting pictures and information on the Lancaster and its splendid military record.

Today the Squadron flies the Vulcan, the largest delta-wing bomber in the world. It is also flown by 27 and 35 Squadrons—also at RAF Scampton.

The aircraft, carrying either nuclear or conventional weapons, weighs up to 95 tons fully laden, and contains enough generating equipment to light up a small town. It forms a major part of the weapons system available to the commander of the Supreme Allied Command Europe (SACEUR) and has the longest radius of action—up to 1,700 miles without refuelling—and the hardest 'punch' of all the aircraft in his armoury.

With the use of its terrain-following radar, the Vulcan is able to fly at low levels and operate in all weathers. It can cruise at high sub-sonic speeds and is particularly manoeuvrable at height.

Vital equipment

The aircraft carries a crew of five: captain, co-pilot, navigator radar, navigator plotter, and air electronics officer, and a vital piece of equipment which warms up the Naafi soup half an hour after take-off.

Flight Lieutenant Roger Honey, the station's press officer, is as enthusiastic about the Vulcan as any of the technical staff: 'The chances of a successful attack with this weapon must be rated in excess of 90 percent' he says.

'Polaris is our major nuclear deterrent, and the Vulcans back them up. Although we no longer have Quick Reaction Alert (where crews are constantly at action stations), we can still get four aircraft in the air within two minutes during the daytime if they have crews in them already. At night, we work on a maximum of 15 minutes from the moment the crew get out of bed until they are airborne.'

The Vulcans of 617 and 35 Squadrons form a major part of the SACEUR strike force, but 27 Squadron performs another important role—as a medium-range maritime radar reconnaissance force.

Until recently, one of this Squadron's main responsibilities was carrying out North Sea oil rig patrols, but now this duty has been taken over by Nimrods. However, the Vulcan remains a formidable high-level reconnaissance aircraft which can spot vessels over a wider area and from higher altitude than Nimrods.

In mid-April when the Russian Navy was on exercise in the north Norwegian Sea, Vulcans of 27 Squadron were flying night and day to keep an eye on them.

230 Operational Conversion Unit is the Vulcan training section at Scampton. Its task is to provide ground and flying training for all Vulcan crews of Strike Command (including those at sister station RAF Waddington, just south of Lincoln). It also provides refresher training for crews and mid-tour training for co-pilots.

The Radar Flying Squadron, part of 230 OCU, flies Hastings aircraft—the last four in the RAF and soon to go out of service. It provides airborne radar training for Strike Command navigators. Although it has no squadron number, it is known affectionately as '1066 Squadron'.

Hive of activity

The operations centre at RAF Scampton is a hive of activity as Vulcan crews are briefed on the day's schedule. A normal sortie, lasting six hours, is actually three hours in the making: two hours discussing manoeuvres in the operations centre and an hour checking instruments in the aircraft prior to take-off.

The sortie takes them to such diverse places as the North Pole, the Middle East, and sometimes to Goose Bay, Canada. On their return the crew spend anything up to an hour on shut-down checks and de-briefing. So an average working day for a crew member on a sortie lasts about ten hours.

In the air traffic control tower, three controllers and three assistants are on duty at any time of the day or night when the station is open. Theirs is a thankless task, but the number of lives they save every week just by their expert guidance is inestimable.

The officer commanding the ATC, Squadron Leader Neil 'Robbo' Robson, said 'In an emergency we can launch all our aircraft in 20 to 30 minutes. Normally they are launched about once every 15 minutes through the day. But because trainee pilots go round and round the airfield making practice overshoots, rollers (where the aircraft just touches the runway and takes off again), and instrument approaches, we might have five Vulcans in a very small area of airspace at any one time.'

Poised to strike: the venomous Vulcan

"Me and Axl are really tight, even with all the stories you've heard about us . . . The biggest fights are between me and Axl, but that's also what makes it happen."

Left: 'Torn' pictures were a feature of this Q article on Guns N' Roses but were nowhere more effective than on this spread.

Below: An intriguing treatment from Europe 20/20 *in which the left half of the cut-out photograph was printed on this right-hand page with a text run-around and the right half appeared on the turnover.*

Automation in Optics

the wind of change breezes in

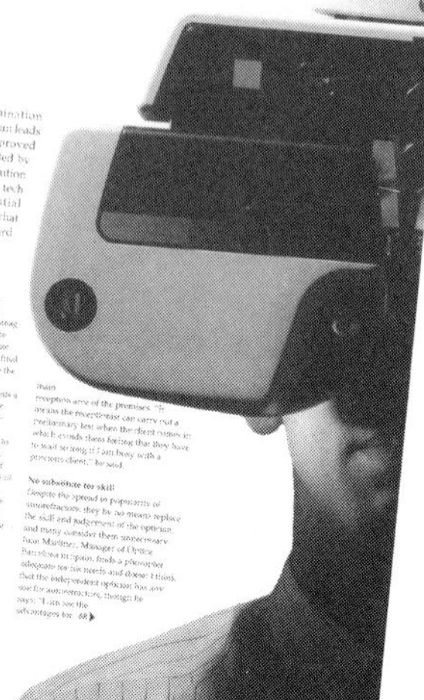

Richard Gilbert's Walking World

Mists and Mountains

Above: Cloud on the Scottish mountain tops allows text to be printed on this photograph in High magazine.

THERE'S A HOT TRADE WIND BLOWING FROM THE COLD STORE

The tremendous growth in Naafi's sales of meat and meat products in recent years received perhaps its greatest impetus from the Deutschmark-saving campaign in Germany. Until only two years ago most of Naafi's retail meat trade on the Continent was limited, by the facilities available, to pre-jointed frozen meat imported from Denmark and the United Kingdom. Sales and foreign currency were being lost to the German high street butchers, so a programme was begun to provide the necessary facilities for the sale of freshly butchered meat. Today 15 large modern shops have been equipped with butcheries and are providing this service and a further three are planned.

The butcheries serve the immediate locality directly but also supply 40 satellite shops throughout the country. Nine refrigerated delivery vans, designed by Naafi's transport department, take daily supplies to those satellite shops, all of which have been equipped with chilled display cabinets and storage cabinets from which the display units can be replenished throughout the day. Three more vans will come into use as the butchery service expands. The butcheries are screened from customer view and, behind the scenes, butchers and their assistants prepare joints, cuts, and chops for the display cabinets and for the daily delivery service to smaller shops. A weighing machine in each production unit automatically produces a descriptive price ticket which gives the weight and price of each cut. Heat sealing machines are used to package the freshly-cut meat at more than six packs a minute.

Above right: In this picture of varying tones, the left side has been ghosted to allow overprinting in a bold sans serif typeface.

THE SEARCH FOR PEARLS

The M&S lingerie group, the land of the rising sun, the world's greatest lace-making centres and British lingerie manufacturers, have all been responsible for creating one of the company's latest ranges of underwear. Alison Young reports on the search for Pearls.

Right: The overprinting on the white curtain evokes a quite different mood on this M&S World *page. The shift left in the second line of the title intrigues the reader's eye and helps lead it to the starting point of the article.*

Above: Cloud on the Scottish mountain tops allows text to be printed on this photograph in High *magazine.*

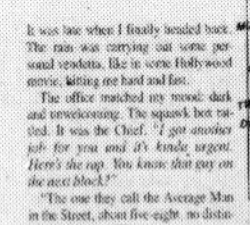

'SAY IT AGAIN SAM'

Jargon phrases like 'conceptual framework' and 'viability orientated' creep into the way we speak, we even learn to accept them, but in reality they bewilder and stun rather than convey a clear message. Writer Rodney Miskin was inspired to find out what happens when the Jargon Junkie's nightmare takes over.

Naafi

Pay NAAFI CUSTOMERS or order

Fifteen Million, Five Hundred Thousand Pounds —— £ 15,500,000

Navy, Army and Air Force Institutes

£ 6.0M DISCOUNT/DIVIDEND TO INDIVIDUAL CUSTOMERS

£ 3.2M REBATE TO UNIT FUNDS

£ 0.6M EXTRA REBATE TO CENTRAL WELFARE FUNDS

PLUS £4.9M TO UNIT FUNDS FROM GAMING MACHINE REVENUE

AND £0.8M TO CLUB IMPROVEMENT FUNDS FROM AMUSEMENT MACHINES

Naafi turnover for 1985/6 was £363.8 Million

Where the money went...

Payment for goods	£241·2m
Operational costs	£ 96·5m
Vat	£ 12·8m
To business reserves	£ 3·5m
To customers	£ 9·8m

Wish you were here...?

Liz Hutton samples the delights of the package holiday

metal would be to commit yourself to third degree burns. Inside it is slightly hotter.

A charming stewardess ushers you to your seat with breakneck speed, the doors close and after another 30 minutes sitting at the end of the runway, you're airborne, sampling the delights of duty-free booze, plastic ham, and limp lettuce. A hostess attempts to entertain you by explaining the complexities of life jackets. You are not amused. There is only one stretch of water on the flight — the 22 miles of English Channel. You passed over that five minutes ago.

Happily, within two hours you're flying over Spain. The warm, soothing voice of the pilot wheedles its way through the intercom to announce that temperatures at the airport are well into the 80s. The passengers 'ooh' in unison.

As the plane touches down, you ignore the futile pleas of the hostess and, standing up, scrabble frantically for your hand luggage in a desperate attempt to be first out. You don't know why you're doing it, but the urge to join the lemming rush is irresistible.

garlic, and knows that you're going to have a wonderful time. He has a fine voice which he demonstrates incessantly during your four-hour drive to the hotel, encouraging you to sing along to 'Una Paloma Blanca'.

You wonder fleetingly if Spanish hit men take travellers' cheques.

At last you arrive. There, in all its splendour, stands your traditional Mediterranean hideaway — the Hotel Miramar — its 600 bedrooms stretching away to infinity.

You check in and deposit yourself and your bags in the 'airy, charming single room' that is heavily disguised as a stuffy, cramped broom cupboard. Nigel rings through and — taking advantage of your, by now, comatose condition — coerces you into signing your savings away on outings: a barbecue, boat trip, vineyard tour, and a day in the city with optional bullfight. Downstairs your companions are meeting for a welcome party. You take a stroll.

Next year, you vow, it will be Barbados or bust. But this year you decide to make the most of it. Just one thought nags at you. If you can afford more exotic climes in 12 months time, isn't there a good chance that everyone else might just manage it too?

providing the outside perspectives and experiences of its members. Chevron has done an excellent job of assembling a Board that not only works well together, but that also has diverse experiences and viewpoints. I also see the committee as a "sounding board" on which management can test ideas.

Q. How do you plan to monitor issues?

A. There are two ways. One is to ask appropriate Chevron officers to study particular issues. The other is for the committee to generate ideas and information out of the experiences and activities of its members. Among us, we have considerable resources with which to look outward and forward. From our perspectives, we may see issues that aren't quite as visible to those within the company.

Q. Could you elaborate on the experience of the committee members?

A. In addition to myself, the committee consists of Ken Derr, Sam Ginn, Chuck Pigott and George Shultz.

Ken Derr, of course, is Chevron's Chairman, and his 30 years with the company give us both Chevron's and the industry's perspective. Sam Ginn is Chairman of the Board and Chief Executive Officer of the Pacific Telesis Group. His special contribution is in community and employee relations. Chuck Pigott, who is Chairman of the Board and Chief Executive Officer of PACCAR Inc, has served on Chevron's Board since 1973. He provides a valuable long-time outside perspective. George Shultz was U.S. Secretary of State from 1982 to 1988, capping 12 years as a U.S. Cabinet officer. There are few persons in the private sector who know more than he does about world affairs. He also has extensive experience in international trade.

Q. What is the World Resources Institute?

A. Briefly, the institute is a not-for-profit organization that does research on envi-

world a better place.

Employees feel the same way. People who invest their lives in a company want to be proud of that company. Pride extends well beyond profitability; it extends to quality, reputation, opportunities. People want to work for a company that "does the right thing."

Q. Do you have a personal goal for the committee?

A. I feel we can be helpful both to the Board and to management. To the extent we are, we also will be helpful in keeping Chevron a company its stockholders and employees can be proud of, one that will contribute positively to the world our grandchildren will inherit.

CHEVRON WORLD WINTER 7

Police • The Voice of the Service • April 1991 • Page 17

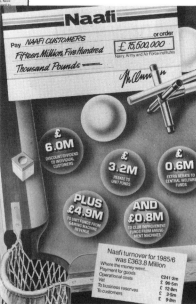

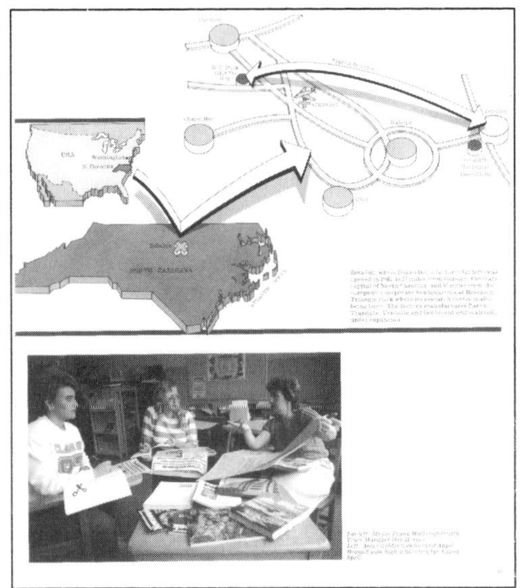

IN SEARCH OF DESTINY

David O'Brien and Ann Smith describe the care of a depressed young woman with great potential, using Peplau's model of nursing

TWENTY-three-year-old Miss Nightingale was admitted to the Rest Home for Gentlewomen suffering from physical and mental exhaustion on December 27, 1843. She was admitted from her home at Embley Park near Romsey, Hampshire, where she lives with her parents and older sister, Parthenope. Her family own an estate in Derbyshire (Lea Hurst) where they usually spend most of the summer. At present, however, the family is visiting Mrs Nightingale's sister at Waverley Abbey, near Farnham. Miss Nightingale felt too ill to join them there.

Miss Nightingale moves in distinguished and intellectual circles, as might be expected of the daughter of a respectable country gentleman and a fashionable society lady. She is well educated, having been taught mainly at home by her father, and has travelled widely in Europe, particularly in Italy and France. She says she enjoys the intellectual stimulation of reading, studying such subjects as mathematics, Greek and philosophy and listening to music, particularly opera. Much of her time, however, is spent meeting family and domestic responsibilities, such as helping to organise the smooth running of the busy household, entertaining and making visits.

Miss Nightingale is considered, by her relatives, to be of a delicate constitution (as are her mother and sister), but there is no history of major illness. She is reported to have a predisposition towards periods of extreme weakness, lassitude and emotional debility with feelings of despondency and irritability. The inability to overcome an exacerbation of these symptoms has led to her hospital admission today.

Fig 1. Peplau's phases of the nurse/patient relationship

Growth and development facilitated by interpersonal relations

Stage	Nurse's role	Focus	Nursing process
Orientation	Stranger	Problem defining	Assessment
	Counsellor	Selection of appropriate nurse	
Identification	Teacher	Therapeutic measures	Planning
Exploitation	Leader	Utilisation of the above measures for problem [illegible]	Implementation
			Evaluation

Nurse — Patient

Miss Nightingale is slightly built, with a pale complexion contrasting with her thick golden-red hair. She looks unhappy and extremely tired. She has a history of loss of appetite. She says her main needs are 'rest and space to think'.

The nursing model advocated for Miss Nightingale (her choice of personal title) was based on Peplau's interpersonal concepts, the central notion of which is that interaction between nurse and patient should be structured, problem-directed and therapeutic[1]. There are four stages in this model, centring on orientation, identification, exploitation and resolution (Fig 1).

Over a period of a few days, through the interaction between nurse and patient, several key issues emerged. These focused on Miss Nightingale's general dissatisfaction with herself, particularly concerning her relationships with others and also her lack of clear ideas over which direction her life should take.

Since childhood, although aware of certain intellectual abilities, Miss Nightingale has often felt a sense of personal failure or 'unworthiness'. She feels that this is mainly her own fault; on the one hand she enjoyed the 'pride of life', and has entered enthusiastically into the glitter of the fashionable world and felt the 'temptation to shine in society' but she is left with a sense of life's lack of purpose and value, and yet has done nothing to rectify this. She has strongly held religious views and senses that God has a purpose for her.

She feels particularly close to her father. Both share the same intellectual interests and enjoy abstract speculation and academic debate. She says they possess the same temperament, sometimes being full of good humour and at other times gloomy and despondent. Her sister and her mother like to spend a great deal of time together, mainly entertaining or visiting the wide circle of relatives and friends. The emphasis given to the intricacies of family life and the time involved on consultations concerning what Miss Nightingale sees as inconsequentials leads to feelings of anger and irritation. Any outward indication of this results in criticism and reproach from her mother and sister and pangs of conscience on Miss Nightingale's part.

26 27 NURSING TIMES MAY 15, VOL 87, NO 20, 1991

A wide variety of art styles, caricatures and cartoons can be commissioned to suit any topic. Opposite page: (top left and right) Billiton Magazine *and* Naafi News, *(centre)* Naafi News *and* Datalog, *(bottom)* Chevron World *and* Police.
This page: (top left) Glaxo World, *(above)* Nursing Times, *(left)* Envoy.

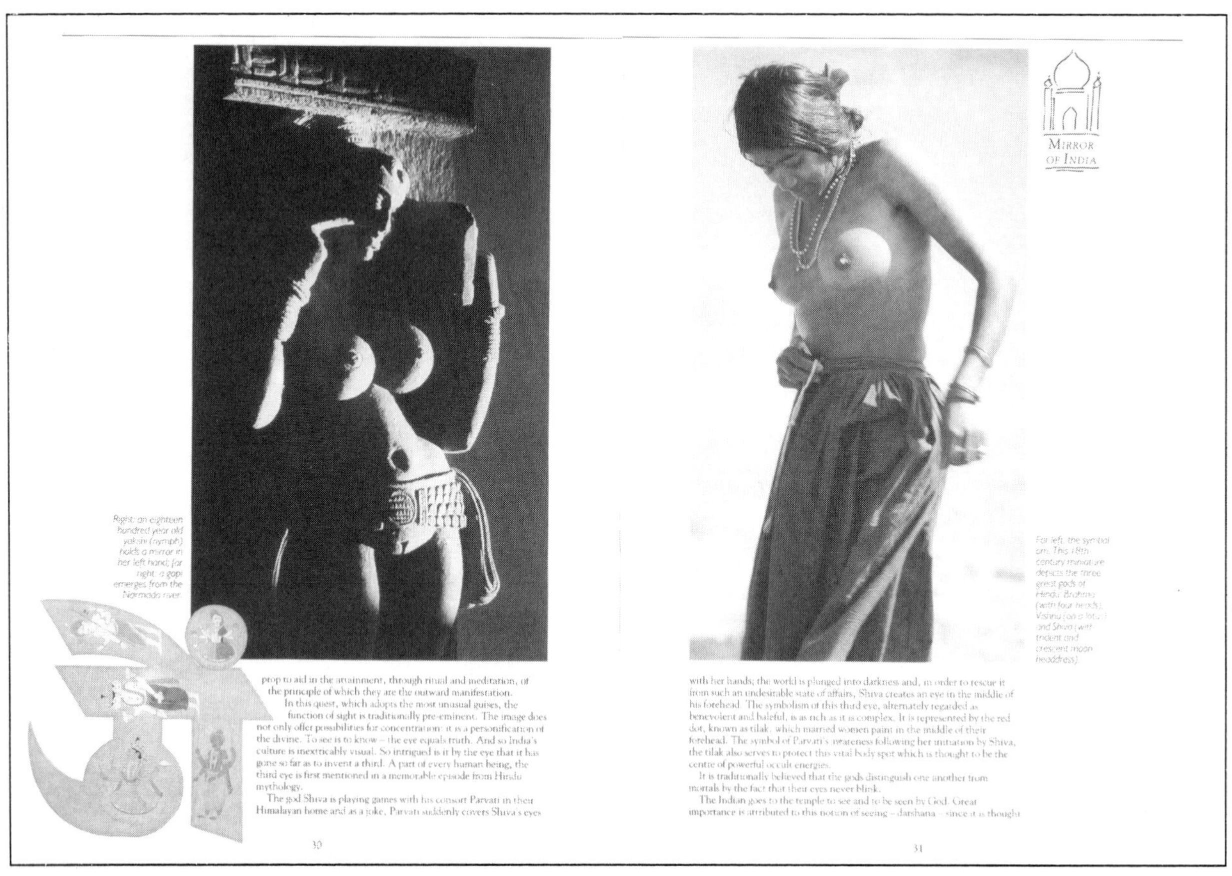

MIRROR OF INDIA

Right: an eighteen hundred year old yakshi (nymph) holds a mirror in her left hand; far right: a gopi emerges from the Narmada river.

prop to aid in the attainment, through ritual and meditation, of the principle of which they are the outward manifestation.

In this quest, which adopts the most unusual guises, the function of sight is traditionally pre-eminent. The image does not only offer possibilities for concentration: it is a personification of the divine. To see is to know – the eye equals truth. And so India's culture is inextricably visual. So intrigued is it by the eye that it has gone so far as to invent a third. A part of every human being, the third eye is first mentioned in a memorable episode from Hindu mythology.

The god Shiva is playing games with his consort Parvati in their Himalayan home and as a joke, Parvati suddenly covers Shiva's eyes

30

with her hands; the world is plunged into darkness and, in order to rescue it from such an undesirable state of affairs, Shiva creates an eye in the middle of his forehead. The symbolism of this third eye, alternately regarded as benevolent and baleful, is as rich as it is complex. It is represented by the red dot, known as tilak, which married women paint in the middle of their forehead. The symbol of Parvati's awareness following her initiation by Shiva, the tilak also serves to protect this vital body spot which is thought to be the centre of powerful occult energies.

It is traditionally believed that the gods distinguish one another from mortals by the fact that their eyes never blink.

The Indian goes to the temple to see and to be seen by God. Great importance is attributed to this notion of seeing – darshana – since it is thought

Far left: the symbol om. This 18th-century miniature depicts the three great gods of Hindu: Brahma (with four heads), Vishnu (on a lotus) and Shiva (with trident and crescent moon headdress).

31

The general rule about contrasting the size and shapes of pictures is broken sensibly on this spread from BBC World *to point up similarities in the two subjects.*

14 More about type

Because typography is such a vast subject, so complex and yet so fundamental to magazine design, I recommend that you read this chapter now without attempting to absorb what is new to you, but simply so that you can begin to fit what you already know about type into an overall picture. You should re-read both chapters on type after you have made a few forays into page design. In due course you can further extend your knowledge with the help of one or two of the many books available on the subject.

If your company (or client) has an established house style, obtain a copy of it. If a house style does not exist then refer to a source such as *Hart's Rules* (Oxford University Press), a copy of which should be on your bookshelf.

A type family consists of a basic design, most often a roman face in medium weight, which has been modified in various ways to provide other weights (the range may include ultra light, light, demi-bold, bold and ultra bold), each of which might also be made available in expanded and condensed styles in roman and italic versions and, perhaps, with other variations such as outline, drop shadow and small caps.

As there are thousands of such type families (many of which have been copied with minor changes and given new names), each of which might consist of 30, 40, or more variations, you cannot expect to be familiar with more than a fraction of them. You would, nevertheless, not so very long ago have been expected, as a designer, to be familiar with the differences which distinguish the broad categories such as old face, modern, slab serif, sans serif, and so on. For the keen student of typography, the history and development of the various styles will still prove necessary and fascinating, but in recent times there have been so many new designs which blur the borders between the various groups that student designers can, at this early stage, find more profitable ways to employ their time and efforts.

Type size is measured from the top of the ascender to the foot of the descender plus a minimal amount of space which has been designed into that particular face. Cap height, x-height and other terms are demonstrated in the illustration on page 14.

All characters typed on a typewriter take up the same width of space on the paper so that the letter-spacing in a word like '`illicit`' will be vastly different from that in '`mood`'. In typesetting the space taken up by the character varies with the width of the character, so that 'illicit' and 'mood' not only look better but are also more legible.

FADS AND FASHIONS

Fashions in typography come and go. The advent of computer typesetting triggered a trend to tighter letter-spacing for display type. Recently the move has been in the opposite direction, often to extremes – indeed, excessive letter-spacing, particularly of all-capital headings, has become something of a design cliché. Words with acres of space between the letters lose all shape and are, in effect, no longer words but simply a series of disconnected letters.

Before slavishly following any new fashion, remind yourself of the purpose of type and your principal objective as designer – to promote communication between writer and reader. We do not read words letter by letter (what a laborious business it would be if we did) but by the rapid recognition of the shapes words make. That is why type set in lower case is easier to read than type set all in capitals; lower case produces more distinctive shapes. We carry mental maps of thousands of these shapes and words which fit those maps are recognized instantly. Unfamiliar words, especially unfamiliar foreign words, bring our rapid progress through text to a temporary halt while we scan the letters. Destroy the shape of familiar words (by distortion, too little or too much letter-spacing, unsuitable backgrounds, and other distractions) and you can quickly lose your reader.

Letter-spacing is based on 'units'. A unit is a division of an em, which, as you already know, is a variable measure based on the square of the width of the letter 'm'. This means that when units of space are added or subtracted the change will always be relative to the type size. Unfortunately, the number of units to an em varies from one system to another, so it is important to discover which figure applies to the system in use.

The letter-spacing designed into a fount cannot account for the designer's every requirement, but modern computer typesetting allows for further adjustment where this is necessary. Thus, units of space can be added to, or subtracted from, the original allocation. The earliest use you are likely to make of this facility is with display type, where kerning (the process of adjusting space between a pair of letters illustrated on page 140) can sometimes greatly improve appearance and legibility.

Computers have bestowed yet more flexibility on the designer in that type can be expanded or condensed at will (the increments varying between systems). This, together with the facility to control letter-space and word-space, and to produce type sizes between the pre-set standard sizes, enables the designer to fit display type to precise measures. Some systems allow type to be rotated, bent to a path, or distorted in a variety of ways – which can be boon or bane.

Some of the distortions now easily and cheaply available via the computer can be truly horrific. On the other hand, it is easy to over-react, as some typographers do, for example, to the expanding and condensing of type. If they are used sensibly and kept within reasonable limits, such effects can help the design of the page and, though an experienced typographer might spot that it is not a purpose-designed face, the average reader would notice nothing amiss.

TOO SPACED OUT FOR WORDS

Perhaps one of the most common errors in text setting is to allow too much space between words. We assimilate words in small groups but if the word-spacing is too wide the eye lurches along picking up one word at a time like a child with a reading primer. The eye travels much more quickly and comfortably along a line where the word-spacing has been kept to a minimum compatible with the ability to distinguish the separate words – something like the space taken by the letter 't' or even, with some typefaces, the letter 'i'.

You will quickly come to appreciate that each designer and typographer has a collection of pet hates. These will undoubtedly include certain typefaces. For some, any letter-spacing at all is an abomination; others cannot abide expanded word-spacing. For myself, I can accept both letter-spacing and word-spacing within reason if their use helps to avoid end-of-line word-breaks. I find carrying over a syllable (or more) from the end of one line to the beginning of the next much more disruptive than an occasional line in which letter- or word-spacing is a little looser than the ideal.

But magazine production is usually ruled to a

greater or lesser extent by economics and deadlines. Somewhere along the line, the designer has to trade off the desire for perfection against the requirement to get the job done on time within the constraints of the money available.

In this chapter, as in others, I have been guilty of oversimplifications, generalizations, and approximations, in my desire to promote understanding but avoid bogging you down in esoteric detail when what you need is to get on with the business of designing pages. For example, I claimed that a point is equal to 1/72 of an inch – in which I have misled you by some hundred-thousandths of an inch. A little further down the road, therefore, with some experience of page design behind you, you should move on to a book or two dealing with typography and other peripheral subjects in much greater depth, detail and exactitude.

Much has been written by typographers and designers in the past few years about the horrors of digital typesetting, the demise of style and the loss of pride in the craft. But typographers and designers of the day said the same sort of thing when Linotype and, later, photosetting arrived on the scene. Of course there are many examples around which could be said to substantiate their claims, but in my view there are also modern examples of typography and design which are superior to anything achieved since the invention of movable type. And, what is perhaps more important, it is now accessible to many more people in both the creation and the enjoyment of it.

SOME GUIDELINES

1. Avoid the temptation to use too many different faces in one design. It would be as well, at first, to use only variations in the size, weight and style of one typeface. Choose a face that offers a wide range of style and weight variations, such as italics, bold, light, extra bold, condensed, expanded, so that titles, captions, crossheads, standfirsts, etc. can be easily distinguished from the body text and from each other. When you are confident in the handling of the variations in that face you can think of adding a contrasting face for titles and other display elements. The easiest and safest way to ensure contrast would be to use a sans serif for display with a serif text face, but with experience you will be able to select two serifs (or two sans) which will work well together. Gradually expand your knowledge of the different type families and build up confidence in handling them.
2. Words set throughout in capitals are more difficult to read than words set in lower case, so restrict all-caps to short titles,

crossheads, bylines (writers' credits), or straps (usually a supplementary line in a smaller size above the main title). Because there are neither descenders nor ascenders, multiple lines of all-caps setting will usually look better with negative leading which reduces the space between the lines.

3. When choosing a body type for sustained reading, look for a large x-height in relation to point size, a wide-set letter with good open counters, probably in the range 9 to 12 pt., depending on column width, with at least 1 pt. of leading.
4. Serif faces are generally thought to give a traditional look, sans serif a modern look, but – for long text passages – serif faces are generally less tiring than sans. Surprisingly, italics have been shown to be more tiring than roman.
5. Large blocks of unjustified setting (ranged left or right or centred) also tend to be more taxing for the reader than justified setting where the eye becomes attuned to the reading rhythm created by the regular length of the lines. Unjustified setting can provide a pleasing contrast, but care is needed to avoid creating unsightly shapes. For both reasons, unjustified setting is best confined to shorter pieces of text (blurbs, captions etc.) where time and attention can be given to ensure ugly shapes are

MILLILITRE

millilitre

Note how much easier it is to recognize 'millilitre' in upper and lower case letters than in all caps if half the word is obscured.

NEGATIVE LEADING
APPLIED TO DISPLAY TYPE
TO PRODUCE
CLOSED-UP LINES

24/20 pt. Helvetica

Helvetica Light	Choose a face that offers a wide range of style and weight variations
Helvetica Light Italic	*Choose a face that offers a wide range of style and weight variations*
Helvetica Medium	**Choose a face that offers a wide range of style and weight variations**
Helvetica Medium Italic	***Choose a face that offers a wide range of style and weight variations***
Helvetica Heavy	**Choose a face that offers a wide range of style and weight variations**
Helvetica Heavy Italic	***Choose a face that offers a wide range of style and weight variations***
Helvetica Light Condensed	Choose a face that offers a wide range of style and weight variations
Helvetica Light Condensed Italic	*Choose a face that offers a wide range of style and weight variations*
Helvetica Cond. Regular	Choose a face that offers a wide range of style and weight variations
Helvetica Cond. Regular Italic	*Choose a face that offers a wide range of style and weight variations*
Helvetica Cond. Bold	**Choose a face that offers a wide range of style and weight variations**
Helvetica Cond. Bold Italic	***Choose a face that offers a wide range of style and weight variations***
Helvetica Cond. Black	**Choose a face that offers a wide range of style and weight variations**
Helvetica Cond. Black Italic	***Choose a face that offers a wide range of style and weight variations***

eliminated. Be cautious about centring text or ranging it right – the eye struggles to pick up the starting point of each line when there is no straight edge to return to. There are comparatively few occasions when the effort this demands of the reader can be justified.

6. Where contrast in tone is required, between title and byline for example, bold and light (or ultra bold and light etc.) will usually prove more effective than bold and medium or medium and light. In other words, miss out at least one intermediate weight to accentuate the contrast.
7. Never use underlining as a means of adding emphasis to words in body text. Italics can provide emphasis and maintain the smooth tone of the text shape. Small caps can also be used – and should be preferred to normal caps. Bold is best used for display purposes or to provide emphasis where continuous reading is not involved, on contents pages, in tables and lists, for example.
8. Always see a test setting of a column of copy on the paper chosen for the publication before committing yourself to a typeface, size, leading and line length.
9. Type printed white out of black (wob), or white out of strong colours, can be eye-catching but should not be used for lengthy text passages.

If you are proposing to underline any straps or headlines be sure to break the lines around any descenders

Ensure sufficient tonal variation between type and its background

Ensure sufficient tonal variation between type and its background

Ensure sufficient tonal variation between type and its background

The variation between this type and its background is obviously insufficient

10. Do not attempt to print type in colour, in black on colour, in colour on colour etc., without testing the colour combination. Some combinations are effective, others will prove disastrous. Where type is to be printed (as a solid or as a tint) on a solid or tinted background of the same colour, ensure that the contrast between the two is sufficient for the text to be readable. Try a difference of 70% as your safe starting point.

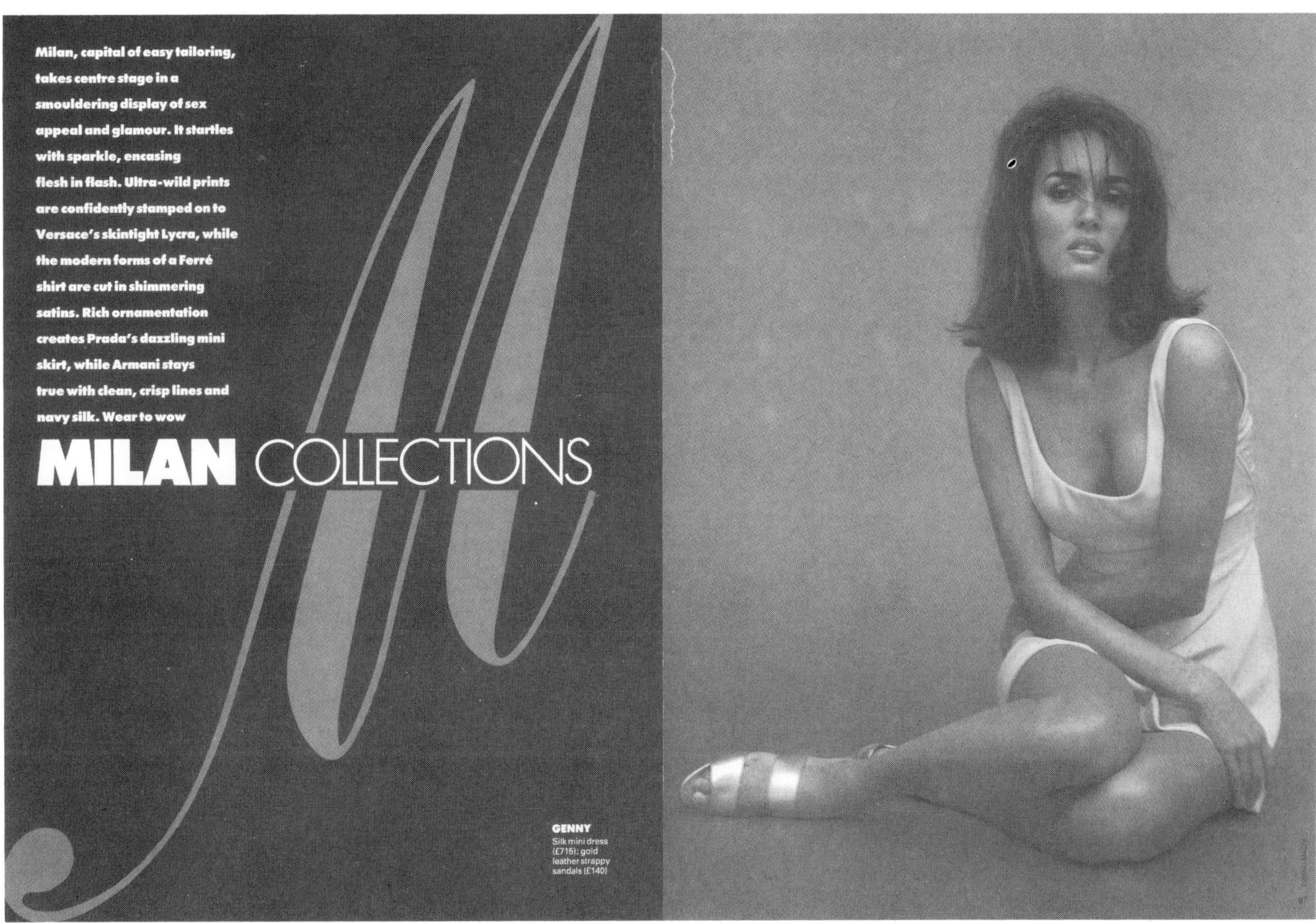

Milan, capital of easy tailoring, takes centre stage in a smouldering display of sex appeal and glamour. It startles with sparkle, encasing flesh in flash. Ultra-wild prints are confidently stamped on to Versace's skintight Lycra, while the modern forms of a Ferré shirt are cut in shimmering satins. Rich ornamentation creates Prada's dazzling mini skirt, while Armani stays true with clean, crisp lines and navy silk. Wear to wow

MILAN COLLECTIONS

GENNY
Silk mini dress (£715); gold leather strappy sandals (£140)

This spread from Elle *demonstrates the sensible use of white out of black text: a short piece set in a bold sans face and well spaced.*

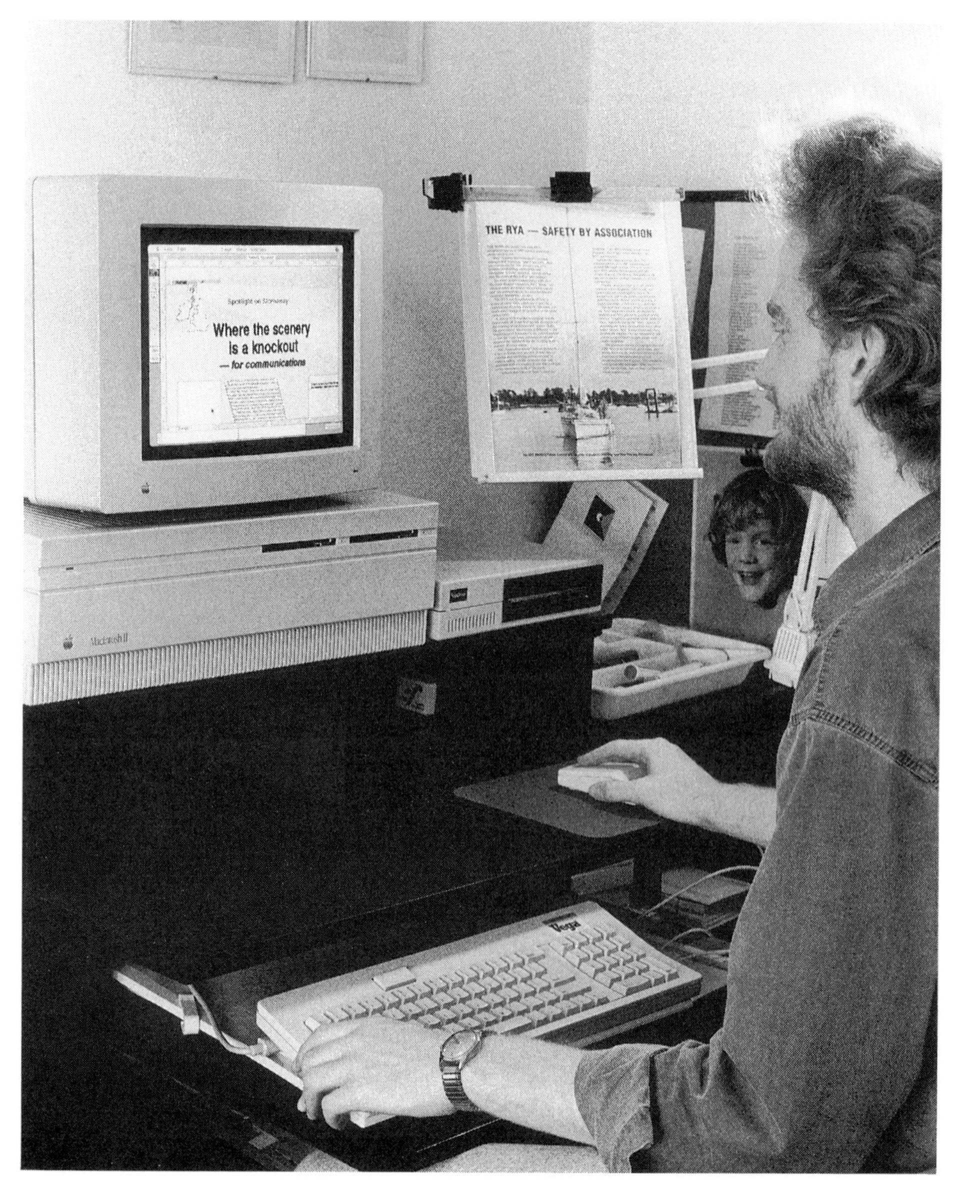

Designing on screen.

15 Designing on screen

Desktop publishing (DTP) means different things to different people. I use the term to mean the computer-based front end of a publishing system which may be all-electronic or may be a mixture of old and new technologies. In essence, it is the hardware and software which make it possible to set type and design pages on a computer. In the magazine world this will usually mean working on Macintosh, IBM or IBM-compatible terminals, which may be stand-alone or networked depending on the size of the operation.

The merits of the various computers and programs available is a subject beyond the scope of this book, but we will consider the advantages and the dangers facing designers who design on screen.

First let me say that those who have developed their skills with pencils, scissors and paste need have no fear of making the transition to on-screen designing. It is true that youngsters tend to take to computers more quickly than more mature adults, but I have provided DTP training to designers and typographers in their fifties and sixties who have later admitted that, despite all their fears, their greatest difficulty proved to be picking up some basic two-finger typing skills.

The most popular page layout programs for magazines use familiar cut-and-paste methodology with electronics replacing scissors, spray booths and waxing machines. The designer has no need to understand how the computer works, merely how to give it orders.

One of the first advantages to strike the designer is that when text is imported into the page and set as required, the amount of space taken up by it is instantly and accurately visible

Type can be stretched

or condensed

shadow can be applied

or outline

ALL CAPS

OR SMALL CAPS . . .

With no kerning applied (top), too much space appears between the 'T' and the 'y'. Kerning (below) tucks the 'y' under the overhang of the 'T'. The intention is, as far as possible, to equalize the amount of space (not the distance) between each pair of letters.

Type

Type

on the screen. No need then for tedious casting off and the counting of lines on grid sheets. This text area can instantly be manipulated into a variety of shapes and moved about the page at will.

SPEED AND FLEXIBILITY

Illustrations (or their keylines) can be enlarged or reduced in proportion without the need to use any of the scaling methods described in Chapters 5 and 13.

Typeface, size, leading and tracking can be changed with a few keystrokes. Type can be stretched, condensed, kerned, and various styles tried. Special characters such as scissors, quads, bullets and many more are available and can be similarly changed at will.

Borders and rules are available in a range of styles and sizes. Tints can be applied and wobs produced. Objects can be moved about the page by the simple expedient of selecting them with the pointer and dragging them to a new position. Each new layout can either be scrapped or saved, so that the most promising design ideas can be printed out for comparison. Parts of these pages can be combined into yet more designs. And all at the modest cost of a little time.

For any periodical designer perhaps the two greatest benefits are the facility to create templates and style sheets. These provide the twin blessings of added speed and relief from much drudgery. At their simplest, templates are similar to the grid sheets we produced in Chapter 7 – but they go much further. Once made up such a master page can be duplicated and adapted in a variety of ways. Any items which are standard to the pages of the publication can be added (datelines, folios, column rules, department headings, etc.) and positioned and formatted so that they appear automatically on each new page and in each new issue.

Appropriate style sheets can be attached to each template. A couple of keystrokes will, thenceforth, instantly put text, captions, crossheads, titling, boxed text into the correct typeface, size, weight, style, leading, alignment, etc. In other words, style sheets can be set up for any regularly appearing setting and, once set, they can, like templates, be duplicated, edited and transferred in practically no time at all.

GETTING FAMILIAR

If, at the outset, you are uncomfortable with designing directly on the screen, continue making your pencil roughs and then transfer your final design to the screen instead of to a full-size paper grid. As you become more familiar with the computer you will eventually regard this step as unnecessary but, while you find it helpful, continue to use it.

CHANGELING

CHANGELING

CHANGELING

CHANGELING

CHANGELING

CHANGELING

CHANGELING

From one typeface (Times bold in this instance) a number of variations are possible within most page layout programs, of which those shown left are merely a sample. Still more variety can be added with the help of graphics software.

Left: A small selection of some of the symbols and devices available and, below, some of the ways in which they can be manipulated.

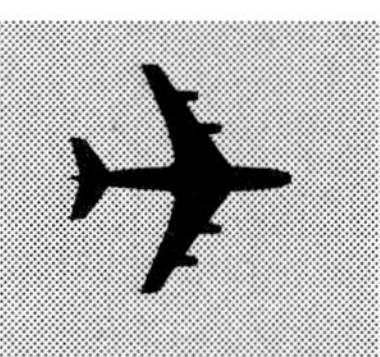

Those who are already computer-literate (and not unduly pressed for time) may find that reading the program manuals and following the prepared tutorials are all they need to get started. But one of the introductory courses (usually about two days) organized by computer distributors and others can provide fast track training, reducing the learning period by weeks. Manuals and training videos cannot answer your questions or tailor their training to your specific needs as a human tutor can. (If you can, find a course which is led by a tutor who uses the program for magazine production.)

If you are planning to convert to on-screen designing do not plan to start serious work involving deadlines immediately after your training course. Having learnt how the program does what, you will need a running-in period to familiarize yourself with the geography of the program before you can build up speed.

CONTROL YOUR URGES

The principal danger posed by DTP is that the novelty, the instant response, the flexibility, and the availability of so many low-cost effects can lead to over-exuberance. Resist the urge to use an effect or a facility simply because it is there, except, of course, while you are familiarizing yourself with the program when you should attempt every experiment that occurs to you, no matter how outrageous. During the learning period you need to learn what is possible rather than what is tasteful.

You can, for example, easily track text to rid yourself of a widow line, but the insertion of a discretionary hyphen (a hyphen which automatically disappears if no longer required), or the cutting of an unnecessary word, might be more appropriate. Although, as I mentioned in the previous chapter, I am not enamoured of end-of-line word breaks, they do sometimes prove to be the lesser of two evils. Designers, too, must learn the art of compromise.

Rotation of text or a graphic to an unusual angle on the page might add interest to a design when the basic ingredients are not exciting. But if rotation is used indiscriminately, simply because it is now easy and inexpensive to do, it loses its capacity to surprise and intrigue.

The designer who is not unduly constrained by budgets will probably find that the computer's main advantages are its speed and the fact that it brings so much control into one's own hand.

The designer who struggles with tight budgets will, in addition, find the range of affordable effects magically increased and, with luck, some of the economies that flow from DTP might find their way into the design budget.

The price, of course, is the time that must be devoted to aspects of the work which might previously have been contracted out.

It is important to recognize that a move to DTP does not require total commitment to electronics. Use those parts of new technology which are appropriate in the circumstances, but if some aspects of the old technologies should offer better quality, greater efficiency, lower cost, quicker production – use them. Don't throw away your scissors and paste: mix and match to get the best of both worlds.

UP THE RESOLUTION

Dots per inch (dpi) is the measure of resolution in DTP. Most monitors have a resolution of 72 dpi. This means that a square inch of monitor screen contains 5184 dots. By making some dots black and some white the screen can represent letters or graphics. It will be obvious from this that the higher the dpi the better the resolution.

Most laser printers have a resolution of 300 dpi (90 000 dots to the square inch) which explains why their output is so superior to what you see on the screen. An imagesetter will have a resolution of 1270 dpi (or greater), producing over 1½ million dots to the square inch.

For some publications the output from the laser printer will provide camera ready artwork of adequate quality. Some improvement on normal output can be achieved by printing out these final pages on a smoother paper than the usual 80 gsm copier, but be wary of using coated papers unless they are specifically for laser printers as coatings can ruin the drum. In the case of magazines smaller than A4 it will pay to set up the pages as large as possible, in proportion, because reduction in the process camera will tighten up the images and effectively increase the number of dots per inch.

It is also possible to print direct to film (positive or negative) from a laser printer and so cut out a processing step, but be sure your film is suitable for the high temperatures generated in the laser printer. Melted film in your laser printer is a sticky and expensive mess you can do without.

There are laser printers now on the market which print at higher resolution (at a higher price, of course); 1000 dpi is possible at the time of writing, which leaves only a small gap between that laser printer and the lower end of the imagesetter range.

OFF TO THE BUREAU

Most designers will, however, be sending a disk to a bureau for output at the higher resolutions which are available from imagesetters. That disk must contain all the relevant files: the pages themselves, the original files of any graphics (whether drawn or scanned) included on the pages, and any necessary data files.

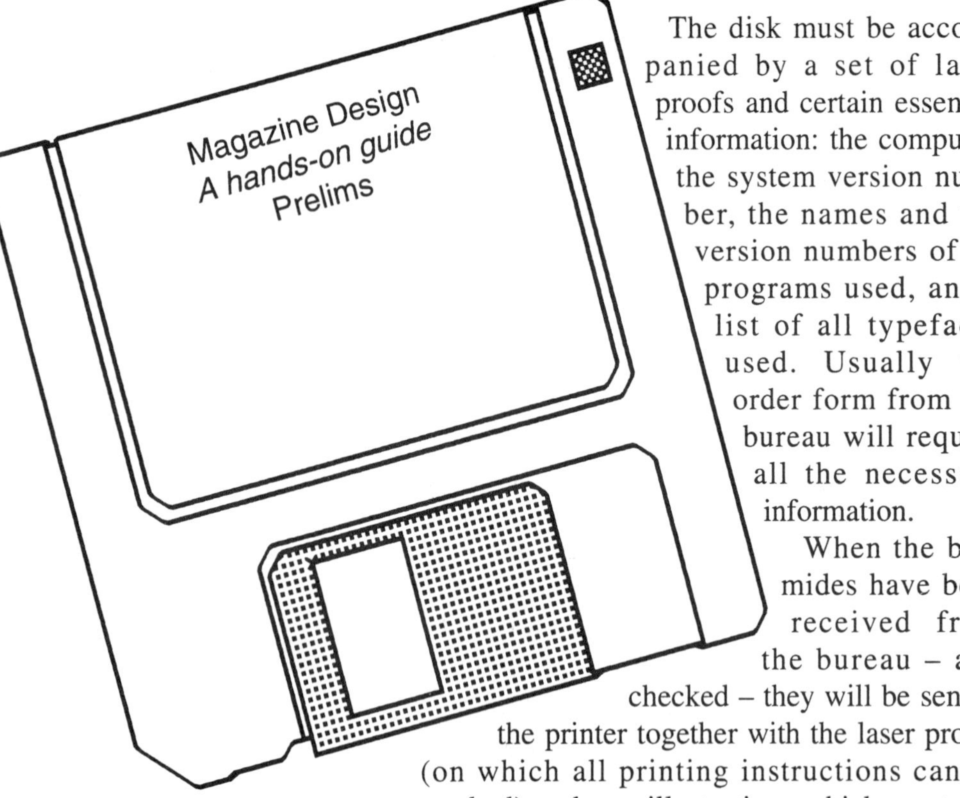

A 3.5in. floppy disk is a common medium for passing data between computers. Information can also be passed directly between networked (linked) computers or, using a modem, down a telephone line.

The disk must be accompanied by a set of laser proofs and certain essential information: the computer, the system version number, the names and the version numbers of all programs used, and a list of all typefaces used. Usually the order form from the bureau will request all the necessary information.

When the bromides have been received from the bureau – and checked – they will be sent to the printer together with the laser proofs (on which all printing instructions can be marked) and any illustrations which are to be dropped in, marked up as suggested in Chapter 8.

A fairly common problem in DTP is that text input is frequently carried out by secretarial staff. In this situation you should try, if possible, to persuade the keyboard operator to unlearn many of the secretarial school conventions (such as two spaces after a full stop) and to learn something about such things as en dashes. Although it is possible to provide codes for tagging styles to the text, it will usually be safer – at least initially – to instruct them to type the text with simple punctuation, one return only at the end of paragraphs, and no attempt to format text in any way. If tables are included, a paper copy should always be produced and marked up with any special instructions.

Ideally a house style booklet – which includes all these new injunctions – should be produced for anyone inputting copy, whether full-time secretarial or editorial staff or freelance writers.

16 Improving your skills

It has been my intention to persuade you that the major hurdle faced by anyone wanting to develop skills as a designer is the first one: putting pencil to paper. To that end I have concentrated on the essential knowledge and skills required to get you started. Enough, I hope, to provide guidance but not so much as to deter. The satisfaction of producing an acceptable, if not brilliant, design at an early stage is, I believe, the strongest spur to further effort and study. It is like that first decent golf shot (or minor success in any sport or game of skill) that convinces the aspiring beginner that the ability is there; a little time, a little practice, and great things will be possible.

The guidelines I have proposed are no more than that – guidelines. Eventually you will want to break away from them, and so you should. For example, I have advocated you should use simple rectangular shapes, but as you study magazines you will see other shapes, some of which will work, some of which won't. To set you on you way; L-shapes (and L-shapes reversed left to right) and U-shapes usually work quite well.

Following my guidelines should keep you out of the worst design bunkers while you are developing your own skill and judgement. Learning how and when to break the rules (but not the prime rule of maintaining communication between the writer and the reader), and gaining the confidence to experiment (but basing such adventures on observation and analysis of design) come with experience and lead to progress as a designer.

To break the rules to good effect one needs not merely to be aware of them but to study and understand them. Fortunately, one of the best

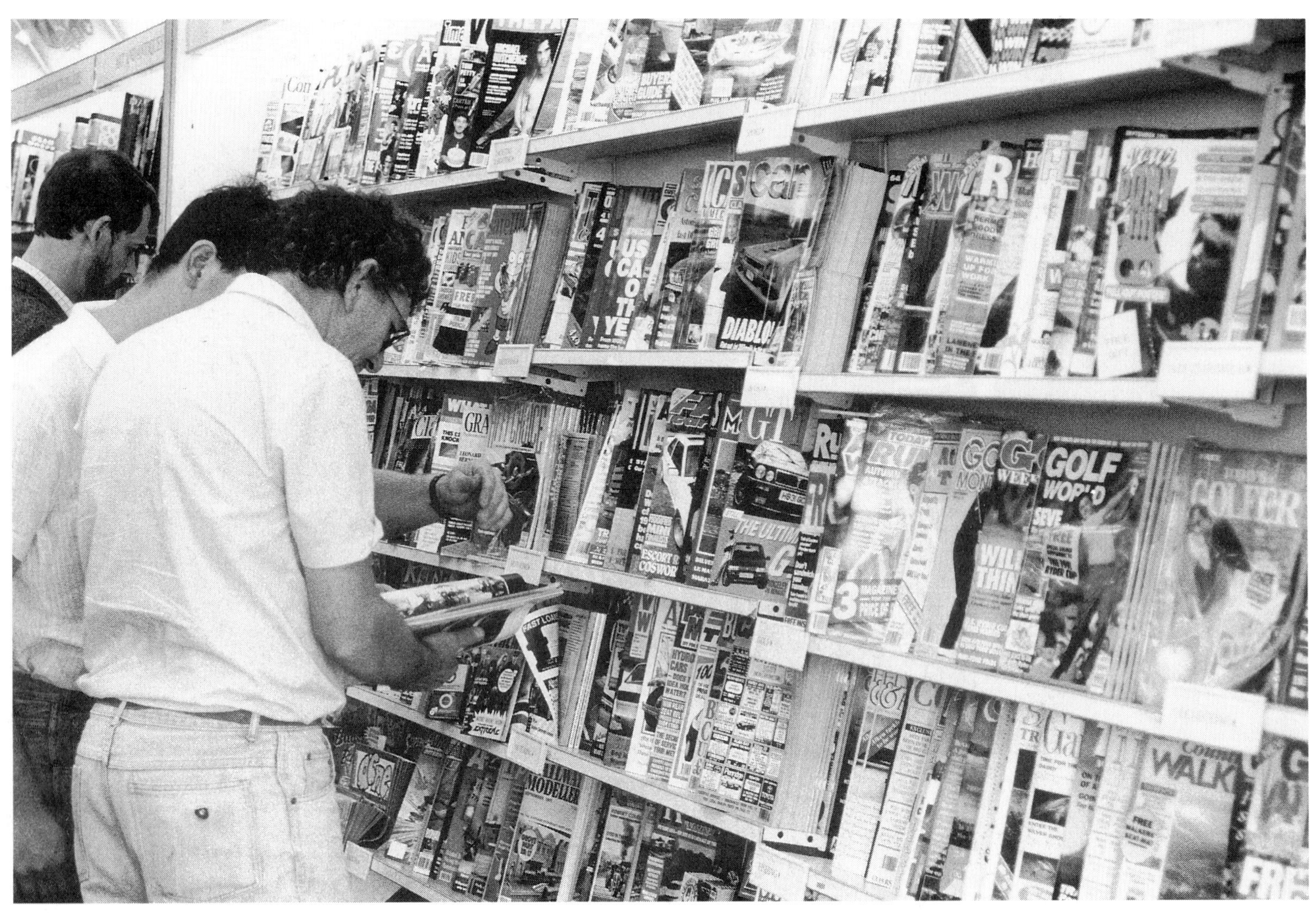

A storehouse of study material is available at most good bookshops.

schools for designers is free: the magazine racks of a handy newsagent. As you browse, some pages will cause you to pause. Why? Was it the impact of a picture? An elegant use of white space. A tweak of the typography? Or was it some design disaster? Learn from other people's failures as well as their successes. A page might demonstrate such a valuable lesson that you decide to buy the magazine. By keeping such pages you can build up a useful tear-sheet file, a file which will spark new ideas when you hit a difficult design problem, or caution you about the dangers inherent in attempting a particular effect.

IMPROVE THE SHINING HOUR

Another attraction of this form of low- or no-cost study is that it can be practised in a variety of places, often in time which would otherwise be wasted. You can study while you wait for an appointment in the reception area of those organizations which provide a scattering of magazines, or in the public library reading room while you wait for your partner to select a novel for the weekend, in the dentist's or doctor's waiting-room, and on the train, tube or bus (yes, you may have to buy that one although you can frequently pick up someone else's discard which might turn out to be a publication entirely new to you).

A serious and detailed study of typography demands rather more dedication, but remember, you need to know how to use type, you do not need to be able to create type.

Evaluate other people's rules but do not get hidebound by them – and that includes mine. Ask yourself that vital question: Are their injunctions aimed at achieving better communication, or do they come from some arcane ideology about 'good' or 'proper' practice?

Do not be tempted to sacrifice the readability of the message in an attempt to impress other designers. The only rule which should never be broken is the one I have now repeated in a variety of ways: the design should never place obstacles between author (and I include artist and photographer here) and reader.

You can afford to be more adventurous with display type than with text (advertisements often lead the way) but you will frequently find that tweaking the rules or conventions works better than shattering them.

Do not ignore type in its other manifestations; posters, newspapers, record and book covers, television ... they can all provide useful lessons and ideas.

THE EVER-READY RESEARCHER

Take whatever opportunities present themselves to study readers' reactions, especially to your magazine but to others as well. If you can, draw them into conversation without letting them know of your connection with the magazine. Lay people can often be persuaded to discuss the worth of a headline or picture and give interesting reasons for their judgements. They usually have more difficulty explaining their reactions to the overall design of pages – which is understandable because of the greater complexity. But value judgments, even without rationalization, tell us something.

The spread of computer cataloguing in our libraries is of great value to the student of design in all its aspects. By setting up searches in the subjects of graphic design, typography, photography, printing, paper, colour and so on, you can see what is available on the shelves (or available at nearby branches and which may be ordered at the cost of a few pence) and how recently it was published.

Short and part-time courses and workshops in design are available: a few are provided by art colleges and a number are offered from time to time by commercial organizations, unions and associations. All of these can be useful in getting started but I believe that, beyond a certain point, design is best learned from practice, subjective study and analysis, rather than from textbook or classroom. Too much theory too early dampens enthusiasm. In the end, experience is the only route to expertise.

The more you study and the more you design the more enthusiastic you will become about design and the more eager to express your own thoughts and ideas. A word of warning, to avoid having that enthusiasm blunted, will not come amiss. The man who pays the piper – whether in salary or freelance fees – has the right and the might to call the tune. You will often find that you must dilute, perhaps – you may think – ruin a good layout to satisfy boss or client. Well, unless or until you reach the dizzy heights of such financial independence that you can pick and choose clients, such is life. Hang on, wait for the next job; there are editors, publishers, corporate clients and others out there who appreciate and encourage good design. Treasure them when you find them.

General reference material

TYPOGRAPHICAL MEASUREMENTS

	Inches	Millimetres
Anglo-American point	0.013837	0.351
Pica	0.166044	4.218
Didot point	0.0148	0.376
Cicero	0.1776	4.511

SCREEN RULINGS

Lines per inch	Nearest equivalent lines per cm	Paper surface
65	26	newsprint
85	34	newsprint
100	40	machine finished (MF)
120	48	MF/matt coated
133	54	MF/matt coated/art
150	60	matt coated/art
175	70	art
200	80	art

PAPER SIZES
‘A’ SERIES SHEETS

Sheet size	Millimetres	Equivalent in inches
4A	1682x2378	66¼x93⅝
2A	1189x1682	46¾x66¼
A0	841x1189	33⅛x46¾
A1	594x841	23⅜x33⅛
A2	420x594	16½x23⅜
A3	297x420	11¾x16½
A4	210x297	8¼x11¾
A5	148x210	5⅞x8¼
A6	105x148	4⅛x5⅞
A7	74x105	2⅞x4⅛
A8	52x74	2x2⅞
A9	37x52	1½x2
A10	26x37	1x1½

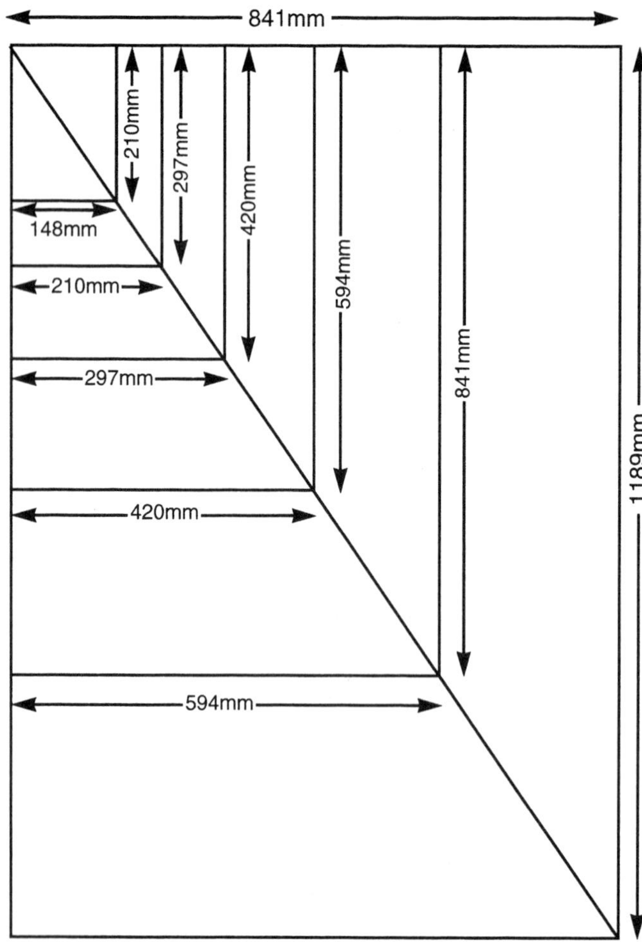

The diagram above shows progressive reductions from A0 to A5, each size being half the previous one.

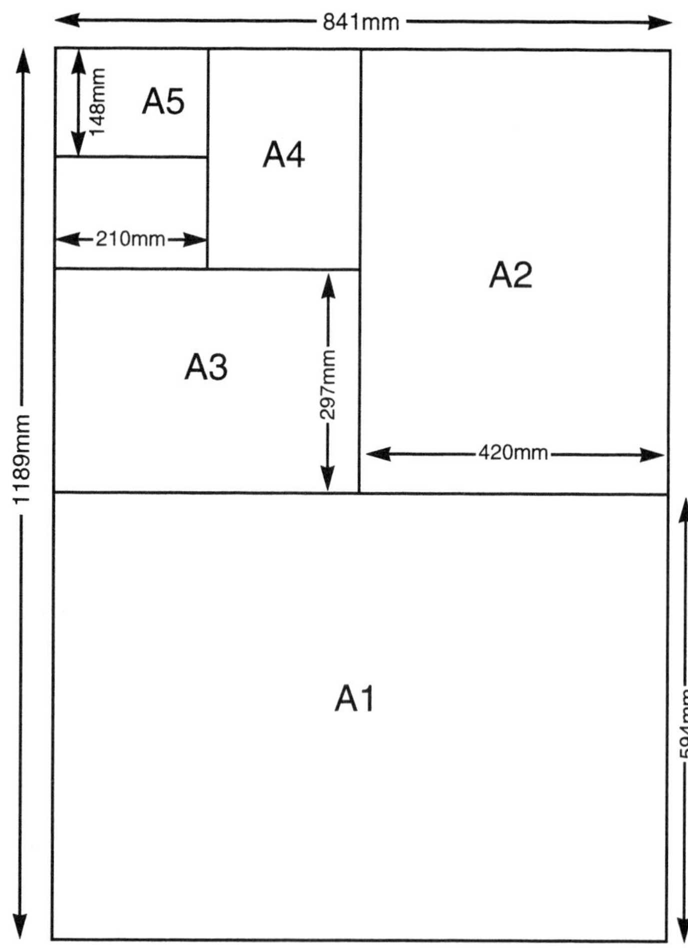

In the above diagram it is clear that the sides in each size are in the ratio of 1:√2.

A SPECIMEN HOUSE STYLE

All magazines should adopt a house style. This may be unique to the magazine or may simply follow Hart's Rules. What follows is an extract from the Naafi house style which may be used as the basis for establishing others. The rules in this extract may be changed, and additions will certainly be required, but they do provide a useful starting point from which a comprehensive and individual house style can be built up to provide the consistency which every magazine should seek to achieve.

ABBREVIATIONS AND CONTRACTIONS

Abbreviations are words shortened but omitting the endings: gal. for gallon, in. for inch. Contractions are telescoped words which begin with the initial letter of the original and end with the final letter: *ft.* for *foot* or *feet*, *Mr.* for *Mister*. Both are invaluable in their proper place – catalogues, recipes, and technical and tabular matter of all kinds would be unwieldy without them.

Some scholars argue, and some house styles rule, that abbreviations should be followed by a full stop or point but that contractions should not. Because this could sometimes cause confusion (not everyone will appreciate that *cwt.* is a contraction while *gal.* is an abbreviation) Naafi has decided to treat them alike.

Abbreviations and contractions using lower case letters take a full stop *(a.m., m.p.h., in., gal., Mr., Messrs.,* etc.) unless, by common usage, they have become accepted as words in their own right (*flu, car, pants, disco*).

Abbreviations for weights and measures do not take *s* to form the plural: *8 gal.*, not *8 gals.*, *5 in.* not *5 ins.* Note the space between the figure and the abbreviation.

Days of the week and months of the year should be spelt out in full. If abbreviation is essential (e.g. for tabular matter) use the first three letters only (see 'Dates').

Initial capital letters do not require full stops between them when used as abbreviations for organisations, decorations, designations and so on: *RAF, USA, OBE, MP.* Full stops must be used after personal initials: *Mr. J. J. Smith.*

AMPERSAND

The ampersand *(&)* should be used only in the titles of those organisations which affect them; *and* is preferred in all other circumstances.

APOSTROPHE

With few exceptions Naafi does not use an apostrophe to form plurals: we write *MPs* not *MP's*, *NCOs* not *NCO's*. We do use the apostrophe to form the plural of individual lower-case characters and would use it when minding our *p's* and *q's* but not for our *whys* and *wherefores*.

In such phrases as *three weeks time*, Naafi follows common usage and uses the apostrophe for the singular *a week's time* but not for the plural (*three weeks* is treated as an adjectival phrase).

CAPITAL LETTERS

Capital letters must be used: to begin a sentence; for the names of persons, streets, towns, counties, countries, ships, regiments, companies, societies and similar organisations; for the titles of books, plays, films, musical works, newspapers and so on; for Government appointments; for the formal titles of persons and for the full ranks of individual officers, NCOs, men and women of the armed forces, the police and similar services.

The practice of using a capital letter for a particular reference but dropping it in general reference is an aid to clarity and is adopted in the Naafi house style. We will use capital letters in writing *Salisbury Cathedral,* and in *the Cathedral* if we are referring back to a named cathedral, but not in a phrase such as *a cathedral is a place of worship*; we will write *Private J. Smith* but *he was a private in the infantry*.

The same rule applies in the plural: *a company of knights* but *Knights of the Garter*, thus *Foreign Secretaries* will never be confused with *foreign secretaries*.

Many words have a concrete and an abstract sense and their meanings are distinguished by the use of capital letters for their concrete form: *State* (organised community), *state* (condition); *Power* (powerful nation), *power* (strength, ability); *Government* (body governing the State), *government* (the function of governing), *Ministry* (political), *ministry* (religious); and so on.

If a title or name requires initial capital letters, the whole of the title should be given initial capitals: *Oxford Street* not *Oxford street, Western Powers* not *western Powers.*

When referring to institutions, corporations, associations and the like, part of the title is commonly dropped after first giving the name in full. In such circumstances the initial capital letter should be retained: *An inspector of the Royal Society for the Prevention of Cruelty to Animals said that the Society . . .*

When a noun which would normally take an initial capital is used as an adjective the capital letter should be retained: *French windows*.

There is nothing to recommend the practice of using capital letters in job descriptions: if *Managing Director* why not *Bus Driver* or *Clerk*? The Naafi style is to use lower case for all such designations except where they are used in addressing letters or envelopes, or in setting up tabular matter.

DASHES

Do not use dashes as a substitute for more appropriate punctuation marks. Never precede or follow a dash with another punctuation mark. See also 'Dates' and 'Numbers'.

DATES

The Naafi style is *25 January 1970* (note that commas are not used) or, for tabular matter, *25.1.70*.

Months and days should usually be spelt out. Where abbreviations are required (as, for example, in tabular matter) use the first three letters: *Jan., Feb., Mar., Apr., May, Jun., Jul., Aug., Sep., Oct., Nov., Dec.*, and *Mon., Tue., Wed., Thu., Fri., Sat., Sun.*

Use the least possible number of figures consistent with clarity to indicate periods of time: *4–18 January 1969*, *1968–9* but *1968–71* not *1968–1, 1914-18* not *1914–8*. If you write *from* you must use *to* (not a dash) and the full year: *from 1914 to 1918* not *from 1914–18* or *from 1914–1918*. Be sure to use an en dash not a hyphen.

EXCLAMATION MARKS

The exclamation mark must not be used merely to give a sentence added emphasis or in a mistaken attempt to inject some excitement.

The exclamation mark is required after interjections such as *Oh!* and *Ah!*, after words and phrases used as interjections *Good heavens! Well! Really!*, after exclamatory sentences *What a glorious day it is! How helpless you are!*, after inversions or ellipses (omissions of words) which express emotion (compare *You liar!* with *You are a liar.*), and for quotations where it is necessary to indicate that the tone of voice is not what might be thought from reading a simple sentence ending with a full stop. *'You missed your train.'* is a simple statement of fact, but *'You missed your train!'* implies sarcasm.

HYPHENS

We cannot attempt to provide here a comprehensive set of rules governing the use of hyphens, but the principles of Naafi's house style (simplicity, economy, clarity) will usually help resolve the problem of whether or not to hyphenate. Ask the question 'If I omit the hyphen am I likely to confuse, mislead, or delay the reader?' If the answer is 'No' leave out the hyphen, if it is 'Yes' put the hyphen in.

The phrase *five year old children* is ambiguous and the writer must mean either *five year-old children* or *five-year-old children.*

For further guidance in matters of

punctuation refer to *Fowler's Modern English Usage*.

INVERTED COMMAS

Single inverted commas are used for quotations. Double inverted commas are used for quotations within quotations.

Follow the logical school of thought and place punctuation marks inside or outside inverted commas according to sense, as in the following examples.

He asked 'Can I call at four o'clock?' The question is contained within the quotation.

Did he say 'Can I call at four o'clock'? The question is not whether he can call at four but whether he said the words quoted.

'Naafi' he said 'is at an interesting stage of its development.' The sentence within the quotation marks is complete in itself. Commas are not required before and after *he said.*

He pointed out that Naafi was at 'an interesting stage of its development'. The quotation is not a complete sentence.

We were stopped by the cry 'Help!' Only the quotation is exclamatory.

How blood-curdling the cry 'Murder'! The whole sentence is exclamatory.

Inverted commas are as often misused as are exclamation marks. When you are tempted to use them for any purpose other than enclosing a quotation ask yourself whether they are needed. They rarely are.

NUMBERS

Numbers under 11, round numbers, and numbers beginning a sentence should usually be spelt out in text setting. Exact numbers (scores, weights and measures, etc.) should usually be expressed in figures. Write *in his fifties* but *he was 53*. Break these rules if necessary to avoid confusing juxtapositions: write *fourteen 400 yd. laps* not *14 400 yd. laps*.

Arabic numerals are preferred to Roman except for such traditional uses as Army corps, legal documents, order of accession, the subsidiary numbering of paragraphs or minutes, and so on.

Roman numerals are not followed by a full stop (except at the end of a sentence) or by *st, nd*, or *th*: *Elizabeth II* or *Elizabeth the Second* but never *Elizabeth IInd*.

The preferred style for dates is *10 September 1971* or, for tabular matter, *10.9.71*.

Use the least possible number of figures consistent with clarity to indicate periods of time (see under 'Dates'), sequences or ranges: *pages 246–9* but *pages 246–51*; *10–15lb.* not *10lb.–15lb*; *8–10°C* not *8°–10°C*. Be sure to use an en dash not a hyphen.

Ordinal numbers, *first, second, third* etc., should usually be spelt out in text. Use *1st, 2nd, 3rd* in tabular matter and for Battalions and Divisions but note: *101 Squadron, Eighth Army*, and *XIII Corps*.

Decimals which are not preceded by whole numbers should be preceded by a nought (*0.4 not .4*) except for gun calibres such as *.303*.

PARENTHESES

Parentheses may be marked by commas, dashes or brackets. Commas should be used where the interruption to the sentence is slight, dashes and round brackets where interruptions are progressively more disruptive or where commas would complicate the punctuation. Square brackets are usually reserved for editorial comment.

PERCENT

Express as one word and prefer it to % except in tabular matter or where many percentages are to be given.

ISE OR IZE

Whether to spell modernise, civilise, and similar verbs with an *s* or a *z* often leads to doubt, delay and the dictionary. There are good scholarly arguments for preferring *z* in some instances but there are a number of verbs (advertise, exercise, supervise . . .) where the *s* MUST be used. In adopting the rule that *s* should always be used, Naafi has also taken into account the merits of consistency and time-saving.

Glossary

Artwork: Elements of the page which are in a finished state (i.e. ready for reproduction).

Ascender: That part of a stroke of a lower case letter which extends above the x-height as in b, d, f.

Bar code: The series of thick and thin black bars (being applied to more and more goods including books and magazines) which can be 'read' by checkout and hand-held scanners to produce price and other information.

Bleed: The area of an illustration, colour panel etc., which prints beyond the page area and will be cut off at the trimming stage.

Body text, body copy: The main text, for continuous reading as opposed to text for display.

Body type: The type to be used for the body text.

Box: Rules formed into a rectangle to contain text or graphics.

Bromide: 1) A photographic print; 2) the printout from an imagesetter.

Bullet: A solid circle (in any type size) often used in listings. An outline bullet is a hollow circle.

Burn-out: Conversion of a half-tone to line by making the lighter tones white and the darker tones black.

Byline: Name of the author, photographer, artist etc., displayed on the page.

Capitals: The upper case letters (A, B, C) as opposed to the lower case letters (a, b, c).

Caption: Text which explains or amplifies an illustration.

Cast off: Calculate how much space will be occupied by a given amount of copy when set in the specified type and size.

Centred (text): Text which has not been forced to justify (q.v.) and is aligned on the middle of the column or type area.

Character: A unit of a type fount, a letter, numeral, punctuation mark etc.

Chinagraph: Pencils (available in a range of colours) which will write on plastic, glass, etc., and (usually) its marks can be removed with a wipe.

Clip art: 'Ready-made' art which can be bought in book or computer disk form and reproduced without further payment.

Continuation pages: Pages to which a feature is carried

over, beyond the opening page or spread.

Continuation symbols: Devices used to indicate that a feature has been carried over from the previous opening.

Copy: 1) Duplicate; 2) the words which make up a story or feature; 3) the manuscript.

Counter: Space partly or totally enclosed in a letter such as o, c, d, n.

Credit box: A box which lists individuals and companies involved in a publication – editor, designer, publisher, printer and so on.

Crop: Indicate a reduced area of an illustration for reproduction, usually by marking on a tracing paper overlay.

Crosshead: A subsidiary heading used to provide breaks in long passages of text.

Cut-out: An illustration in which all or part of the background around the main element has been removed.

Dash: Longer than a hyphen, usually specified as an en-dash or em-dash.

Descender: The stroke of a lower case letter which extends below the baseline as in g, j, p.

Display text: The words which make up straplines, headlines, standfirsts, etc., which are to stand out from the body text.

Display type: The face and size specified for text which is to be displayed.

DPI (dots per inch): Defines the resolution of computer screens, scanners, printers, etc.

Drop cap, drop letter: A large initial letter, usually at the beginning of the text, which may be two three or more text lines deep.

Drop shadow: See 'shadow'.

Duotone: Obtaining a two-colour effect from a monochrome illustration by creating two half-tone copies, with differing screen angles (q.v.), one for each colour, which then overprint one on the other.

Em: The square of the width of the letter 'm'.

Emulsion: The light-sensitive coating on photographic paper and film.

En: Half the width of an em (q.v.).

Flat plan: See 'Imposition'.

Folio: Page number.

Font: See 'Fount'.

Footer: Text (e.g. page numbers) placed in the margin at the foot of the page.

Fount: Strictly, all the characters of one size of one design of type; now frequently used (particularly 'font') to refer to all sizes of one design.

Galley proof: A first proof of the text from the typesetter, usually in single column form.

Ghosting: A darkroom or studio camera technique (also used in vignetting) in which part of a photograph is reduced in density to allow overprinting.

Grid: Outline of a page or spread showing margins, columns, gutters, etc.

Gutter: The space between the columns.

Half-tone: An illustration with varied tones which may range from black through greys to white.

Hanging cap: An enlarged initial capital letter, similar to a drop cap (q.v.) but placed immediately outside (to the left) of the text area.

Header: Text (e.g. the date, publication name, etc.) placed in the head margin (at the top of the page).

Headline (also 'heading'): Text set and positioned for display to attract the reader to the main text. ('Headline' is usually associated with news stories.)

Hood: In essence, a box with one side removed to link the contents of the hood with another element (e.g. a caption with its picture).

Imposition: A plan showing the relative positions of pages on the printed sheet to ensure the correct sequence of pages is achieved after folding and trimming.

Indent: Set in from the usual left or right edge.

Intro: Common abbreviation for 'introductory paragraph'. Unlike a standfirst (q.v.), the intro is an integral part of the main text.

Justified: Each line of text is of equal length (with the possible exception of first and last lines of paragraphs).

Kerning: Adjusting the space between a pair of letters to produce letter-spacing which is visually (as opposed to mechanically) uniform.

Keyline: An outline indicating the position and size of a half-tone, drawing, advertisement, etc.

Landscape: The width is greater than the height.

Layout: Design, usually in sketch or outline form, of a page or spread.

Leading: The space between consecutive lines of type in a column.

Letraset: 1) A transfer system for applying type (usually display type) to artwork; 2) the company which supplies the above transfer sheets (and much more).

Letter-spacing: Controlling the space between letters over a selected range of text. See also 'Tracking'.

Light box: A box with a ground glass (or similar) top above a cold light source. Principally used for viewing transparencies but has many other uses.

Line artwork: Artwork in black and white (no in-between tones).

Lower case (l.c.): The small letters in a fount (a, b, c) as opposed to upper case (A, B, C).

Make-up: See 'Page make-up'.

Margins: The (largely) blank borders around the page enclosing the type area.

Mark up: To write instructions (to printer, typesetter, etc.) on copy, layout, overlays etc.

Masking tape: Preferred to other sticky tapes because it is less likely to cause damage as it is removed.

Ornamentation: The use of type ornaments (rules, borders, etc.) and other devices to embellish a design.

Outline: Hollow type or object (e.g. 'quad') defined by a line.

Overlay: Transparent or semi-transparent paper fixed in place over artwork and marked with instructions.

Page make-up: Assembly of the various elements before proceeding to plate-making etc.

Pica: A unit of measure, approximately $^1/_6$ in.

Point: The most common unit of measure for specifying type sizes in the USA and UK (12 pt = 1 pica).

Portrait: See 'Upright'.

Pulled quote: A quotation from the main body of the text and printed (perhaps larger, bolder, within a box or rules . . .) as a device to brighten up the page.

Quad: A solid square.

Reflective artwork: Artwork which is reproduced by light reflected from it (c.f. 'Transparent artwork').

Repro house: A company which undertakes reproduction of artwork, usually to film or plate.

Reverse out: To make type (or graphic) appear as white out of a colour or tint.

Roughs: Preliminary sketches of design ideas.

Rule: A line (or combination of lines) generally used to separate items (hence, column rules separate columns).

Run-around: To make the line ends of text follow the shape of an object (such as a cut-out photograph or drawing).

Sans, sans serif: A typeface without serifs (q.v.).

Scale: To calculate the area which will be covered by an illustration when it is proportionately enlarged or reduced.

Scanner: An electronic device which 'reads' photographs, drawings, etc., and records the information digitally.

Screen: 1) The glass surface of a computer monitor on which type etc. is displayed; 2) a fine grid through which continuous tone images are photographed to break the tones down into printable dots.

Screen angle: When screened images are to be printed in more than one colour, each colour requires its own plate. To avoid the ink dots of one colour overprinting another colour, the angle of the screen (and therefore the position of the dots) must be changed for each colour plate.

Serif: A small stroke at the end of a main stroke of a letter and in opposition to it.

Shadow: Usually a tinted duplicate of type or an object, printed beneath and offset from the original to give a three-dimensional effect.

Sideheads: See 'Crossheads'.

Solid: Colour printed at full density as opposed to a tint (q.v.).

Spot colour: A colour other than black used as a solid or tint to embellish a page.

Spread: A pair of facing pages.

Standfirst (occasionally 'blurb'): Text, usually placed between the heading and the main text, which gives a brief insight into the subject matter and, unlike an intro (q.v.), it can stand alone.

Strap, strapline: A line of display type leading into but smaller than the heading.

Style sheet: 1) Information on the publication's preferred method of dealing with style variables; 2) a type specification which can be stored in a page make-up program and be instantly applied to selected text whenever required.

Tabular matter: Information set out in columns or cells.

Tagline: A word (or two) followed by a number which helps identify the pages and sequence of a news story or feature.

Teaser: Brief, enticing reference on a cover to an inside feature.

Template: A grid or pattern (particularly in page layout software) which can be used again and again.

Tint: 1) A reduced density of ink; 2) a pattern of dots (or lines, etc.) which has the effect of reducing the colour density of the ink. More properly a 'mechanical tint'.

Tracking: Adjusting the letter- and word-spacing across selected text.

Transparent artwork: Artwork which is reproduced by passing light through it (c.f. 'Reflective artwork').

Type horizon: An imaginary line across a page or spread above which the body type is not allowed to protrude.

Typeface: A single, distinctive design of a set of characters (q.v.).

Type-scale (sometimes 'type-gauge'): A device which facilitates the measuring of printed type, counting lines etc.

Typesetting:1) The printed text produced by the typesetter; 2) the act of setting text in type.

Typography: The study of type.

Upper case: See 'Capitals'.

Upright: Being deeper than it is wide.

Widow: A short line of text at the top of a column.

Wob: White out of black.

Wrap-around: A cover picture (or drawing etc.) which is continuous over front and back covers.

X-height: The height of a lower case letter without ascender or descender, as a, c, and, of course, x.

Index